IMMIGRATING TO CANADA

IMMIGRATING TO CANADA
Who is allowed? What is required? How to do it!

Gary L. Segal, B.A., LL.B.

Self-Counsel Press
(*a division of*)
International Self-Counsel Press Ltd.
Canada U.S.A.

Printed in Canada

First edition: July, 1975
Second edition: January, 1977
Third edition: April, 1980
Fourth edition: August, 1981
Fifth edition: July, 1983
Sixth edition: June, 1986
Seventh edition: October, 1987
Eighth edition: June, 1990
Ninth edition: October, 1990; Reprinted: March, 1992

Canadian Cataloguing in Publication Data
Segal, Gary L., 1946-
    Immigrating to Canada

    (Self-counsel legal series)
First-2nd eds. published as: How to immigrate into Canada
    ISBN 0-88908-951-5

1. Emigration and immigration law - Canada - Popular works. 2. Canada - Emigration and immigration - Handbooks, manuals, etc. I. Title. II. Series.
KE4454.Z82S44 1990a   342.71'082   C90-091656-7

Self-Counsel Press
(*a division of*)
International Self-Counsel Press Ltd.
Head and Editorial Office
1481 Charlotte Road
North Vancouver, British Columbia V7J 1H1

U.S. Address
1704 N. State Street
Bellingham, Washington 98225

CONTENTS

APPENDIXES

LIST OF SAMPLES

LIST OF TABLES

NOTICE TO READERS

Laws are constantly changing. Every effort is made to keep this publication as current as possible. However, neither the author nor the publisher can accept any responsibility for changes to the law or practice that occur after the printing of this publication. Please be sure that you have the most recent edition.

NOTE: At the time of this printing, the occupational demand list shown as Table #4 on page 52 had been changed. As well, the category of "retired persons" has been eliminated. For the most up-to-date information, please contact Canada Immigration.

Also, legislation is currently before the Canadian government that would change the definition of a "dependant" as it applies to family class members (see chapter 4). Under the new legislation, only children under the age of 19 will qualify as dependants unless they are in full-time attendance in school and wholly dependent on their parents for financial support. This legislation is expected to become law in Spring, 1993.

These changes do not affect the basic procedures outlined in this book, and you should be able to successfully process your immigration procedure by carefully following the explanations provided.

-The Editors 02/92

1
SO YOU WANT TO MOVE TO CANADA?

Immigration to Canada has increased steadily since the end of World War II. A country with one of the world's highest standards of living, relatively uncrowded, and with many opportunities for new-comers, Canada offers much to would-be immigrants from all over the world.

At the same time, immigrants to Canada form a multicultural mosaic that has great-ly enhanced the cosmopolitan character of Canada and has helped it to step beyond its image as one of Britain's oldest colonies. Today, cities such as Toronto, Montreal, and Vancouver have large immigrant populations from all over the world, often rivalling in number the largest cities in their homelands.

Since the beginning of this century, Canada's population has increased from just over 5 million to almost 27 million. Of this number, over 9.5 million were im-migrants. More than 5 million people have come to Canada since the end of World War II. While the average yearly immigra-tion has been 140 000, the range has been from a low of 47 000 in 1947 to highs of 282 000 in 1957 and 249 000 in 1973.

The large waves of immigration to Canada have followed periods of economic growth, especially in the period from 1954 to 1972. These waves of im-migration have come from various parts of the world. In 1956, almost 58% of Canada's immigrants came from western Europe in-cluding the United Kingdom (31%) and only 2.1% came from Africa, India, and Asia combined. In 1956, the U.S.A. ac-counted for 6% of our immigrants and the Caribbean and all of South America ac-counted for less than 2%. By 1977, United Kingdom immigrants were less than 16% and western Europe less than 12.5%, while Asia, India, and Africa had increased to more than 27% and the Caribbean and South America to almost 19%. Today over 50% of our immigration comes from the Far East, Southeast Asia, and the Sub-Con-tinent.

Since World War II, almost 2 million people have left Canada to emigrate to other countries, mostly during 1960 to 1961 and 1967 to 1968 in periods of economic slow-down. The bulk of this emigration was to the United States and this flow les-sened considerably during the 1970s. Cur-rent projections place Canada's population between 27 and 31 million by the year 2001 depending on the levels of immigration allowed and the birth rate.

Beginning in 1973, the Canadian govern-ment began to cut the flow of immigration. In 1975, there were 187 881 immigrants to Canada, a drop of 14% from the 218 465 in 1974. In 1976, immigration fell again to 149 429 and in 1977 to 114 914. As a result of the tightening of immigration laws fol-lowing the proclamation of the new Im-migration Act, 1976, on April 10, 1978, the number of immigrants fell again in 1978 to a very low 86 313.

Immigration increased slightly to 143 117 in 1980 but has fallen steadily due to government policy that set levels to lows of 89 157 in 1983 and 85 000 in 1985.

An analysis of immigration to Canada between 1973 and 1983 shows that immigration has dropped from just under 250 000 to approximately 90 000 in 1983. Most important, however, is to note that in 1973, the immigrants were composed of approximately 50 000 in the family class, 5 000 refugees, and 195 000 in the assisted relative and independent immigrant classes. These 195 000 people represented some 65 000 families.

Recent changes in the law and especially in the requirement for approved employment offers for all but family class immigrants, refugees, and independent immigrants on the job demand list (see chapters 6, 9, 10 and Table #4) meant that the 85 000 immigrants in 1985 included about 63 000 family class and 10 000 refugees (a figure set by the government) leaving only 14 000 to 15 000 independent class and assisted relative immigrants, a mere 5 000 families from approximately 900 000 applicants worldwide that year.

As can be seen from the above, not only was total immigration reduced in an 11-year period by 60%, but the crucial independent category was reduced by over 90%.

This was due, in large part, to the federal government actively discouraging immigration to Canada prior to 1986. This policy evolved because immigration is tied directly to the needs of Canada's labor force and to national population goals. Thus it is essential that prospective immigrants to Canada follow closely and comply with all the regulations established by the Employment and Immigration Commission.

Starting in 1986, the federal government announced the first increase in immigration levels in 13 years. For 1986, immigration to Canada was targeted at a range of 105 000 to 115 000 people in all categories. This 25% increase in the overall levels was felt most in the assisted relative and independent categories where the number of families increased from about 5 000 to approximately 12 000.

The federal government has continued this policy for the past four years, setting levels of 115 000 to 125 000 (1987), 140 000 (1988), 160 000 (1989) and 175 000 for 1990 — an 84% increase since 1985.

The 175 000 immigrants in 1990 will include approximately 21 000 family class families, 10 000 refugee families, 4 300 entrepreneur and business families, 3 000 retiree families, and 20 000 independent immigrant families based on needed job skills in Canada.

These 20 000 families will be chosen from almost 1 500 000 families who will apply in 1990 at Canadian embassies and consulates — a success rate of about 1.3%.

To accomplish these objectives there has been a relaxing of the requirements for an approved job offer in 116 job classifications. See chapters 6 and 9 for more information on this new policy.

This book is intended as a guide to immigration into Canada. It will deal with who can come and how to go about making an application to immigrate. It will also cover the deportation from Canada of both visitors and immigrants who are permanent residents. It is not intended as a complete legal text on the subject of immigration law, nor is it intended to replace a competent lawyer.

However, it will give prospective immigrants to Canada, or people in Canada wishing to sponsor their relatives from overseas for immigration, a working knowledge of the complexities of immigrating to Canada and help them avoid the all-too-often unscrupulous tactics of many so-called "immigration consultants" and travel agents who promote easy immigration to Canada for a substantial fee.

It has become essential during the past five years for a prospective immigrant to

Canada complete his or her application form with as much accurate and detailed information as possible and for the application to be accompanied by as much supporting documentation as the applicant can obtain.

Often, however, prospective immigrants to Canada have difficulty understanding the complex forms and documents that have to be completed in full. If, after reading this book and speaking to a Canadian immigration officer, you still feel lost and in need of expert advice, you should consult a qualified lawyer.

If you do not have a lawyer or if you cannot afford one, you should contact your local bar association or law society which may be able to assist you in finding both free legal advice and lawyers knowledgeable in the area of immigration law.

2
CANADIAN IMMIGRATION POLICY

On April 10, 1978, Canada's new immigration act was proclaimed into law. It is known as the Immigration Act, 1976, since it was first presented to the Canadian Parliament in that year. Following study, suggestions from the public, lawyers, and others, and the resulting amendments from those representations, Canada's new immigration act became law in the spring of 1978.

The effects of the new law are now being both felt and seen.

For the first time, our immigration law sets forth objectives defined in section 3 of the act itself. In that section, Canada declares that our law shall be designed and administered to —

(a) promote the domestic and international interests of Canada including the setting of immigration levels from time to time based on Canada's needs — nationally, provincially, and locally,

(b) enrich Canada's cultural and social fabric and especially the bilingual nature of Canada (English and French),

(c) facilitate the reunion of Canadian citizens and landed immigrants with their close relatives abroad,

(d) co-operate with other levels of government (especially the provinces) with respect to the settlement and admission of immigrants,

(e) assist the entry of visitors into Canada for trade, commerce, tourism, and cultural and scientific exchanges,

(f) ensure visitors and immigrants to Canada are subject to non-discriminatory standards in accordance with the Canadian Charter of Rights and Freedoms,

(g) fulfil Canada's international obligations to refugees and the persecuted,

(h) foster a strong economic Canada,

(i) protect the health, safety, and good order of Canada, and fulfil Canada's international legal obligations to refugees and the persecuted while affording no haven to those who would use Canada for criminal purposes.

All the above sound very idealistic. The reality is another matter. As you will learn as you read the remainder of this book, the re-unification of families does not mean you can bring your brother to Canada if he cannot fit within the very strict definition of "family class" as defined by our law.

Similarly, while immigration levels to Canada have been set by the federal government at 175 000 in 1990, the implications of which will be discussed in chapters 4, 9, and 10, independent immigrants will only total about 20 000 families from the whole world or 1.3% of 1.5 million applicants.

This book will try to explain, with concrete examples and in easy-to-understand language, the complexities of Canadian immigration law. It will look at the reality of the law rather than the way it is often perceived from the general principles stated above.

No individual or group has yet taken the government to court in an attempt to have a judge say that the Canadian government is not living up to the policies outlined in section 3 of the Immigration Act, 1976. It is not likely that such an attempt would succeed in our courts, because the general idealism of section 3 must give way to specific law as outlined in the 123 other sections of the Immigration Act, the many interpreting regulations passed, and the policies established to carry out and explain the law.

3
VISITORS AND IMMIGRANTS

The immigration law of Canada is a federal law. All those seeking to come into Canada, whether they are Canadian citizens, immigrants, people previously admitted to Canada as immigrants, or non-immigrants, such as tourists or business people, are subject to an examination by a federal immigration officer at the point of entry.

The object of this examination is to determine whether or not you should be allowed to enter the country. While the specific questions will vary from crossing to crossing and from officer to officer, the following is typical of what you will be asked.

(a) What is your name?

(b) Where do you live?

(c) What is your citizenship?

(d) Why do you wish to come into Canada?

(e) What is your destination in Canada?

(f) Whom do you intend to see in Canada?

(g) How long do you intend to stay in Canada?

Obviously, people who are Canadian citizens and can prove it by showing a passport, birth certificate, or naturalization papers come into Canada by right. This right is afforded to them under section 4(1) of the Immigration Act.

Also included in this category of people who have a right to enter Canada, with certain exceptions, are permanent residents of Canada. A permanent resident is a person who has been admitted into Canada as a landed immigrant and who has not as yet become a Canadian citizen, has not lost his or her landed immigrant status as outlined in chapter 23, and has not become a prohibited individual as discussed in chapter 24.

a. WHO ARE VISITORS?

"Visitor" is a legal term in Canadian law used to describe a person who seeks to come into Canada or is in Canada for a temporary purpose usually, but not always, for a relatively short period of time and who is not a Canadian citizen, a permanent resident, or a person who has been granted special permission by the immigration authorities or by the Minister of Employment and Immigration to enter Canada.

You are a visitor if you are — a tourist; a student coming to study; a business person temporarily in Canada; a member of a ship's crew; a member of a dramatic group; an artist; an athlete; or a musician temporarily in Canada to give a performance; a worker in Canada on an employment authorization; a diplomat — to mention a few (see chapter 20).

b. WHO ARE IMMIGRANTS?

An "immigrant" is a person who seeks admission to Canada as a permanent resident — a person who wishes to make Canada his or her home and who wants to work and live in Canada and become part of the fabric of Canadian life. There are essentially four categories of immigrants under the Immigration Act:

(a) Independent applicants
(b) Family class relatives (who are dependent on their sponsors)
(c) Assisted relatives (who are non-dependent relatives of Canadian citizens or landed immigrants whose relatives agree to assist them)
(d) Refugees

4
THE FAMILY CLASS AND ASSISTED RELATIVE CLASS

The "family class" and "assisted relative" categories have been established to allow Canadian citizens and permanent residents of Canada an opportunity to bring their relatives to Canada.

The application either to sponsor a family class member or to assist a relative must be made in Canada by a Canadian citizen or by a permanent resident on behalf of someone abroad. In part c. below, there is a detailed discussion of the procedures for applying for either family class or assisted relatives.

The only exceptions to the policy of having to apply to sponsor your relative while he or she is outside of Canada appear to be the case of a husband or wife sponsoring his or her spouse, situations involving hardship such as illness, and cases involving the care of elderly parents or grandparents where going "back home" would mean hardship and dislocation. In these cases (at least until recently), the Employment and Immigration Commission has been allowing applications to be made from inside the country.

The policy in this area may change at any time and you should consult the Employment and Immigration Commission or a lawyer familiar with immigration law for up-to-date information. Such contact should be by phone and not in person if your close relative is already in Canada since, if you identify yourself, the government might begin deportation proceedings against your relative, who might be in Canada illegally.

Other than in situations involving spouses, there are indications that the Immigration Commission will require the immigrating relative to leave Canada and apply in the ordinary way from outside the country unless there are strong humanitarian and compassionate reasons for not leaving. Such grounds could include inability to support oneself, long distance to travel to homeland for the elderly, the need to care for children, and the like.

Since 1984, the federal government has allowed the sponsorship of a spouse within Canada provided that the marriage takes place in Canada and that the marriage is found to be a legitimate, *bona fide* marriage and not one contracted merely for the purpose of assisting in immigration to Canada.

a. WHO ARE FAMILY CLASS MEMBERS?

A Canadian citizen or permanent resident over the age of 18 and living in Canada may sponsor an application to immigrate by a family class member. A family class member is one of the following people:

(a) A husband or wife of the sponsor

(b) A fiancé or fiancée of the sponsor

(c) An unmarried (never married) son or daughter of the sponsor (including adopted children; see chapter 5)

(d) A grandparent of the sponsor over the age of 60

(e) A grandparent of the sponsor under the age of 60 if widowed or unable to work

In the case of parents:

(f) A Canadian citizen living in Canada or a permanent resident who has been living in Canada for three years or more since receiving permanent resident status and who is over 18 years old may sponsor a mother and/or father of any age

(g) A permanent resident who has been living in Canada less than 3 years who is at least 18 years old may sponsor a mother and/or father over age 60 or under age 60 if widowed or unable to work

(h) Orphans, unmarried, under the age of 18 years who are the grand-children, brothers, sisters, nephews, or nieces of the person sponsoring them

(i) Any child under the age of 13 whom you intend to adopt and who is an orphan, abandoned without parents, or has been placed with a child welfare agency for adoption

(j) One other relative, on the condition that you do not have any person either *in Canada* or outside Canada who is your spouse, child, parent, grandparent, brother, sister, aunt, uncle, niece, or nephew who is available to sponsor as a family class member.

People often misunderstand this last category of individuals. It means that you cannot have any of the named relatives either in Canada or abroad that you could otherwise sponsor. *None* of these relatives can be living in Canada or elsewhere or be a Canadian citizen. For instance, if you are married and your spouse is living in Canada with you, this last section does not apply. In the past 21 years I have seen only 3 cases in which Canadian widows have complied with section (j).

In December, 1984, the government announced a policy change allowing the sponsorship on humanitarian and compassionate grounds of a last remaining son or daughter unmarried (never married) of any age or a last remaining brother or sister unmarried of any age if both parents were deceased. This policy was cancelled when sponsorships were allowed for all unmarried children of any age.

The effect of this means that the sponsorship of unmarried brothers and sisters both over and under the age of 21 *will be tied* to the sponsorship of parents who must be immigrating to Canada. These children will come as dependants of their parents or, if the parents are already Canadian citizens or permanent residents living in Canada, as sponsored dependants in the family class.

The practical result is that older unmarried brothers and sisters cannot immigrate on their own in the family class as they could under the December, 1984 policy if both parents were deceased.

Also under the new regulations, unmarried brothers and sisters who are older than 21 *must* come with their parents and be on their application to immigrate. If they choose not to come at the same time, the parents will be required to sign a document *giving up forever* their right to immigrate in the family class.

Note: For children over 21 this is a once-only chance to immigrate in the family class. Thereafter they will be independent immigrants or assisted relatives as the case may be and subject to the rules and policies applying to those categories.

If you have relatives who fit into any one of the categories, they can be sponsored by you for immigration to Canada provided that you, the sponsor, are over the age of 18 and living in Canada.

While there is no specific limit to the number of people you can sponsor in the family class, there are financial guidelines used by immigration officials. These guidelines will not normally be used when sponsoring a spouse who has no children or when sponsoring a child under 21 who has no children, but will be used when sponsoring your parents and grandparents and any dependent (under 18 and unmarried) brothers and sisters accompanying your parents. If you earn insufficient income to support your family, they will be refused (see Table #1 at the end of this chapter).

b. THE SPONSOR'S OBLIGATIONS

As a sponsor, you have certain ongoing obligations toward the people on whose behalf you apply. You will be required to provide for the accommodation, care, and maintenance of the person you sponsor for immigration to Canada and to ensure that in the future he or she will not become a burden on Canadian taxpayers. This means that if your dependants are unable to support themselves, you will be called upon to do so.

Your sponsored dependants will not normally be eligible for welfare or other similar public assistance in Canada. Such assistance, however, does not include things like unemployment insurance, the Canada Pension Plan, and workers' compensation for which your sponsored dependant will be eligible if he or she contributes to them.

The sponsor is usually made responsible for the well-being of the family member for a period of 10 years. Although the period may be shorter, it cannot be longer. In my experience, I have not seen a sponsorship period for less than 10 years for family class and 5 years for assisted relatives.

c. APPLYING TO SPONSOR A FAMILY CLASS MEMBER

In order to obtain an interview to sponsor a family class member, you should go to your nearest Canada Immigration Centre and tell them you wish to make an appointment to sponsor your husband, wife, parents, etc. You will be provided with the documents which appear on the following pages.

Sample #1 shows sample instructions you, as sponsor, will receive. This form will give you a time and place for the interview and tell you to bring with you proof of your status in Canada, proof of income such as a letter from your employer, your bank book, your medical insurance card (the Ontario certificate is specified in this form, but of course this would change according to which province you live in), and proof of relationship to your relative.

The proof of relationship to your relative would include a marriage certificate for your spouse, a birth certificate for your parents (it must be the long form showing the names of your parents), and a birth certificate for your children showing you as the parent of the child. A father can now sponsor a child even if he was not legally married to the mother of the child. The major problem will be proof of relationship if the father's name is not on the birth certificate. This can be overcome by very sophisticated and expensive blood tests of the child, mother, and father.

A recent decision in the Federal Court of Appeal should make it easier for the children of second, third, or fourth wives and of concubines to be sponsored for immigration if the relationship was *legally* recognized in the country of birth at the time of birth.

In cases of sponsorship from parts of the Third World, especially India, Pakistan, the Caribbean, and South America, there are often problems of proving relationships since records are often incomplete or non-existent. If your application for a family class member is refused, you have a right of appeal to the Immigration and Refugee Board (see chapter 25). In addition, there are often problems proving the age of children when there is a lack of accurate, reliable records.

Fortunately, two recent cases have resulted in the acceptance by the higher courts and the Immigration Appeal Board

SAMPLE #1
INSTRUCTION SHEET FOR FAMILY CLASS MEMBER
AND ASSISTED RELATIVES

CANADA EMPLOYMENT AND IMMIGRATION COMMISSION
CANADA IMMIGRATION CENTRE

INSTRUCTIONS FOR COMPLETING IMMIGRATION APPLICATIONS:

You have been given an appointment for interview in regard to your application at _____ on _____ . Every effort will be made for the interview to be held at the above-mentioned time, but some delay may be encountered due to the volume of work.

You are requested to complete every item on the attached application form by typewriter or in clear block letters.

If the prospective immigrant(s) have been known by, or use any other names, or if there are variations in spelling, please specify.

On the above appointment date, please present this application to:

RECEPTION COUNTER
443 UNIVERSITY AVENUE
MAIN FLOOR
TORONTO, ONTARIO
M5G 1V2

When calling for interview, please bring the following documents:

1.   Your passport, travel document, or Canadian Citizenship Certificate.

2.   A letter from your employer and if you are married, also a letter from your spouse's employer, showing the nature of employment; present salary; length of time employed; and whether income tax is being deducted. If self-employed, a statement of income tax from a bookkeeper or accountant, or a copy of income tax filed.

3.   Your bank book brought up-to-date.

4.   Your Ontario Hospital Services Commission Registration Certificate.

5.   If you are married, your husband/wife should accompany you.

6.   If will be necessary to prove your relationship to your relative.

(now the Immigration and Refugee Board) of genetic blood testing to prove relationships between parents, children, and siblings and of skeletal x-rays to prove age under 21. The blood tests are very expensive, about $250 (Canadian) per person tested, and fees for the Canadian medical experts required to interpret the full skeletal x-rays are also fairly expensive. You will require a lawyer to properly prepare this kind of medical evidence for court presentation.

Sample #2 is a copy of the application you must complete to sponsor a dependant for immigration to Canada. The form is one page long and three copies of the page are required. The application form and the attached copies can be obtained from a Canadian Immigration office, and where there is no such office, usually from a Canada Employment office.

The form for sponsoring your dependants is known as an Undertaking of Assistance Immigration Form IMM #1344. As you can see from the form, the sponsor is required to provide the following information: full name, date of birth, complete address and telephone number, and the name and address of your employer. In addition, you, the sponsor, must indicate whether you are a Canadian citizen or a permanent resident and if the latter, the day, month, and year you became a permanent resident and where the visa was issued.

You must provide the names, relationship, date, place, and country of birth, marital status, and citizenship of the person(s) you wish to sponsor. You must also make a declaration that you will be responsible for the dependant(s) and that you have told the truth on the application.

The application then must be signed in front of an immigration officer. If you are married, your husband or wife must go with you because he or she will be required to sign the form as well.

You will also be required to complete an Evaluation of Guarantors' Financial Circumstances, IMM #1283 (see Sample #3). In this form you must show all your income as well as your debts and obligations and the number of people you are currently sponsoring. You should take all these forms unsigned to the immigration office since they must be signed in front of a government official.

Following the interview, your application, once accepted, will be sent to the Canadian immigration office abroad that is closest to where your dependant lives. Your dependant will be interviewed and will be required to take a medical examination and pass a security check (see chapter 13) and will probably have to fill out the applicable sections of an Application Form IMM #8E (see Sample #8 and the detailed discussion in chapter 11).

Note: A family class member is not assessed under the point system and is not required to obtain a certain number of points in order to immigrate to Canada.

Chapter 14 deals with the situation in which you may be allowed to apply for a family class member while he or she is in Canada as a visitor; chapter 17 describes the particular situation of refugee applications.

If your sponsorship of a family class member is refused, a Canadian citizen or permanent resident sponsor can appeal this decision to the Immigration and Refugee Board (see chapter 25 section **e**).

Note: A new program being tried in Toronto only is experimenting with mail-in sponsorships for family class. You pick up a package of documents and instructions, return the completed forms by mail along with the appropriate filing fee, and, if acceptable, your copy of the Undertaking (IMM #1344) is returned to you by mail with an acknowledgment that the documents have been sent to the appropriate embassy or consulate abroad.

SAMPLE #2
UNDERTAKING OF ASSISTANCE FOR FAMILY CLASS

Employment and Immigration Canada / **Emploi et Immigration Canada**

UNDERTAKING AND ASSISTANCE

U- 0090001

CANADIAN RESIDENT COMPLETES AREA WITHIN RED BORDER - PLEASE PRINT OR TYPE

SPONSOR / GUARANTOR (PLEASE SEE REVERSE)			RESIDENTIAL ADDRESS (NO. AND STREET)		POSTAL CODE
FAMILY NAME	GIVEN NAMES		1 St. Albert Street		A1A1A1
NORMAN	BARRY LAWRENCE				

MAIDEN NAME — SEX: [X] MALE [ ] FEMALE

CITY: CALGARY   PROVINCE: ALBERTA   TELEPHONE NO.: 555 2222

DATE OF BIRTH	COUNTRY OF BIRTH	CITIZEN OF
25 01 44 D M Y	ENGLAND	CANADA

MARITAL STATUS: [ ] NEVER MARRIED [X] MARRIED [ ] DIVORCED [ ] ENGAGED [ ] SEPARATED [ ] WIDOWED

IF YOU WERE EVER ISSUED A CANADIAN IMMIGRANT VISA, COMPLETE THE FOLLOWING:

MY CANADIAN IMMIGRANT VISA WAS ISSUED AT (NAME OF OFFICE): LONDON U.K.

I BECAME A CANADIAN PERMANENT RESIDENT IN: 1 2 7 2 (M Y)

MY NAME ON MY CANADIAN IMMIGRANT VISA WAS: [X] SAME AS ABOVE OR

LIST PERSON YOU WISH TO ASSIST AND ALL OF HIS/HER ACCOMPANYING DEPENDANTS
NOTE: A DEPENDANT IS THAT PERSON'S SPOUSE AND/OR NEVER MARRIED SONS AND DAUGHTERS OF ANY AGE (INCLUDING THEIR NEVER MARRIED CHILDREN, IF ANY), USE SEPARATE SHEET IF NECESSARY.

FAMILY NAME	GIVEN NAMES	RELATIONSHIP TO SPONSOR/ GUARANTOR	DATE OF BIRTH D M Y	COUNTRY OF BIRTH	CITIZENSHIP	MARITAL STATUS
NORMAN	LAWRENCE	FATHER	15 08 16	England	U.K. & C.	Married
NORMAN	JOAN	MOTHER	21 09 20	England	U.K. & C.	Married

THE PRESENT COMPLETE MAILING ADDRESS OF PERSON(S) NAMED ABOVE IS:

1 CRITCHELEY CRESCENT

LEEDS

COUNTRY: ENGLAND   TELEPHONE NO.: 666 - 1111

I HAVE READ AND UNDERSTAND THE WARNING ON THE BACK OF THIS FORM.

I WILL PROVIDE OR ASSIST IN PROVIDING (AS REQUIRED) ADEQUATE LODGING, CARE AND MAINTENANCE TO THE ABOVE-NAMED PERSON(S) DURING THE PERIOD OF SETTLEMENT IN CANADA, AS DETERMINED BELOW BY THE IMMIGRATION OFFICER AND WHICH MAY BE FOR AS LONG AS 10 YEARS.

I WILL PROVIDE FINANCIAL ASSISTANCE TO THE ABOVE-NAMED PERSON(S) SO THAT SUCH PERSON(S) SHALL NOT REQUIRE FINANCIAL MAINTENANCE SUPPORT, INCLUDING SUBSIDIZED HOUSING, FROM ANY FEDERAL OR PROVINCIAL ASSISTANCE PROGRAM PRESCRIBED BY REGULATION UNDER THE IMMIGRATION ACT.

SIGNATURE OF SPONSOR/GUARANTOR   DATE

SIGNATURE OF SPOUSE   DATE

OFFICIAL USE ONLY	[ ] FAMILY CLASS	[ ] ASSISTED RELATIVE

CIC	P/S CODE	CIC FILE NO.	SETTLEMENT ARRANGEMENTS:

- MET FOR _____ PERSON(S)
- NOT APPLICABLE FOR _____ PERSON(S)

LENGTH OF UNDERTAKING _____ YEARS

SIGNATURE OF IMMIGRATION OFFICER

COST RECOVERY CODE

PROCESSING OF APPLICATIONS AT _____ CURRENTLY TAKES
A MINIMUM OF _____ DAYS

RECEIPT NO.   DATE SIGNED D M Y

INQUIRIES MAY DELAY THE PROCESSING OF YOUR RELATIVE'S APPLICATION. PLEASE CHECK WITH YOUR RELATIVE BEFORE CONTACTING YOUR LOCAL CANADA IMMIGRATION CENTRE FOR A PROGRESS REPORT.

THIS FORM HAS BEEN ESTABLISHED BY THE MINISTER OF EMPLOYMENT AND IMMIGRATION

Canada

IMM 1344 IP-P (06-88) E   C.I.C. FILE   1

Employment and Immigration Canada Emploi et Immigration Canada

EVALUATION OF GUARANTORS' FINANCIAL CIRCUMSTANCES
ÉVALUATION DE LA SITUATION FINANCIÈRE DU GARANT

(Family Class and Assisted Relatives) — (Membres de la catégorie de la famille et parents aidés)

IMM 1344 – Undertaking Serial No. IMM 1344 – N° de série de l'engagement d'aide	**U 089810**
File No. — Référence	**55555555**	Office — Bureau	**Toronto East**

1. Guarantor's Surname — Nom du garant
NORMAN

Given Names — Prénoms
BARRY LAWRENCE

2. Number of relatives you are now seeking to support or assist:
Nombre de parents que vous désirez aider ou aux besoins desquels vous désirez pourvoir: **2**

3. Number of family members (husband/wife and children) dependent upon you for support:
Nombre de membres de la catégorie de la famille (mari, femme et enfants) aux besoins desquels vous pourvoirez: **3**

4. Number of relatives (other than those in questions 2 & 3) for whom you have previously given a guarantee of support
Nombre de parents (autres que ceux visés aux 2 & 3) pour lesquels vous avez déjà donné une guarantie portant que vous pourvoirez à leurs besoins **0**

5. List below the names of those relatives included in questions 3 & 4 for whom you have previously given a guarantee of support.
Nommez ci-dessous les parents visés aux 3 & 4 pour lesquels vous avez déjà donné une guarantie portant que vous pourvoirez à leurs besoins.

A) **NONE**

B)

C)

D)

E)

F)

6. List total gross family income (for working family members, include only that portion of their income which is contributed directly to the operation of the household) — Specify whether amounts listed are weekly, monthly or yearly.
Indiquez le revenu brut de la famille (pour les membres actifs de la famille, n'indiquez que la partie de leur revenu qui contribue directement à payer les dépenses du ménage) — Précisez si les montants indiqués sont hebdomadaires, mensuels ou annuels.

7. List your debts and obligations – Specify whether amounts listed are weekly or yearly.
Énumérez vos dettes et obligations – Précisez si les montants indiqués sont hebdomadaires ou annuels.

		Amount Montant	Per Par	Nature of debt/obligation Nature de la dette et (ou) obligation	Amount Montant	Per Par
A)	Wages Salaires	☒ N/A OR S/O OU $ 32 000	yr		$	
B)	Self-employed earnings Gains : travailleur autonome	☐ N/A OR S/O OU				
C)	Rental Income Revenu provenant de loyers	☐ N/A OR S/O OU				
D)	Pension Income Revenu provenant de pensions	☐ N/A OR S/O OU				
E)	Spouse's Income Revenu du conjoint	☒ N/A OR S/O OU 18 000	yr			
F)	Family Allowance Allocations familiales	☒ N/A OR S/O OU 660	yr			
G)	Other (Specify) Autres (préciser) interest dividends	☐ N/A OR S/O OU 2 500	yr			

8. Name your occupation and, if applicable, your spouse's occupation
Indiquer votre profession et, s'il y a lieu, celle de votre conjoint

Guarantor Garant **Systems Analyst**

Spouse Conjoint **Legal secretary**

9. Employer's name (or name of company) — Nom de l'employeur ou de l'entreprise
Compusearch Canada Ltd.

Address No. and Street — Adresse (N° et rue)	City or Town — Ville	Province	Postal Code — Code postal	Telephone No. — N° de téléphone
347 Bay St.	Toronto	Ontario	M 5 R – 2 B 5	8 6 2 – 8 8 6 9

10. Guarantor's Comments — Observations du garant

11. I, Je, **BARRY LAWRENCE NORMAN**

(Name of guarantor) — (Nom du garant)

declare that the information I have provided above is accurate and correct to the best of my knowledge.
déclare par les présentes que les renseignements que j'ai donnés ci-dessus sont, au meilleur de ma connaissance, exacts.

Signature of Guarantor — Signature du garant

Signature of guarantor's spouse – if applicable
Signature du conjoint du garant – s'il y a lieu

Dated at Fait à ___ this , ce ___ day of jour de ___ 198___

12. Provincial endorsement (if applicable)
Approbation des autorisés provinciales (s'il y a lieu)

13. Signature of Immigration Officer
Signature de l'agent d'immigration

14. Comments of Immigration Officer — Observations de l'agent d'immigration

The information to be provided on this form is required for the purpose of determining, under the authority of the Immigration Act, 1976 and the regulations thereunder, your ability to guarantee support of your relatives, should they be granted landing in Canada, for the period indicated on the undertaking of assistance. For more details on uses and the rights for inspecting and correcting the information, refer to the Federal Information Bank Index available in Canada at Post Offices and most libraries.

Les renseignements qui devront figurer sur le présent formulaire visent à établir si, aux termes de la Loi sur l'immigration de 1976 et du règlement qui s'y rattache, vous serez en mesure de subvenir aux besoins de vos parents s'ils obtiennent la résidence permanente au Canada et ce, pendant la période indiquée sur l'engagement d'aide. Si vous désirez obtenir des précisions quant à l'utilisation des renseignements et au droit de les vérifier et de les corriger, veuillez consulter le catalogue des Banques fédérales de données que vous pouvez vous procurer au Canada dans les bureaux de Poste et la plupart des bibliothèques.

THIS FORM HAS BEEN ESTABLISHED BY THE MINISTER OF EMPLOYMENT AND IMMIGRATION
FORMULAIRE ÉTABLI PAR LE MINISTRE DE L'EMPLOI ET DE L'IMMIGRATION

IMM 1283 (4-82)

Canada

d. APPLYING FOR A FIANCE OR FIANCEE

A special word should be said concerning the sponsorship of a fiancé or fiancée. If you wish to sponsor a fiancé(e), both of you will be required to be legally capable of marrying at the date of the filing of your application. In addition, you must agree to marry within 90 days of your fiancé(e)'s arrival in Canada. If you do not marry within the 90 days, your fiancé(e) will be subject to loss of permanent resident status and removal from Canada. There can be no extension of the 90-day requirement.

Sample #4 shows the declaration each party to the marriage must sign. The sponsor will sign the form in Canada, and it will then be forwarded to the Canadian embassy or consulate abroad where the fiancé(e) will also be required to sign.

e. WHO ARE ASSISTED RELATIVES?

An "assisted relative" may be one of the following people:

(a) A son or daughter of the nominator of any age who is married or previously married or widowed

(b) A brother or a sister of the nominator

(c) A parent or grandparent of the nominator under 60 years old not widowed and able to work (where the nominator is a permanent resident living in Canada less than 3 years)

(d) A nephew, niece, uncle, aunt, or grandchild of the nominator

As in the case of the family class member, the application will also cover the immediate family of the assisted relative. This means a husband or wife and any unmarried sons or daughters.

The assisted relative category allows a Canadian citizen or permanent resident to assist in bringing their more distant relatives to Canada. As will be discussed

below, this advantage is not great and is, actually, almost non-existent.

f. OBLIGATIONS TO ASSISTED RELATIVES

It will be your obligation as a nominator to accept the responsibility for the accommodation, care, maintenance, and assistance in locating employment for your assisted relative, for a period of five years.

This means that your assisted relative will not be entitled to government welfare programs or similar government programs during the five-year period. Again, this prohibition does not apply to those programs such as unemployment insurance, the Canada Pension Plan, and workers' compensation if your nominated relative contributes to them. (See also g. below.)

g. APPLYING FOR AN ASSISTED RELATIVE

The Canadian government requires your assisted relative to go to the nearest Canadian embassy or consulate with an immigration division (see Appendix 1) and first apply as if he or she were an independent applicant (see chapter 6). If your relative is refused as an independent applicant, he or she will be assessed as an assisted relative *provided that he or she reveals your existence in Canada* to Canada's immigration officer overseas.

Your relative overseas must be told by you to list all his or her close relatives in Canada. If the immigration officer believes that your relative may succeed with your assistance, then a letter will be sent to your assisted relative telling him or her of this decision.

It is the responsibility of your relative to send this letter to you in Canada asking you to go to the Canada Immigration Centre nearest to you to complete an application for your assisted relative.

SAMPLE #4
DECLARATION OF INTENTION TO MARRY

 Employment and Immigration Canada   Emploi et Immigration Canada

DECLARATION OF INTENTION TO MARRY — *DÉCLARATION D'INTENTION DE MARIAGE*

Name of sponsor — *Nom du garant*	Name of fiancé(e) — *Nom du (ou de la) fiancé(e)*
BARRY GROOM	BRENDA BRIDE

PART 1: TO BE SIGNED BY SPONSOR

I, the above named sponsor do hereby declare that I am free to marry, and that if my fiancé(e), named above, is admitted to Canada our marriage will take place within ninety days of her/his arrival in Canada.

PARTIE 1: CETTE SECTION DEVRA ÊTRE SIGNÉE PAR LA GARANT

Je soussigné(e) déclare par les présentes que je suis libre de me marier et que si mon(ma) fiancé(e) est admis(e) au Canada notre mariage aura lieu dans les quatre-vingt-dix jours suivant son arrivée au Canada.

Barry Groom
Signature of sponsor — *Signature du garant*

Declared before me at _____Toronto_____

this __30th__ day of _November_ 19____.

Déclaré devant moi, à _____

ce _____ *jour de* _____ 19___.

_____
Immigration officer — *Agent d'immigration*

PART 2: TO BE SIGNED BY SPONSORED FIANCÉ(E)

I, the above named fiancé(e) do hereby declare that I am free to marry and that I am the fiancé(e) of the above named sponsor. I further declare that if I am admitted to Canada our marriage will take place within ninety days of my arrival in Canada.

I understand that if the marriage does not take place I may be liable to removal from Canada.

PARTIE 2: CETTE SECTION DEVRA ÊTRE SIGNÉE PAR LE (OU LA) FIANCÉ(E)

Je soussigné(e) déclare par les présentes que je suis libre de me marier et que je suis fiancé(e) à la personne précitée qui parraine mon admission. Je déclare aussi que si je suis admis(e) au Canada notre mariage aura lieu dans les quatre-vingt-dix jours suivant mon arrivée au Canada.

Je comprends parfaitement que si le mariage n'a pas lieu je peux être renvoyé(e) du Canada.

Brenda Bride
Signature of sponsored fiancé(e) — *Signature du (ou de la) fiancé(e)*

The above was interpreted to in her/his own language.

_____Brenda Bride_____
Name

Declared before me at _____Paris, France_____

this __26th__ day of _December_ 19___.

Ce qui précède a été interpréter dans sa langue à l'intention de

_____
Nom

Déclaré devant moi à _____

ce _____ *jour de* _____ 19___.

_____
Visa officer — *Préposé aux visas*

IMM. 243 (11-77)

16

The purpose of this policy is clearly to make it difficult for you to bring your assisted relative to Canada. In the past, you could initiate the process; now your relative must apply in writing, then go to the expense of travelling to the nearest embassy or consulate without first knowing whether or not you are prepared to assist or whether or not you will satisfy the financial requirements.

The application form for an assisted relative (see Sample #5) is the same as that used for the family class. It is also known as an Undertaking of Assistance, Immigration Form IMM #1344. You will also be required to provide all the information requested in the instructions (see Sample #1) for completing immigration applications: letter from employer, bank books, proof of relationship, passport or birth certificate, medical insurance, etc.

If you are self-employed, your last income tax return or a statement of income from an auditor will suffice.

You must also bring a list of any property you own and a list of any stocks, bonds, mortgages, or other valuables.

When you go to the office, you should be accompanied by your spouse, who will be required to sign the application as well. Again, Form #1344 (Sample #5) should not be signed until the interview, since it must be signed in front of, and witnessed by, an immigration officer.

As in the case of family class members, proof of relationship is required and in some situations this can be very difficult as outlined earlier in this chapter.

Your assisted relative will also be asked to complete Form IMM #8E (see Sample #8 in chapter 11). In addition, your relative will have to pass a medical examination and security check (see chapter 13).

Unlike the family class member, the assisted relative has to obtain a certain number of points on a reduced point system.

Compare the following short description of this reduced point system with the detailed explanation of the point system in chapter 9.

h. THE ASSISTED RELATIVE AND THE POINT SYSTEM

An assisted relative does not require the same number of points that an independent applicant does. Recent changes in the rules have resulted in brothers, sisters, and married children requiring only 55 points (a bonus of 15 for the undertaking) while the other assisted relatives need only 60 points (a 10-point bonus for the undertaking).

Of course, the assisted relative will obtain 10 or 15 bonus points for your undertaking of assistance and, therefore, must effectively obtain an additional 55 or 60 points. Sometimes this can be very difficult to accomplish because if no points are awarded for occupational demand, immigration is automatically disallowed. In my opinion, only those assisted relatives who have occupations included in the 116 job categories or those entering family businesses will have some hope of immigrating to Canada. You should refer to chapter 9 for an explanation of the criteria involved in each of the categories.

Two additional criteria are added to the requirements for both assisted relatives and most independent applicants.

First, your assisted relative will *not* be approved for immigration to Canada unless he or she obtains at least one point in the experience category. The only exception to this requirement is if your relative is trained in one of the very few designated occupations set by Employment Canada as being jobs for which there is such a large demand in Canada that there is no need for experience. (See chapter 9 for a full explanation of designated occupations and the experience factor.)

SAMPLE #5
UNDERTAKING OF ASSISTANCE FOR ASSISTED RELATIVES

Employment and
Immigration Canada

Emploi et
Immigration Canada

UNDERTAKING AND ASSISTANCE

U- 0090002

CANADIAN RESIDENT COMPLETES AREA WITHIN RED BORDER - PLEASE PRINT OR TYPE

SPONSOR / GUARANTOR (PLEASE SEE REVERSE)

FAMILY NAME	GIVEN NAMES		RESIDENTIAL ADDRESS (NO. AND STREET)	POSTAL CODE
NORMAN	BARRY	LAWRENCE	1 St. Albert Street	A 1 A 1 A 1

MAIDEN NAME		SEX [X] MALE [ ] FEMALE	CITY CALGARY	PROVINCE ALBERTA	TELEPHONE NO. 5 5 5 2 2 2 2

DATE OF BIRTH (D 2 5 M 0 1 Y 4 4)	COUNTRY OF BIRTH ENGLAND	CITIZEN OF CANADA	MARITAL STATUS [ ] NEVER MARRIED [X] MARRIED [ ] DIVORCED / [ ] ENGAGED [ ] SEPARATED [ ] WIDOWED

IF YOU WERE EVER ISSUED A CANADIAN IMMIGRANT VISA, COMPLETE THE FOLLOWING:

MY CANADIAN IMMIGRANT VISA WAS ISSUED AT (NAME OF OFFICE) LONDON U.K.	I BECAME A CANADIAN PERMANENT RESIDENT IN: M Y 1 2 7 2	MY NAME ON MY CANADIAN IMMIGRANT VISA WAS [X] SAME AS ABOVE OR

LIST PERSON YOU WISH TO ASSIST AND ALL OF HIS/HER ACCOMPANYING DEPENDANTS
NOTE: A DEPENDANT IS THAT PERSON'S SPOUSE AND/OR NEVER MARRIED SONS AND DAUGHTERS OF ANY AGE (INCLUDING THEIR NEVER MARRIED CHILDREN, IF ANY), USE SEPARATE SHEET IF NECESSARY.

FAMILY NAME	GIVEN NAMES	RELATIONSHIP TO SPONSOR/ GUARANTOR	DATE OF BIRTH D M Y	COUNTRY OF BIRTH	CITIZENSHIP	MARITAL STATUS
NORMAN	FRANK	BROTHER	1 6 0 8 4 5	England	U.K. & C.	Single

THE PRESENT COMPLETE MAILING ADDRESS OF PERSON(S) NAMED ABOVE IS:	I HAVE READ AND UNDERSTAND THE WARNING ON THE BACK OF THIS FORM.
10 SUNSET BLVD.,	I WILL PROVIDE OR ASSIST IN PROVIDING (AS REQUIRED) ADEQUATE LODGING, CARE AND MAINTENANCE TO THE ABOVE-NAMED PERSON(S) DURING THE PERIOD OF SETTLEMENT IN CANADA, AS DETERMINED BELOW BY THE IMMIGRATION OFFICER AND WHICH MAY BE FOR AS LONG AS 10 YEARS.
MANCHESTER	I WILL PROVIDE FINANCIAL ASSISTANCE TO THE ABOVE-NAMED PERSON(S) SO THAT SUCH PERSON(S) SHALL NOT REQUIRE FINANCIAL MAINTENANCE SUPPORT, INCLUDING SUBSIDIZED HOUSING, FROM ANY FEDERAL OR PROVINCIAL ASSISTANCE PROGRAM PRESCRIBED BY REGULATION UNDER THE IMMIGRATION ACT.

COUNTRY ENGLAND	TELEPHONE NO. 4 4 4 - 3 3 3 3	SIGNATURE OF SPONSOR/GUARANTOR	DATE
		SIGNATURE OF SPOUSE	DATE

OFFICIAL USE ONLY [ ] FAMILY CLASS [ ] ASSISTED RELATIVE

CIC	P/S CODE	CIC FILE NO.	SETTLEMENT ARRANGEMENTS:
			• MET FOR _____ PERSON(S)
		SIGNATURE OF IMMIGRATION OFFICER	• NOT APPLICABLE FOR _____ PERSON(S) / LENGTH OF UNDERTAKING _____ YEARS
COST RECOVERY CODE			PROCESSING OF APPLICATIONS AT _____ CURRENTLY TAKES
RECEIPT NO.		DATE SIGNED D M Y	A MINIMUM OF _____ DAYS
			INQUIRIES MAY DELAY THE PROCESSING OF YOUR RELATIVE'S APPLICATION. PLEASE CHECK WITH YOUR RELATIVE BEFORE CONTACTING YOUR LOCAL CANADA IMMIGRATION CENTRE FOR A PROGRESS REPORT.

THIS FORM HAS BEEN ESTABLISHED BY THE MINISTER OF EMPLOYMENT AND IMMIGRATION

IMM 1344 IP-P (06-88) E

Canadä

C.I.C. FILE   1

The government has also provided that if your relative's prospective employer states he or she will take a person without experience, you do not need the one point in experience; however, as soon as an employer makes such an admission the government is then able to fill the job with any unemployed Canadian of which there are many. In effect, you *must* get at least one point under the experience factor.

Second, your relative *must* obtain at least one point in the occupational demand category (see chapter 9).

The regulations also provide that Canada's immigration representative abroad, a visa officer, has a final overriding personal discretion (not reviewable in the courts) to reject anyone who obtains sufficient points and to accept anyone who does not obtain enough points.

As stated above, this final decision, in the case of an assisted relative, cannot be challenged in the courts. Only the Canadian citizen sponsor of a family class member who has been refused a visa may appeal to the Immigration Board and Refugee (see chapter 25).

The only possible method of bringing an assisted relative to Canada who does not have an approved job offer (see chapters 9 and 10) is by having your assisted relative join an already existing and established small family business in a position of trust (see chapter 7).

i. DEFINITIONS

The immigration regulations provide the following definitions of relatives as related to you, a nominator or sponsor.

(a) *Aunt* means a sister of your father or mother.

(b) *Brother* includes a half-brother who is a son of your father or mother.

(c) *Daughter* means a female who is the issue of the sponsor not adopted by someone else or adopted by you before she attains 13 years of age.

(d) *Nephew* means the son of a brother or sister of yours.

(e) *Niece* means the daughter of a brother or sister of yours.

(f) *Sister* includes a half-sister who is a daughter of your father or mother.

(g) *Son* means a male who is the issue of the sponsor not adopted by someone else or adopted by you before he attains 13 years of age.

(h) *Uncle* means a brother of your father or mother.

(i) *Unmarried* means that the person is not married and has never been married.

j. FINANCIAL REQUIREMENTS FOR FAMILY UNITS

Table #1 shows an approximate minimum income required by an individual and his or her spouse in order to sponsor a member of the family class or help an assisted relative. You should note that if you have previously given an undertaking of assistance (IMM #1344) for someone else, the total number of people sponsored will be used in calculating your minimum financial requirement. For example, if you are married with no children and brought your parents to Canada two years ago and now want to bring your brother, his wife, and one child to your family business in Toronto, you will be assessed under Column A for seven persons *not* for five because you are required to support yourself, your wife, your parents, and now the three new prospective immigrants — your brother, his wife, and child.

TABLE #1
MINIMUM INCOME FINANCIAL REQUIREMENTS FOR FAMILY UNITS

SIZE OF FAMILY UNIT	SIZE OF AREA OF RESIDENCE				
	A	B	C	D	E
	500 000 and over	100 000- 499 999	30 000- 99 999	Less than 30 000*	Rural areas
1 person	$11 569	$10 987	$10 307	$ 9 529	$ 8 555
2 persons	15 263	14 487	13 516	12 540	11 181
3 persons	20 418	19 348	18 083	16 821	14 972
4 persons	23 528	22 361	20 903	19 444	17 308
5 persons	27 417	25 960	24 209	22 556	20 127
6 persons	29 945	28 292	26 446	24 597	21 973
7 persons	32 960	31 209	29 168	27 125	24 209
FOR EACH ADDITIONAL PERSON	$ 2 800	$2 600	$ 2 500	$ 2 300	$ 2 000

*Includes non-metropolitan cities (with a population between 15 000 and 30 000) and small urban areas (under 15 000)

20

5
ADOPTIONS

Many people ask whether or not they can adopt a child and sponsor the child to Canada as a permanent resident in the family class category. Often the person wishes to adopt a niece, nephew, or cousin.

They are often disappointed, for the immigration regulations define an "adopted" person as any person adopted before his or her thirteenth birthday. Thus, in order to sponsor a child, the adoption must be completed before the child reaches the age of 13. Adoptions can take place either in Canada or overseas in the country of origin or residence of the child.

In Canada, adoption comes under the jurisdiction of the provinces. Each of the provinces has different laws and procedures relating to adoption. In general, however, adoptions will only be allowed when the child has been in the actual care of and supported by the prospective parents in their home for a period of time.

For instance, in Ontario, this time period is six months. Following this probationary period, there are investigations of the prospective parents' home by various agencies of the provincial government. A lawyer must first complete the necessary applications for the adoption. To obtain the final adoption order, a lawyer must appear in court before a judge with all the various reports from the government agencies.

The total procedure in Ontario averages 10 to 12 months. Following the final order of adoption, you will be allowed to apply for the immigration of your child as a family class member provided the child was adopted prior to his or her thirteenth birthday (see chapter 4).

Although the regulations of the Immigration Act define "adopted child" as one adopted prior to the age of 13 years, there is a legal argument to be made that this regulation is beyond the power of the federal government since under the Canadian constitution adoption of children in Canada is the responsibility of the provincial governments. Most provinces allow adoption of children prior to their eighteenth birthday.

This apparent conflict seems to be the result of a difference in priorities between the federal and provincial governments in Canada. The federal government is in charge of controlling immigration and appears to want to prevent immigration of adopted children older than 13; however, provincial governments are concerned with adoption and most of them allow adoption until the age of 18.

To my knowledge, this apparent conflict has never been completely tested in a Canadian court, and the question arises as to how the federal government can deny the relationship created by a *bona fide* adoption made anywhere in the world prior to the eighteenth birthday of the child (and perhaps even the twenty-first birthday of the child) if unmarried due to the definition of sponsored dependant (see chapter 4).

I know I would like to have a case someday of a child of 15 or 16 who has been properly adopted either in Canada or elsewhere who is denied admission as a family class member. The constitutional and legal arguments would be both intriguing and precedent setting.

What about the adoption itself? In Ontario, for instance, an adoption of just anyone you wish to adopt will not be approved by the authorities. You must prove, in the case of an older child, that the child has been your responsibility; that the parents are unknown or if known, have not cared for the child; and that there is no longer anyone to care for the child. Thus, for example, if you have a 10-year-old nephew who has lived with his parents all his life, you cannot adopt him just to get him into Canada.

Second, if you wish to adopt in Canada, the child must be present in the province where the adoption is to take place and be able to remain there for the long period of waiting for the final adoption order. You cannot adopt in a Canadian court a child who is not in Canada.

Of course, you can adopt a child outside of Canada depending on the laws of the country where the child was born. Recently, for example, several people of Jamaican origin who are Canadian citizens were able to adopt a child in Jamaica according to the laws of that country and bring the child back to Canada.

Provided that the Canadian and provincial authorities are satisfied with the adoption laws and proceedings in a foreign country, there appears to be no reason why children adopted in this manner could not immigrate to Canada as family class members. The problem in adopting outside of Canada is that there are as many laws as there are countries and states. However, most countries require that you be a resident or at least present in the country to adopt a child born there. This means leaving Canada — often for a considerable period of time — in order to comply with the foreign country's law. This is not always easy to do!

All the processing requirements concerning the adoption of children overseas may not apply to babies in some jurisdictions (e.g., the requirement for a home study). The major problem in the adoption of babies abroad is getting the baby to Canada quickly. Canadians and permanent residents adopting babies abroad do not want to wait the six to twelve months of processing until the baby receives an immigrant visa to Canada.

In addition, depending on the country, there may be the need to co-ordinate between provincial and federal authorities in Canada as well as the appropriate authorities in the country from which the baby is coming. It is impossible in this book to cover the rules and regulations concerning adoption for over 100 countries as well as 10 Canadian provinces and 2 territories. It has been my experience that if you are contemplating adopting a child or baby who has a Canadian immigration problem, you require the services of a lawyer who is knowledgeable in adoption in Canada and/or abroad as well as in Canadian immigration laws.

The immigration regulations also provide that you may sponsor as a member of the family class a child you *propose* to adopt (i.e., a child whom you have not as yet actually adopted). This is somewhat similar to the fiancé(e) situation in which you may sponsor for immigration someone you *intend* to marry.

Under this regulation, the child you propose to adopt *must* be under 13 years old and also be an orphan, abandoned by his or her parents, born out of wedlock and in the care of an agency, or placed with an agency for adoption. I seriously question whether or not this regulation could withstand a strong challenge in the Canadian courts. To date, to my knowledge, no extensive challenge has been made, which leads me to conclude that the immigration authorities are not refusing cases such as these if a court challenge is commenced or threatened.

The Immigration Section of the Canadian Bar Association has presented a brief to the Minister of Employment and Immigration about their concerns, both legal and moral, about the position taken by the federal government. In this presentation, the association urged the minister to allow children who are to be adopted to remain in Canada while their cases are being processed, which often is not the case since processing can take a year or longer. At the time of writing, the government had not as yet made any change in the regulation or the law other than to allow fathers to sponsor children born out of wedlock (see chapter 4).

In summary, while adoption is possible, it is not simple. In my experience, it is often done for orphan relatives or illegitimate children of Canadian citizens or permanent residents. Remember, though, that it will take at least nine months to complete the immigration procedures after adoption and a total of eighteen months to two years to complete both adoption and immigration.

6
INDEPENDENT APPLICANTS

An independent applicant for immigration to Canada is anyone who is not eligible for either the family class or assisted relative categories described in chapter 4. The independent applicants can be conveniently organized into the following groups:

(a) Independent workers based on skills

(b) Entrepreneurs

(c) Investors

(d) Self-employed

(e) Family business applications

(f) Retired

Chapter 7 deals with the entrepreneurial, self-employed, and family business categories. Chapter 8 deals with the investor category. This chapter describes the retired and all other independent applicants.

a. REQUIREMENTS FOR INDEPENDENT APPLICANTS

Independent applicants are required to apply at a Canadian embassy, consulate, or immigration office in either their homeland, their country of residence abroad, or in some country other than Canada where the applicant can remain if necessary while the application is being processed. For example, an Australian with a permit to work in the United States who wishes to immigrate to Canada as an independent applicant should be able to remain in the United States while the application is being processed.

You *must* apply from outside Canada. However, you should carefully read chapter 14 dealing with situations relating to the sponsorship of family class members only from inside Canada and chapter 17 dealing with refugees.

In order to be an independent applicant for immigration to Canada, you must be 18 years of age or older; you can be either male or female. You will be assessed on the nine areas detailed in chapter 9 and you will be required to obtain a minimum of 70 out of a possible 100 points. While you might think it will be easy to obtain 70 points, many people are surprised to find that they are just short of the required number — that they have somewhere between 60 and 69 units of assessment. You must read chapter 9 very carefully to understand the point system.

Independent applicants include anyone from a manual laborer to a company president, from a butcher to a doctor, from an engineer to a salesperson. Canada does not specifically categorize groups or quotas by occupation. If you do not fit into the family or assisted relative classes, you are an independent applicant.

The federal government, in consultation with the provinces, has set immigration levels at approximately 175 000 individuals in all categories for 1990. This number is a target, not a specific quota, and it may be exceeded or not met at all. It is an increase from 160 000 in 1989.

The regulations currently provide that immigrants to Canada shall be processed in the following orders of priority:

(a) Family class and convention refugees

(b) Entrepreneurs/investors

(c) Designated occupations

(d) Individuals with approved employment

(e) Self-employed and retired

(f) Independent applicants awarded more than 8 units of assessment under occupational demand in the point system

(g) Independent applicants awarded from four to eight units of assessment under occupational demand in the point system

(h) All other independent applicants

As you can see, the lowest priority is given to independent applicants. As outlined in chapters 9 and 10, an independent applicant must obtain an approved offer of employment in writing in advance or be a member of a designated occupation.

In my opinion, unless an independent applicant has such an approved offer or is in one of the 116 occupations currently in demand in Canada (see chapter 9 and Table #4), he or she stands almost no chance of final approval. Even if you have the necessary 70 points, you still will likely be rejected on discretionary grounds.

For all practical purposes, there is no appeal from such a rejection to any court or tribunal in Canada except as mentioned in chapter 26.

b. RETIRED PERSONS

The regulations define a retired person as an immigrant who is "at least 55 years old and does not intend to seek or accept employment in Canada." There has not been, as yet, much law or policy in this area. An individual who wishes to retire to Canada must show that he or she has sufficient funds to support himself or herself and any accompanying dependants (family class members — spouse and unmarried children).

There is no particular dollar amount set by law; however, a good rule of thumb would be a minimum income of $12 000 to $15 000 (Canadian) per person before taxes. This would require a minimum capital sum of approximately $300 000 to $500 000 depending on size of family or a combination of interest, investment, and pension income equivalent to that sum. Some people would argue that my figures are too high, but I believe them to be realistic and practical.

Remember, a retired person is saying to the government that he or she is capable of supporting himself or herself without any government assistance and without working. The cost of living in Canada is high and the rate of inflation is currently about 5% per year.

The key issue for the retired category is the requirement that the person have a *substantial connection* with Canada. This means family, close friends, business ties, or perhaps you went to school in Canada. Unless you have visited often and can prove close connections with Canada, you will not qualify in the retired category. Canada expects to take in between 2 000 and 3 000 only in this category in 1990.

Recently, a chartered accountant asked me whether or not a person who has entered Canada as a permanent resident in the retired person category is prohibited from taking employment subsequent to arrival.

After researching the law, I came to the conclusion that there is no such prohibition and a retired person can later take employment. My opinion is merely that — an opinion — and has not as yet been tested in a court of law.

c. THE APPLICANT'S FAMILY

The close family members of any independent applicant — spouse and unmarried children — are entitled to accompany the successful applicant to Canada.

Remember that the head of the family need not necessarily be the husband. If the

wife has an occupation which is on the list of 116 jobs in demand, which will obtain more points, or for which an approved offer of employment is more readily obtained, then the wife should make the application and not the husband.

7
ENTREPRENEURS, SELF-EMPLOYED, AND FAMILY BUSINESS APPLICATIONS

a. INTRODUCTION

Under the current legislation, a sophisticated selection and processing system has been established to determine which business people will be allowed to immigrate to Canada. This process, which is described below, almost necessitates hiring a lawyer and probably an accountant if you intend to use the entrepreneurial category to immigrate to Canada.

Entrepreneurs come to Canada because of its relative stability, its lack of violence, and its opportunities in the future for those who are prepared to work hard and long.

During 1981, almost 1 900 entrepreneurs and self-employed immigrants came to Canada bringing in excess of $400 million dollars. This number reached 2 200 by 1984, 3 700 in 1988, and is expected to be over 4 000 in 1990 (including investors).

The advantages to Canada of entrepreneurial immigration can easily be summarized:

(a) The establishment or expansion of businesses or industries and the creation or extension of job opportunities for Canadian citizens and permanent residents

(b) The expansion of general economic growth and development in the community or region through the "spin-off" effect of increased demand for products and services

(c) The visible testament to the general benefits to Canada of the immigration program particularly in times of employment difficulties.

The key aspect of Canada's attempt to encourage entrepreneurial immigration is the creation of new jobs or the maintenance of already existing jobs.

b. WHO IS AN ENTREPRENEUR?

The regulations of the Immigration Act define an entrepreneur as follows:

> "entrepreneur" means an immigrant
>
> (a) who intends and has the ability to establish, purchase or make a substantial investment in a business or commercial venture in Canada that will make a significant contribution to the economy and whereby employment opportunities will be created or continued in Canada for one or more Canadian citizens or permanent residents, other than the entrepreneur and his dependants, and
>
> (b) who intends and has the ability to provide active and on-going participation in the management of the business or commercial venture;

Note: The creation of only one job is virtually always insufficient to be classified as an entrepreneur (see below).

As you can see from this definition, a business person must "intend" and have the "ability" to establish or buy a business where he or she will employ at least one Canadian citizen or resident not including the entrepreneur or the family members who accompany him or her to Canada.

The Immigration Section of the Canadian Bar Association succeeded in having the old definition of entrepreneur changed from ownership of a "controlling interest" to a "substantial investment." There is as yet no definition of substantial investment, but practice seems to indicate that a minimum investment in excess of $150 000, purchasing an interest no smaller than perhaps 25% of a large company would meet the requirement.

c. CRITERIA FOR ENTREPRENEURS

While on the surface it appears that the federal government encourages the immigration of entrepreneurs to Canada, the process has become increasingly difficult and complex since 1981, and recent recommendations of a parliamentary sub-committee to increase entrepreneurial immigration from approximately 2 200 families per year to between 7 500 and 8 500 families per year have apparently been rejected by the current government in favor of a range of 4 000 to 5 000.

In my view, entrepreneurial immigration is a many-layered bureaucratic maze subject to the discretion of federal and provincial public servants.

The government recently released a long policy statement concerning potential entrepreneurial immigrants to Canada. This statement can be used to justify the acceptance or refusal of any potential entrepreneur.

Great emphasis will be placed on the background, expertise, and entrepreneurial spirit of the business immigrant. The visa officer overseas will be concerned with the applicant's proven track record in business, financial resources, and intent to participate actively in a business activity that contributes to significant economic development and the creation of jobs for Canadians.

Note: Care will be taken by Canadian officials to ensure that the source of the entrepreneur's funds is legitimate and that the funds are those of the entrepreneur and do not belong to some other individual.

Financial statements must be supported by accurate documentation: tax returns (personal and corporate), independent real estate evaluations, financial statements, and the like.

d. CATEGORIES OF ENTREPRENEURIAL ADMISSION

There are two categories or methods of immigrating to Canada as an entrepreneur: unconditional and conditional.

1. Unconditional landing

An unconditional immigrant visa means that permanent residence will be granted with no terms or conditions on the establishment of the entrepreneurial enterprise. This will occur following consultations between the visa officer and the provincial authorities and when the visa officer is fully satisfied and confident in the abilities of the entrepreneur and the province is satisfied about the viability and desirability of the business plan.

The unconditional landing will normally be granted only where the business is already in operation and the monies invested and committed.

2. Conditional admission

Conditional admission is granted when the applicant has a solid, verifiable business track record owning his or her own business and financial resources sufficient to carry out a range of activities but where there is no firm business the entrepreneur proposes to establish and no firm commitment behind any business plans.

A conditionally admitted entrepreneur receives permanent residence status conditional on him or her establishing a business in Canada within two years of receiving permanent residence status. The business must employ one or more Canadians or permanent residents who are not members of the entrepreneur's family, and must provide significant economic benefits to the province of destination.

If you fail to establish the business within two years, you will be subject to removal from Canada. Monitoring has been greatly increased recently and all entrepreneurs who have immigrated since 1987 are tracked in a new computer system. In Toronto, a business immigration office has been established to counsel, deal with, and especially monitor entrepreneurial and family business immigrants to confirm compliance with the law.

e. PRESENTATION OF YOUR BUSINESS PROPOSAL FOR PROVINCIAL APPROVAL

As an entrepreneur, you will be required to present your business proposal to both the federal immigration department and the appropriate provincial industry department for approval.

Presentations prepared in my office include a wide variety of information about the prospective business person, his or her background, training, ability, finances, and proposed business. In addition, in almost every situation, a Canadian or provincial corporation will have been established, materials and machinery may have been ordered, and a market study for the business and possible locations prepared.

All of this work is usually done in advance of the entrepreneurial immigrant actually receiving a visa to come to Canada. This is why a lawyer is almost always required by the prospective entrepreneur to prepare the presentation (often 40 to 50 pages in length), set up a company, deal with the normal legal problems of leases, and handle the myriad of laws that might apply to the business.

The business proposal is then submitted to the provincial authority that is responsible for reviewing all proposed entrepreneurial immigrants (see list in section g.). If you present your proposal to one

of Canada's offices abroad, it will be forwarded to the province where you intend to establish your business.

Our embassies and consulates have also been advised to assist you in selecting a province and area for your business. If your proposal is prepared in Canada, then your lawyer will submit it to the proper provincial office.

The provincial authorities will review the proposal and hear any submissions made in addition on your behalf.

Almost all the provincial authorities wish to interview the prospective entrepreneur, which will require a trip to Canada. Federal immigration officials overseas will also recommend an exploratory visit to Canada to meet with both federal and provincial officials. Where it is felt necessary, permission to work in Canada while establishing the business and getting it off the ground or when purchasing and expanding an existing business *may* be granted in rare circumstances to entrepreneurs but *not* usually to the self-employed.

The provincial authorities will then decide if your proposal is viable. That means they will decide, using all the information you have prepared, whether or not your business is likely to succeed. Whether the decision is in your favor or against you, this decision will be sent to the office to which you applied.

Note: About one and a half years ago, the Province of Ontario decided to stop requiring long business proposals in advance and to devote their resources to follow-up after the entrepreneur had arrived in Ontario. Today Ontario *will only approve conditional visas* in those areas of interest outlined in section g. Other provinces still require business proposals.

The final decision is that of the immigration officer who interviewed you abroad. He or she will be guided by a committee made up of federal trade and commerce officers and others, as well as by the provincial recommendation. If you have received a favorable report from the provincial authorities, it is unlikely you will be refused, but it can happen. Similarly, if you have received a negative report from the provincial authorities in Canada, you will likely be refused. There is no formal appeal in law from such a refusal.

It is, therefore, most important that your business proposal is complete, sophisticated, and accurately presented. The following is an example of an index from a typical entrepreneurial proposal prepared by my law firm, showing what should be included.

PROPOSAL INDEX

1. Letter from Gary L. Segal outlining the business proposal

2. Names and addresses of applicants

3. Proposals to establish and operate a private high school and heritage program

4. Location of project including an Agreement of Purchase and Sale

5. Background of applicants

6. Proposed cultural program

7. Approval from government authorities

8. Employment created

9. Survey of existing institutions

10. Financial information

11. Copies of applications for permanent residence of applicants

12. Proof of funds

Sample #6 represents examples of financial statements prepared in our office for the private high school project and for a car wash/gasoline station proposal. Financial statements similar to these should be included in proposals submitted by entrepreneurial applicants to provincial and federal authorities where required.

f. SELECTION CRITERIA AND FOLLOW-UP

If you apply as an entrepreneur, you will be required to obtain only 25 points out of a maximum of 80 points based on the following seven factors:

(a) Education (up to 12 points)

(b) Specific vocational preparation (up to 15 points)

(c) Experience (up to 8 points)

(d) Levels control (up to 10 points)

(e) Age (up to 10 points)

(f) English/French (up to 15 points)

(g) Personal suitability (up to 10 points)

Unlike relatives and independents, an entrepreneur does not have to obtain any points for pre-arranged employment or occupational demand.

In my opinion, if you are in good health and have obtained provincial and federal approval for your proposed business, you should have no difficulty in obtaining the necessary 25 points. (For a discussion of the point system, see chapter 9.)

Once you have arrived in Canada as a permanent resident/entrepreneur, you will likely be visited by a government official. If you are in Ontario, both a federal government representative *and* a provincial government official may visit you. In British Columbia and Quebec, you will be visited by a provincial official only, and in the other seven provinces, it will be a federal official.

If you have not carried out your plans, or substantially so, in the two years after your arrival, it is possible that your permanent resident status will be revoked and you will be ordered removed from Canada. Such a revocation of status could be appealed to the Immigration and Refugee Board (see chapter 25).

ENTREPRENEURIAL FINANCIAL PROPOSAL

THE PRO FORMA STATEMENT OF INCOME AND EXPENSES
FOR THE FIRST THREE YEARS OF OPERATION
OF THE PROPOSED PRIVATE SCHOOL
INCLUDING CULTURAL ENRICHMENT PROGRAM

	1ST YEAR	2ND YEAR	3RD YEAR
REVENUE	120	140	150
TUITION/STUDENT	@6 000	@6 400	@6 800
TUITION FEES	720 000	896 000	1 020 000
CULTURAL PROGRAM	@1 000	@1 100	@1 200
ACADEMIC FEES	120 000	154 000	180 000
TOTAL FEES	840 000	1 050 000	1 200 000

EXPENSES			
SALARIES—			
TEACHERS (6, 7, & 8)	240 000	308 000	384 000
PRINCIPAL	1 500 000	56 000	60 000
REGISTRAR	130 000	32 000	36 000
TEACHERS' CULTURAL PROGRAM (4, 5, & 6)	48 000	64 000	82 000
SECRETARY	120 000	22 000	24 000
CARETAKER	120 000	22 000	24 000
REALTY TAXES	26 000	28 000	30 000
UTILITIES	16 000	18 000	20 000
TELEPHONE & TELEGRAM	6 000	8 000	10 000
LEGAL & ACCOUNTING	20 000	22 000	24 000
PROMOTION & RECRUITMENT	10 000	10 000	12 000
OFFICE EXPENSES	40 000	42 000	44 000
SUPPLIES FOR CULTURAL PROGRAM	20 000	22 000	24 000
TOTAL EXPENSES	546 000	656 000	774 000
NET INCOME BEFORE INCOME TAX	294 000	394 000	426 000

CAR WASH/GAS BAR
PRO FORMA BALANCE SHEET
AS AT AUGUST 6, 198-

ASSETS

Cash on hand or in banks	$ 30 000.
Inventories	10 000.
Fixed assets	
Land	
Buildings	
Equipment	1 170 000.
Automobile	10 000.
Other	30 000.
Total Assets	**$1 250 000.**

LIABILITIES

Mortgage payable		
1st, due April 198-	$295 000.	
2nd, due Aug. 198-	300 000.	
3rd, due Oct. 198-	50 000.	
		645 000.

OWNER'S EQUITY

Mr. and Mrs. Clean	605 000.
Total Liabilities and Owner's Equity	**$1 250 000.**

CAR WASH/GAS BAR

CAPITAL REQUIREMENTS

The following expenditures are required to commence operations:

Legal — including land transfer tax, etc.	$ 25 000.
Equipment — including fixtures	
Land	
Building	1 170 000.
Automobile	10 000.
Working capital	20 000.
Reserve for contingencies	25 000.
TOTAL	$1 250 000.

To be financed by:
1st mortgage loan	$295 000.	
2nd mortgage loan	300 000.	
3rd mortgage loan	50 000.	
Owner's Capital		$ 645 000.
		605 000.
		$1 250 000.

CAR WASH
PROJECTED CASH FLOW
FOR THE YEAR ENDED JULY 31, 198-

	Quarter Year Ended Oct. 198-	Quarter Year Ended Jan. 198-	Quarter Year Ended April, 198-	Quarter Year Ended July 31, 198-	Total
RECEIPTS					
Sales					
— Car wash	$ 28 000.	$ 72 000.	$ 94 000.	$ 30 000.	$ 224 000.
— Contract	1 800.	1 800.	1 800.	1 800.	7 200.
— Wax sales	3 000.	7 500.	9 500.	3 000.	23 000.
— Gasoline	198 000.	223 000.	237 000.	263 000.	921 000.
Rental income	9 700.	10 200.	10 200.	10 200.	40 300.
Advances by owners	50 000.	—	—	—	50 000.
Mortgage loan	—	—	600 000.	—	600 000.
	$290 500.	$314 500.	$952 500.	$308 000.	$1 865 500.
DISBURSEMENTS					
Purchase					
— Gasoline	$182 000.	$205 000.	$218 500.	$242 000.	$ 847 500.
— Car wash supplies and materials	1 500.	2 500.	2 500.	1 500.	8 000.
Labor and employees' benefits	18 500.	26 000.	30 000.	21 000.	95 500.
Realty taxes	4 500.	4 500.	4 500.	4 500.	18 000.
Utilities	2 750.	6 000.	6 000.	3 000.	17 750.
Insurance	1 500.	1 500.	1 500.	1 500.	6 000.
Repairs and maintenance	500.	1 000.	1 000.	500.	3 000.
Licence and business tax	600.	600.	600.	600.	2 400.
Mortgage payments					
— Principal and interest 1st	9 000.	9 000.	303 000.	27 000.	348 000.
2nd	11 700.	11 700.	311 700.	—	335 100.
3rd	50 000.	—	—	—	50 000.
Legal and accounting	500.	500.	500.	500.	2 000.
Advertising and promotion	500.	500.	500.	500.	2 000.
Telephone	250.	250.	250.	250.	1 000.
General and office	250.	250.	250.	250.	1 000.
Management fee	3 000.	3 000.	3 000.	3 000.	12 000.
*Improvement — capital	10 000.	10 000.	10 000.	—	30 000.
	$297 050.	$282 300.	$893 800.	$306 100.	$1 779 250.
Excess or (deficiencies) before owner's drawing and income tax	(6 550.)	32 200.	58 700.	1 900.	86 250.
Accumulated excess — before owner's drawing and income taxes	(6 550.)	25 650.	84 350.	86 250.	

*One time capital expenditure for new paving, signage and painting if necessary will be covered by capital input by owner.

**CAR WASH/GAS BAR
PROJECTED INCOME STATEMENTS
FOR THE YEAR ENDED JULY 31, 198-**

REVENUE
  Sales
    — Car wash · · · · · · · · · · · · · · · · · $224 000.
    — Contract with metro police · · · 7 200.
    — Wax · 23 000.
    — Gasoline · · · · · · · · · · · · · · · · 921 000.
  Rental income · · · · · · · · · · · · · · · 40 300.

                                                    $1 215 500.

COST OF SALES
  Gasoline · · · · · · · · · · · · · · · · · · · $847 500.
  Wash supplies and materials · · · 8 000.
  Labor and employee benefits · · · 95 500.

                                                    951 000.

GROSS PROFIT · 264 500.

EXPENSES
  Advertising and promotion · · · · · $ 2 000.
  Management fee · · · · · · · · · · · · · 12 000.
  Interest · 88 000.
  Realty taxes · · · · · · · · · · · · · · · · 18 000.
  Utilities · 17 750.
  Insurance · · · · · · · · · · · · · · · · · · 6 000.
  Repairs and maintenance · · · · · · 3 000.
  Licence and business tax · · · · · · 2 400.
  Legal and accounting · · · · · · · · · 2 000.
  General and office · · · · · · · · · · · · 1 000.
  Telephone · · · · · · · · · · · · · · · · · · 1 000.

                                                    153 150.

NET PROFIT BEFORE DEPRECIATION · · · · · · $111 350.

g. SPECIFIC PROVINCIAL GUIDELINES

All the provinces have now established guidelines for entrepreneurs intending to establish business and reside in their provinces. These guidelines are in addition to the requirements established by federal legislation and are reproduced here.

1. Alberta

Alberta seeks to attract entrepreneurial immigrants with the necessary skill and investment to enter into active business ventures that will result in long-term job creation and economic benefits to the province. Alberta is most interested in proposals dealing with high technology (medical research, food processing, electronics, communications, software, etc.), manufacturing, and energy. Alberta will assist in expediting established business people in coming to Alberta on conditional visas; however, it will monitor them very closely.

2. British Columbia

Entrepreneurs and self-employed business people who have visas to establish their futures in British Columbia will be asked to initiate contact with the Ministry of Economic Development within six months of arrival. This will provide an opportunity for business counselling to aid in the successful establishment of the business and allow follow-up. Visa officers are asked to supply the ministry with the local addresses and estimated arrival dates of these successful applicants.

Entrepreneurs and self-employed people with more than $100 000 to invest in their projects should prepare and submit business proposals according to the format described earlier.

3. Manitoba

Manitoba actively promotes and encourages entrepreneurial proposals across the full spectrum of business investment activity and reviews the merits of each proposal on a case-by-case basis. Of special interest to the province are entrepreneurs proposing projects that will manufacture products or provide services with potential to replace imports or develop export markets; extend or introduce new technologies and engineering systems; upgrade or create new facilities in the manufacturing and tourism industries; or develop new or expanded business and commercial activity with emphasis on regional benefits in rural Manitoba.

Certain types of businesses in some urban areas have reached, or are approaching, the saturation point in the market. In these cases, unless there are unusual circumstances, the province is likely to decline support, or may encourage the prospective entrepreneur to consider a different location. Businesses in this category include, for example, grocery stores, gift shops, bakery shops, small restaurants, or travel agencies in Winnipeg.

4. New Brunswick

New Brunswick is primarily interested in advanced technology and small scale manufacturing industries. This includes entrepreneurs who would contribute to industrial craft production such as the manufacture of items that have a high artistic or design value and that are easily transported. Examples include glassware, high quality ceramic products, and, especially, steel production.

Also, tourist-oriented proposals are of interest to the province. Examples include accommodation and resort facilities and attraction products.

5. Newfoundland

Proposals under the following categories are considered:

(a) New manufacturing that meets at least one of these criteria: it uses primary resources; it replaces imports; it brings new technology; it produces an exportable product; or it relates to the needs of major capital projects such as oil and gas, fisheries, and marine-related equipment.

(b) Investment in existing manufacturing companies. The proposal should be a joint venture with existing management in order to strengthen existing companies by giving them access to new skills. It should also protect existing jobs or expand the employment base.

(c) Proposals that diversify the manufacturing base, such as high technology equipment or product manufacturing.

(d) The development of tourist facilities that will have a significant impact on a local region or community.

(e) Services related to the industrial base such as repair or overhaul of capital equipment or knowledge industries such as research and development.

Business proposals in other areas such as restaurants, retail stores, travel agencies, etc. are not encouraged except in selected circumstances.

6. Nova Scotia

Nova Scotia has a special interest in attracting manufacturing, high technology, and ocean-related business ventures, but it does not discourage the establishment of any promising business with the exception of small retail businesses in areas already well serviced.

7. Ontario

Ontario places business proposals from entrepreneurs in three categories and offers a different range of services to each category, as follows:

(a) Category A: Proposals that will create 25 or more jobs. Proposals in this category will be given top service. They will receive in-depth study by a senior committee within the Ontario Ministry of Industry and Trade and, if deemed viable, the ministry will follow up regularly with the entrepreneur during the pre-immigration process and do everything required to assist. The ministry will ensure all government services are available to assist the immigrant and spare no effort to ensure successful establishment of the venture.

(b) Category B: Proposals that will create 10 to 24 jobs. Proposals in this category will be granted limited assistance except in cases where the proposal has significant implications for a local economy.

(c) Category C: All other proposals. Proposals in this category will not receive assistance during the pre-immigration process and will be examined when time permits.

The ministry has upgraded its post-arrival services and, for this reason, has asked that posts be reminded of the necessity to advise the ministry of visa issuance and address or contact for entrepreneurs on arrival.

In line with its new policy of putting most of its efforts into monitoring and working with entrepreneurs after their arrival in Ontario on a conditional visa, Ontario sees no necessity to file a business proposal with this province prior to applying to immigrate at a Canadian visa office abroad. Ontario has asked the federal government to apply its rules for cash, track record, etc. and to give a conditional visa to the immigrant with a legal requirement that the entrepreneur report to provincial authorities within 30 days of arrival in Canada.

Ontario has indicated little or no interest in entrepreneurial proposals involving small retail or service businesses, franchises, import/export agencies, fast food outlets, investment companies, construction or land development projects, and distribution agencies.

8. Prince Edward Island

Prince Edward Island encourages firms that engage in food processing; manufacture equipment and supplies for agriculture, fisheries, and forestry; design and produce various crafts; provide professional services to off-shore industries; relate to the shipbuilding industry; produce wool yarn and woven cloth products; manufacture and develop high technology products; produce metal rolling, casting, and extruding projects; produce light metal products; complement a major veterinary college; or produce pharmaceuticals and health-related products.

9. Quebec

Offices overseas will submit cases involving entrepreneurs or self-employed workers who wish to settle in Quebec to the responsible office of the Services d'immigration du Quebec abroad. Canada Immigration Centre offices must submit cases involving self-employed workers and entrepreneurs who intend to settle in Quebec to the provincial ministry in Montreal. The ministry in Montreal will forward its views on each case to the responsible Canada Immigration Centre as quickly as possible. Acceptance by Quebec *will* result in federal approval, subject to medical and security clearance. See also chapter 15.

10. Saskatchewan

Saskatchewan is interested in projects that will manufacture products to replace imports or increase export potential, introduce new technology or expand existing technology, upgrade tourist facilities, or provide needed retail or service businesses in rural communities.

For a list of offices that offer publications relating to starting a business in Canada, see Appendix 5. For a list of the addresses of provincial government ministries or departments responsible for approving entrepreneurial applications, see Appendix 6.

h. WHO IS A SELF-EMPLOYED PERSON?

The "self-employed" person category includes an immigrant who intends and has the ability to establish a business in Canada that will create opportunities for employment in Canada for himself or herself and will make a significant contribution to the economy or the cultural or artistic life of Canada.

This category is intended to allow immigration of individuals who do not qualify as entrepreneurs or who are well known in the arts. This category also includes small business people, those intending to establish family businesses, and artists, and may include professionals such as doctors, engineers, and similar professionals who intend to establish their own businesses.

i. HOW DOES THE SELF-EMPLOYED DIFFER FROM AN ENTREPRENEUR?

The self-employed applicant is required to obtain 70 out of a possible 90 points on the 9 factors listed below (see chapter 9 for a detailed description of each factor) plus a 30-point bonus (see below).

(a) Education (up to 12 points)

(b) Specific vocational preparation (up to 15 points)

(c) Experience (up to 8 points)

(d) Occupational demand (up to 10 points)

(e) Levels control (up to 10 points)

(f) Age (up to 10 points)

(g) English/French (up to 15 points)

(h) Personal suitability (up to 10 points)

In addition, the regulation provides that the immigration officer has the discretion to award an additional 30 points to a self-employed independent applicant if he or she believes the prospective immigrant will be able to become successfully established in an occupation or business in Canada.

Since you will not likely be approved unless the officer believes you will successfully establish yourself, you really must obtain 40 out of 90 points plus the 30 points for being likely to succeed. In addition, unlike the entrepreneur, the self-employed applicant *must* obtain at least one point in experience. The entrepreneur has no such requirement.

The self-employed person will be required to make a presentation of his or her proposed business to the federal government immigration division and to the provincial authorities in the manner outlined for entrepreneurs. While the presentation might not be as extensive, all the same requirements exist, except that the self-employed's business will be smaller and, therefore, will require less initial capital — perhaps in the $150 000 to $200 000 range.

Professionals who wish to immigrate in the self-employed category will have to satisfy all licensing and training requirements prior to applying. This means you cannot intern or article or apprentice here in Canada and then apply. If your professional organization in Canada requires you to return to school or work for someone here before qualifying and licensing you, you will not normally be able to immigrate in the self-employed category.

j. FAMILY BUSINESSES — POSITION OF TRUST

In 1981, the Immigration Department instituted a special program for processing job offers given to relatives coming to work in family businesses in Canada. While the first program was experimental and was to expire in 1982, the program was in fact extended and has now become a permanent program within the Immigration Department.

At the present time, the program, as it appears in immigration policy manuals, is clearly defined as relating *only to those relatives who fit within the assisted relative class or the family class.*

The object of this program is to expand the opportunities for family reunification. Therefore, this small family business project should be seen as a means for members of the assisted relative class, who would otherwise not be able to obtain an approved job offer, to immigrate to Canada if they are joining a business already in existence run by their families in Canada.

In this program, the existence of available Canadian workers to do the particular job required in the family business is *not* the primary question. Rather, this project provides an opportunity for relatives in Canada to bring a family member to this country when it can be demonstrated that it is more sensible to employ a family member than someone else.

Overseas offices of immigration have been instructed that at least equal if not more weight should be given to family reunification than to whether or not other Canadians are available to do the work.

The unique and special feature of this program is that the relative from overseas must be going to a family business in a position of trust. Family members are usually more committed to the success of a business venture than are people who are not members of the family. In this situation only, normal job approval requirements as outlined in chapter 9 do *not* apply.

The processing of family business job offers will be conducted both overseas and in Canada. In Canada, the local Canada Immigration Centre will interview the Canadian relatives to determine that the person overseas falls within the family class or assisted relative definitions given in chapter 4. The local immigration office in Canada will also determine that the job offer made by the family business is legitimate and offers reasonable prospects of continuity, *that wages and working conditions being offered to the relative overseas are normal for the occupation in the area where the family business is located, and that the family business has been a viable operating business for a minimum period of one year prior to the application for the relative abroad.*

The only time that the one-year requirement will not be followed is where the job offer is associated with the expansion of an already existing business that is opening a new branch when the main operations has been in existence at least one year.

In addition, the nearest Canada Employment Centre may also be required to determine that the job offer to a relative is a logical and commonsense choice for the position; that is, it involves a position of trust, a close relationship, and a working environment that has unusual aspects such as long working hours.

The Canadian embassy or consulate where your relative applies for immigration has the responsibility to verify the relationship between you and your relative abroad and to determine through an interview that your relative has the work experience and aptitudes necessary to indicate that he or she could successfully fill the position in your family business in Canada.

The following are some situations where you would likely succeed in having your relatives join an already existing family business in Canada:

(a) You have a family business that you want your assisted relative to take over, to become a partner in, or to inherit upon your death.

(b) The family business in Canada is expanding by opening a new outlet or introducing a new product. Because it is a family business, a relative in whom you have trust is the logical person to assume the new responsibilities, which you cannot do because of the amount of work involved.

(c) The family business involves combinations of duties that, despite reasonable pay and conditions, are unattractive to many Canadian workers. This is likely to apply in the service-oriented fields such as small family restaurants, grocery stores, farms, etc.

Some of the situations in which you are *unlikely* to receive approval in this category are as follows:

(a) The job requires no special relationship of trust but seems designed only to facilitate entry to Canada.

(b) The job has nothing about it that makes a relative a commonsense choice.

(c) The relative to whom the job offer is made does not have and cannot reasonably be expected to acquire within a reasonable time the skills demanded for the job.

Note: In my opinion, at the present time, given the circumstances outlined earlier in this book, this is the only method by which an assisted relative can come to Canada unless that relative has sufficient job qualifications that he or she would be able to obtain an approved job offer without reliance on relatives in Canada.

8
THE INVESTOR CATEGORY

On January 1, 1986, the federal government announced the creation of a new category of business immigrant to be known as the "Investor." In addition, the government also announced that the new category was part of an attempt to increase the numbers of business persons immigrating to Canada yearly from approximately 2 200 in 1985 to 4 000 in 1986.

The old category of entrepreneur and of self-employed remained the same and the criteria regarding their immigration remained unchanged as outlined in chapter 7.

The move to entice new capital to Canada through immigration includes new promotional efforts on the part of several federal government departments including Investment Canada, the Canadian Employment and Immigration Commission, the Department of Regional and Industrial Expansion, the Department of State for External Affairs, and others.

At the time of writing the previous edition of this book, I predicted that the total of all business immigrants — entrepreneurs, investors, and self-employed — would not exceed 3 000 families in 1986 and that the government would be hard pressed to reach 4 000 such families in any year. I was correct and, in fact, total business immigration to Canada in 1985, 1986, and 1987 was 2 136, 2 404, and 3 602. In 1989 it was expected that the 4 000 business immigrant families would finally be reached for the first time. The investor component of this total was less than 25% or 1 000 families and while I predict it will grow over the next five years, I do not expect it to exceed one-third of the business immigrant total.

The investor category addressed the problem of individuals possessing significant resources who wished to immigrate to Canada but who did not wish to become involved in the day-to-day management of the business in which they invested or which they started in Canada. Often these individuals had investments and companies in a number of countries and were not prepared to give up these interests to participate on a near full-time basis in a business in Canada.

Other potential business immigrants have significant assets which they are prepared to invest in Canada in a business venture with others. Some of these potential investors might have little or no knowledge concerning the business and yet still be prepared to invest money in Canada. It was to entice just such individuals to Canada that the new investor category was created.

The investor category requires the potential immigrant to have operated, controlled, or directed a financially successful business or commercial undertaking, but does not require him or her to be actively involved in the management of the investment in Canada.

The investor must have acquired by his or her own endeavors a personal net worth of $500 000. This means that the young, 24-year-old second son of a wealthy Hong Kong family who is given $500 000 to come to Canada as an investor will *not* be approved since the money was not acquired by his own efforts. You *must* be able to trace the sources of these funds.

The investor must be prepared to make an *irrevocable* investment of at least $150 000, $250 000, or $500 000 for at least three years in a business, private investment syndicate, or government-managed capital venture fund.

This investment must result in the creation or continuation of employment for Canadians and the investor must have sufficient other funds to maintain himself or herself and family in Canada.

When writing the last edition just after the creation of the investor category, I predicted that there would be no government-run investment/venture capital funds under the program and no private venture capital funds and that only private single investment projects would be approved such as hotels, factory expansions, and the like. Boy, was I wrong!

Today there are probably between 300 and 400 venture capital funds of which approximately 50% are private venture capital funds pooling millions of dollars and investing like a mutual fund in various ventures. There is also one provincial Crown Corporation (soon to be two) owned and operated by a provincial government and hoping to raise $36 000 000 from 240 investor immigrants in its first phase.

The program has evolved dramatically in the past four years. The first year, 1986, was very slow especially until the autumn when regulations and definitions were published and the federal and provincial governments sorted out their respective responsibilities under the investor program.

In 1988 there were significant changes in both the program and in the levels of investment. At the outset, the investor/

immigrant had to have a net worth of $500 000 (Canadian) and be prepared to invest $250 000 *irrevocably* for a minimum of three years in a government-approved immigrant investor project. "Government approved" does *not* mean government guaranteed. It means a project approved for immigrant investors (i.e., if they put their money in and pass securities, medicals, and the like, they and their immediate families can immigrate to Canada).

All these investor projects involve *risk capital*. That means they have no guarantees (and can have none under federal law) that your money will be safe or returned at the end of three years. Nor is there any guarantee that there will be a market or purchaser for your shares in a venture capital fund or your interest in a hotel in Vancouver, Moncton, or Charlottetown.

In 1988, the six smaller, less prosperous provinces of Canada complained to the federal government that they were getting no investor projects in their provinces and these projects were all going to the four wealthier provinces — Ontario, Quebec, British Columbia, and Alberta — which was true. After months of negotiations and several federal/provincial meetings, a new structure was approved in which the six less prosperous provinces — Newfoundland, Nova Scotia, New Brunswick, Prince Edward Island, Manitoba, and Saskatchewan — would be permitted to approve investor projects in which the investment required would only need to be $150 000 (Canadian); the four wealthier provinces would still require a minimum investment of $250 000 and all investors in these two categories would continue to require a net worth of $500 000 earned by their own efforts.

In addition, a third level of investor was created, one who had a minimum net worth of $700 000 and was prepared to invest a minimum of $500 000 (Canadian) on an approved immigrant investor project *irrevocably for five years.* Such an investor would be permitted to be given a third party guarantee (i.e., from a bank or other financial institution) with respect to the return of their capital after the five years. Almost no investments of this size have been made to date probably since most people would rather risk $150 000 or $250 000 for three years than give up the use of $500 000 for five years.

Although projects under the new proposed rules have existed since the spring of 1988, the regulations creating these $150 000 projects are only now coming into force and in fact were proclaimed on January 22, 1990.

There has been a great deal of criticism in the press and otherwise of the investor program. People have been accused of buying permanent residence status and eventually Canadian citizenship. Some immigrants (and Canadians who have assisted them) under both this program and the entrepreneurial program have abused our laws and failed to open businesses or to live in Canada while having Canadian status. There have been accusations that some investor projects are extremely tenuous (risky) financially.

Others argue that the process of having to put your money up when you first apply to immigrate to Canada, waiting twelve or more months of processing your application until you receive your permanent residence visa, and waiting three to five years before being eligible to get your money back is far too long and convoluted. It is better, these critics argue, to come in as an entrepreneur with a conditional two-year visa because you do not have to open a business and employ Canadians until two years after your arrival here. You will be opening and controlling your own investment and not giving your money to people you do not know in highly risky ventures.

On the other hand, the investor need not start his or her own business or invest in an existing business and be prepared to work in it. The investor receives an *unconditional visa* and is a permanent resident without any conditions from the day of his or her arrival in Canada.

In my opinion, the investor category is appropriate for a select, small number of potential immigrants. They are people with significant assets (not merely $500 000); who do not want to start, own, or operate a business or a joint venture in Canada; who want an unconditional visa as soon as possible; who can afford to put $150 000 or $250 000 into a project and not worry about how successful it will be or how long it will take to get their investments or some percentage of it back in the future. For these persons, the investor program may be the best route to Canadian immigration. For others — be very cautious. Do not become an investor if you cannot afford the potential losses as well as profits.

9
THE POINT SYSTEM

Anyone may apply to come to Canada as an immigrant. You must apply at the Canadian embassy or consulate nearest to your home or place of residence.

Each applicant for admission to Canada as an independent applicant or an assisted relative is graded on a point system.

As you have read in chapters 4, 6, and 7, the number of points required and the various factors applicable to you depend on the category under which you are applying. Only independent applicants who are not entrepreneurs, investors, or self-employed have all nine categories applicable to them. You *must* remember, however, that the nine factors do not change under any circumstance — thus, the points for age or education are the same whether you are an assisted relative, entrepreneur, self-employed, or independent applicant.

On January 1, 1986, the point system was revised. The categories of location (5 points) and relatives (5 points) have been eliminated. The age factor has been changed, the points for English and/or French have been increased, and a new factor, "levels control," has been created. The most important change is that *an independent immigrant must now obtain 70 out of 100 points*.

a. EDUCATION

One unit of assessment (i.e., one point) will be awarded for each year of primary and secondary education successfully completed up to a maximum of twelve points.

Technically, these points are awarded on the basis of equivalent Canadian standards, and the official position is that you must not assume that a certain level of education in your country will be recognized in Canada. However, in practice, at least for the countries with a generally recognized acceptable level of education, you will be awarded points as though the two educational systems were equivalent.

For some idea of the Canadian equivalents, the Jamaican sixth standard would be grade 8 in Canada; the British "O" levels (nine papers) would be grade 12 in Canada; and the British "A" levels would be grade 13 in Ontario.

Unfortunately, some countries (especially India and Pakistan) offer university degrees that do not correspond with the equivalent levels at North American and European institutions. Care should be taken in these cases not to overvalue the points for education and training. A preliminary enquiry about the evaluation of your education at your nearest Canadian embassy or consulate would be a very helpful first step prior to completing and submitting your application.

b. SPECIFIC VOCATIONAL PREPARATION

Before attempting to explain this category, for which a maximum of 15 points may be awarded, I think it would be best to reproduce the actual regulation defining specific vocational preparation:

> To be measured by the amount of formal professional, vocational, apprenticeship

in-plant, or on-the-job training specified in the Canadian Classification and Directory of Occupations, printed under the authority of the Minister, as necessary to acquire the information, techniques and skills required for average performance in the occupation in which the applicant is assessed under item 4. Units of assessment shall be awarded as follows:

(a) when the amount of training required is less than thirty-one days, one unit;

(b) when the amount of training required is thirty-one days or more and less than three months, three units;

(c) when the amount of training required is three months or more and less than six months, five units;

(d) when the amount of training required is six months or more and less than twelve months, seven units;

(e) when the amount of training required is twelve months or more and less than two years, nine units;

(f) when the amount of training required is two years or more and less than four years, eleven units;

(g) when the amount of training required is four years or more and less than ten years, thirteen units; and

(h) when the amount of training required is ten years or more, fifteen units.

What this regulation is saying is that you will be awarded points on the basis of your training — the more training, the more points. The points are not awarded on the number of months or years of training you may actually have taken, but rather on the amount of time that would be spent on training for your occupation in Canada. The amount of time spent on training in Canada may be far shorter than that spent by you in your homeland.

As far as evaluating trade, technical, and professional certificates is concerned, their value depends on their acceptability or non-acceptability to the particular profession, society, or union under whose jurisdiction you hope to work. Most of these bodies are organized provincially, and so you have to tackle the particular one in your selected province. There are three ways of doing this.

If you have a friend or relative living in the same province (or even better, in the same city) where the governing body is located (you can find addresses through your nearest immigration office), you can send that person a list of your qualifications and have him or her follow it up for you. It is generally of no use writing directly yourself because foreign inquiries are often not answered.

Second, you can arrange an interview with an immigration officer who will give you a preliminary opinion on the acceptability and worth of your certificate. If it looks as if you have a reasonable chance of becoming a successful immigrant, he or she will provide you with follow-up information on ascertaining your status through the services of the immigration office.

Third, your trade organization, society, or professional body may have had past contacts with its foreign counterparts and may be able to advise you on your acceptability to them. You should inquire through your local organization.

c. EXPERIENCE

Up to a maximum of eight points will be awarded for experience in the occupation you are applying under, or, in the case of an entrepreneur/investor, for experience in the occupation that the entrepreneur is qualified for and is prepared to follow in Canada, as follows:

(a) when the specific vocational preparation time needed is less than three months, two units for the first year of experience;

(b) when the specific vocational preparation time needed is three months or more and less than twelve months, two units for each year of experience not exceeding two years;

45

(c) when the specific vocational preparation time needed is one year or more and less than four years, two units for each year of experience not exceeding three years; and

(d) when the specific vocational preparation time needed is four years or more, two units for each year of experience.

This category is based on middle-class, North American values which rate a professional more highly than an unskilled laborer. It is a demonstrated fact that, for example, a surgeon or lawyer with more than four years' experience will be given eight points under this category, while an unskilled laborer will be given only two points or maybe no points. This is an inequitable category since, in my opinion, the unskilled ditch digger or manual laborer is often equally — or even better — equipped to survive in Canadian society.

Be that as it may, a person who has received specific training in excess of four years will receive eight points in the experience category and either thirteen or fifteen points under the specific vocational preparation category.

If the experience category applies to you, YOU MUST OBTAIN AT LEAST ONE POINT IN THIS CATEGORY IN ORDER TO IMMIGRATE TO CANADA, OTHERWISE YOU WILL BE REFUSED.

d. OCCUPATIONAL DEMAND

On May 1, 1982, all occupational demand points for all job classifications were reduced to zero points.

On January 1, 1986, the federal government designated 100 job classifications that would have occupational demands of either 5 or 10 points. This list has been revised five times since then with the points going up and down. Many occupations have only 1 or 3 points for demand while some have 8 or 10 points. Also some occupations have been dropped from the list and others added to it. Some — such as Specialty Chefs — have been dropped and then come on again.

The most recent list came into effect on October 19, 1989, and appears as Table #4 at the end of this chapter. It contains 116 occupational categories out of a list of about 2 500. Ten occupations were added to this most recent list; 17 were dropped; 17 occupations had their points increased while 16 had their points decreased.

ALL OTHER JOB CLASSIFICATIONS WILL CONTINUE TO RECEIVE ZERO POINTS, WHICH IS AN AUTOMATIC BAR TO APPLYING TO IMMIGRATE TO CANADA UNLESS YOU HAVE AN APPROVED JOB OFFER; SEE **e.** BELOW.

The points for occupational demand are based on the demand for your occupation or skill in Canada. These points are changed every three or four months, depending on Canadian government surveys of current labor needs, both on a national and local basis.

Occupational demand is a very important category, not only because of the number of points involved, but also for the type of treatment you will receive at the immigration office. The policy is usually to encourage those with the desired skills and experience and to discourage applications from those with low-demand occupations. In fact, a person with a low-demand occupational category stands virtually no chance of being accepted, unless he or she has a pre-arranged job (see chapter 10 for a discussion of this) or a relative to sign an Undertaking of Assistance. Therefore, before bothering to complete the application, find out the demand for your particular skill or trade by referring to Table #4 or by arranging an appointment with an immigration officer, or by writing to an immigration office (see Appendix 2 for a list of addresses).

The application form only provides sufficient space to list one or perhaps two occupations. However, many people can do more than one job well. For example, one individual may have experience as an automobile mechanic, diesel engine mechanic, punch press operator, and draughtsman. You should be careful to list all possible occupations — on a separate sheet of paper if necessary — in order to provide the immigration officer with all the information necessary to make an assessment under this category.

It is important to provide complete details of all the work you can do because the points for occupational demand are given for *only one* occupation: you are entitled, however, to obtain the highest number of points allotted among the occupations you list under the section "Intended Occupation in Canada" on the application form (see Sample #8 in chapter 11).

The points for occupational demand are broken down into a great number of categories. It is possible that when you apply there may be little demand for automobile mechanics, but a great demand for heavy equipment, diesel mechanics. If you are qualified to do both jobs and list only one (the former), you would likely be rejected as a prospective immigrant to Canada.

The policy followed by immigration officials is to attach great significance to the applicant's employment possibilities in Canada. Therefore, the primary factor in determining the acceptability for an applicant is the existence of a written job offer from a Canadian company. Such an offer should be obtained by every applicant if possible; this includes assisted relatives but not family class members.

While written offers of employment on the prescribed form (see Sample #7 in chapter 10) can sometimes be obtained directly from companies in Canada or through immigration offices overseas offering employer contracts to immigrants, it is far more likely that you will have to obtain an offer of employment as a result of your own direct efforts. Here you should use the services of any relatives or friends you have in Canada to help you obtain a written job offer. (For more suggestions, see chapter 10.)

If you are employed in a high occupational demand area, you will have no trouble receiving an offer from a Canadian company, and many of them conduct interviews overseas. However, it is impossible to determine these high-demand areas in advance. For example, only a few years ago, engineers were very much in surplus and the demand from employers low. Later, the situation was somewhat reversed and certain industrial and technical engineers were in short supply. Your best bet is to check with your nearest immigration office regarding employment possibilities. Also, watch the want ads of your newspaper.

With the exception of entrepreneurs/investors, self-employed, and a family business job offer, if the occupational demand category applies to you, YOU MUST OBTAIN AT LEAST ONE POINT IN THIS CATEGORY IN ORDER TO IMMIGRATE TO CANADA, OTHERWISE YOU WILL BE REFUSED.

ALSO, PEOPLE IN THESE JOB CATEGORIES LISTED IN TABLE #4 ONLY WILL HAVE AN OPPORTUNITY TO IMMIGRATE TO CANADA WITHOUT AN APPROVED JOB OFFER.

e. ARRANGED EMPLOYMENT

Ten points will be awarded to you if you have a pre-arranged job, in writing, in Canada. This job must offer a reasonable prospect of being a permanent position based on information provided by the employment division of the Employment and Immigration Commission. In addition, it must be found that your employment will not adversely affect employment opportunities for Canadian citizens, and permanent residents already here, and that you meet all federal, provincial, and other (professional) licensing and regulatory requirements relating to your job.

This means that even if you have an offer in writing from a Canadian employer, you will not get 10 points unless the employment division decides that you are likely to maintain the job for a reasonable length of time. In addition, the employment division must declare that it is unable to find a qualified Canadian citizen or permanent resident to do the work that you have been offered.

Chapter 10 is devoted to the topic of employment clearance, and you should read it before awarding yourself 10 points under this category.

A large and complex bureaucratic process has now been established, and all immigration to Canada is controlled and determined in the first instance, not overseas in a Canadian consulate or embassy, but in a Canadian employment centre, where an official will either approve or disapprove the job offer.

f. DESIGNATED OCCUPATIONS

Similar to occupational demand, all designated occupations were "temporarily" abolished on April 30, 1982; therefore, *all* jobs are required to have approval (see chapter 10). I include this section on designated occupations for the day when they once again exist.

Designated occupations are determined by the Canadian government and change every couple of months or so. These are occupations for which there is a great demand in Canada and in which the government believes the prospective immigrant will not have any difficulty obtaining employment, and will, in fact, be eagerly sought out by Canadian employers. The list of "designated occupations" is not available to the public and is, in fact, a restricted document.

If you are in a designated occupation, you will receive high points on specific vocational preparation, occupational demand, and experience. If you are in a designated occupation, you will *not* require an approved job offer.

g. AGE

Ten points are assigned for applicants between the ages of 21 and 44 upon the date of application for immigration. If you are under 21 or over 44, 2 points will be subtracted for each year. Table #2 illustrates the number of points received for age. Remember, an independent applicant must be at least 18 years old.

TABLE #2
ALLOCATION OF POINTS FOR AGE

Age	Points
18	4
19	6
20	8
21-44	10
45	8
46	6
47	4
48	2
49 and over	0

h. KNOWLEDGE OF ENGLISH AND FRENCH

A maximum of 15 points is awarded for proficiency in both of Canada's official languages (English and French). In order to receive the maximum 15 points, you must be able to speak, read, and write fluently in both languages.

The following list outlines the points you will receive if your degree of proficiency to read, write, or speak is not perfectly fluent.

(a) Fifteen units of assessment will be awarded if you read, write, and speak fluently both English and French.

(b) Nine units of assessment will be awarded if you read, write, and speak fluently only one of English or French.

(c) Six units of assessment are available for the second official language you read, write, and speak fluently.

(d) If, in your first official language, you either read, and/or write, and/or speak only you will receive two points for what you do well (as opposed to what you do fluently) and one point for what you do with difficulty.

(e) If, in your second official language, you do something well you will receive one point, but zero points if you do it with difficulty.

Thus, for example, if you spoke and read English fluently and wrote it well you would receive 8 points (3 + 3 + 2), and if, as your second language, you spoke French well and read French fluently but wrote only with difficulty, you would receive 3 points (2 + 1 + 0) for a total of 11 out of 15 points.

You should expect to be tested in your ability to read, write, and speak Canada's two official languages.

i. PERSONAL SUITABILITY

Up to a maximum of 10 points is awarded for personal suitability by the immigration officer. This is based on the officer's assessment of your ability to adapt to the Canadian way of life, your motivation to succeed and work, your initiative, and your personality. This assessment will be made when the immigration officer interviews you.

The average number of points awarded for personal assessment is six or seven out of ten. It is not very often that an applicant will receive more than eight points.

j. LEVELS CONTROL

Levels control is a method that gives the government some leeway or discretion in the number of people immigrating to Canada. At present all persons will receive five points out of a maximum of ten. If after six months there are too many people coming to Canada (based on the current target of 175 000) the levels control figure will be reduced. Conversely it will be increased if the number of immigrants is too low.

k. BONUS POINTS

Bonus points will be awarded as follows:

(a) Ten bonus points if you are in the assisted relative category and the relative assisting you is your aunt, uncle, niece, or nephew

(b) Fifteen bonus points if you are in the assisted relative category and the relative in Canada assisting you is your mother, father, brother, or sister

(c) Forty-five bonus points if you are approved as an entrepreneur

(d) Forty-five bonus points if you are approved as an investor

(e) Thirty bonus points if you are approved as self-employed.

l. HOW POINTS ARE ALLOCATED

Table #3 shows how points could be allocated to four people with varying backgrounds.

Even if you get more than 70 points as an independent applicant, it does not mean you will automatically be allowed to immigrate to Canada. The immigration officer has discretion to accept people who have less than 70 points or deny those with more than 70 points.

However, if you have less than 70 points and you are not sponsored or assisted, you should try to increase your points before applying. You can do this by improving your English or French, or especially by taking school courses in the evening in order to upgrade your qualifications, or by obtaining qualifications in areas of employment needed in Canada.

This point system makes it very difficult for prospective immigrants to come to Canada. Not only are approved offers of employment or assisted relative undertakings a virtual necessity, but also the discretionary rejection of even otherwise approved applicants is high. It is my understanding that the final approval rate in some countries is as low as 1% or 2% of all independent and assisted applicants and that even in highly industrialized western Europe, the approval rate today is around 25%.

In summary, while Canada is now taking more immigrants, the demand to come here is *very* high and Canada will continue to choose only the most highly skilled workers in demand to fulfil our immigration requirements along with close family members such as spouses, parents, and never-married children.

TABLE #3
SAMPLE ALLOCATION OF POINTS FOR ALL FACTORS

Maximum points	Category	APPLICANT A Stenographer, dicta-typist, legal secretary. High school, grade 12, 2-year legal secretary course. Age 25. Assisted relative offer in writing. Four years' experience.	APPLICANT B Dye tool machinist. Public school, 5 years' apprenticeship. Age 38. Approved job offer.	APPLICANT C Public school teacher, university degree (B.A.), 4 years' professional training, bilingual. Age 30. Assisted relative offer in writing not approved.	APPLICANT D Electrical engineer. University degree (B.Ch.E.). Age 45. No offer of employment.
		Applicants			
		A	B	C	D
12	Education	12	12	12	12
10	Occupational demand	5	5	0	1
15	Specific vocational preparation	9	11	11	13
10	Approved job offer	0	10	0	0
8	Experience	6	6	6	8
10	Age	10	10	10	8
15 (9+6)	English and/or French	9	9	15	9
10	Personal suitability	7	6	8	7
10	Levels control*	5	5	5	5
100	SUBTOTAL	63	74.	67	63
	BONUS POINTS				
10	Assisted relative	10	0	10	0
45	Entrepreneur	0	0	0	0
45	Investor	0	0	0	0
30	Self-employed	0	0	0	0
	TOTAL	73	74	77	63
		Accepted	Accepted	Refused	Refused
				Did not receive at least 1 point for occupational demand.	Did not obtain 70 points. Might be approved if prepared to go to an area where he can obtain approved job offer.

* Levels control currently set at 5 points for everyone as of January, 1990. It can be changed at any time by the government.

51

TABLE #4
POINTS DESIGNATED FOR JOB CATEGORIES

Note: Occupations on the list can be removed at any time by the government; similarly new occupations can be added to the list. Points can be increased or decreased at any time. Consult Canada Immigration to determine if there have been any changes. This list is accurate as of the date of publication.

MANAGERIAL & ADMINISTRATIVE OCCUPATIONS	POINTS
Managerial, natural sciences, engineering & mathematics	1
Managers, social sciences	10
Administrators, medicine & health	10
Financial management occupations	5
Personnel & industrial management occupations	3
Sales & advertising management occupations	1
Purchasing management occupations	3
Services management occupations	1
Production management occupations	1
Management, construction operations	1
Transport & communications operations, management operations	1
Financial officers	1
Organizational & methods analysts	5
Personnel management occupations	5
Industrial, commercial purchasing officers	5
Inspectors & regulatory officers non-government	10
OCCUPATIONS IN NATURAL SCIENCE, ENGINEERING & MATHEMATICS	
Chemists	1
Geologists and related occupations	1
Physicists	1
Meteorologists	1
Physical science technologists	1
Agriculturalists & related scientists	1
Biologists & related scientists	1
Life science tech.	1
Architects	1
Chemical engineers	1
Civil engineers	1
Electrical engineers	1
Industrial engineers	1
Mechanical engineers	1
Metallurgical engineers	1
Mining engineers	1
Petroleum engineers	1
Aerospace engineers	1
Nuclear engineers	1
Draughtpersons	1
Architectural & engineering technologists	1
Statisticians & actuaries	1
Systems analysts	1
OCCUPATIONS IN SOCIAL SCIENCES	
Economists	1
Psychologists	5

TABLE #4 — Continued

Social workers	10
Occupations in welfare & community services	10
Librarians, archivists & conservators	5
OCCUPATIONS IN MEDICINE & HEALTH	
Veterinarians	1
Non-supervisory graduate nurses	10
Physiotherapists & other therapists	10
Pharmacists	8
Dieticians & nutritionists	1
Optometrists	10
Dispensing opticians	10
Radiological technicians	5
Medical laboratory technologists	5
Denturists & dental technicians & hygienists	10
Other occupations in medicine & health	10
ARTISTIC, LITERARY, PERFORMING ARTS OCCUPATIONS	
Product & interior designers	1
Advertising & illustrating artists	5
Publication writers & editors	1
ACCOUNT RECORDING OCCUPATIONS	
Executive & specialized secretaries	5
Production co-ordinators	1
Claim adjusters & service representatives	8
SALES OCCUPATIONS	
Scientific & technical commodities salespersons/advisors	1
Manufacturing & pharmaceutical commercial salespersons	1
Group insurance representatives	3
Appraisers & business valuators	10
Securities salespersons	5
Advertising salespersons	8
Buyers, wholesale & retail trade	1
SERVICES OCCUPATIONS	
Fire fighting occupations	10
Police agents & investigators, private	8
Chefs & cooks	5
Funeral directors, embalmers & related occupations	10
PROCESSING OCCUPATIONS	
Metal smelting, converting & refining occupations	10
Moulding & metal casting occupations	10
Metal processing inspectors	10
Forming occupations: clay, glass, stone	10
Chemical distilling & carbonizing occupations	10
Cellulose pulp preparing occupations	10
Papermaking & finishing occupations	10

TABLE #4 — Continued

MACHINING OCCUPATIONS	
Tool & die making occupations	5
Machinists & machine tool occupations	5
Inspecting & testing occupations, metal machining	8
Forging occupations	10
Mould & pattern makers	5
PRODUCT FABRICATING & ASSEMBLING OCCUPATIONS	
Industrial machinery fabrication and assembly occupations	5
Metal products — inspectors	10
Precision instruments fabrication and assembly occupations	5
Electrical equipment fabricating & assembly	10
Electrical repairing & installation occupations	1
Other electronic repairing & installation	1
Electronic equipment inspectors	8
Electronic equipment repairers	1
Pattern making	5
Upholsterers	5
Motor vehicle mech. & repair	5
Aircraft mechanics & repairers	1
Industrial machinery mechanics	5
Business machine repairs	8
Inspecting & testing occupations, equipment repair	5
Watch & clock repairs	1
Precision instrument installers & repair	5
Paper product fabricating & assembly	10
ELECTRICAL POWER, LIGHTING, COMMUNICATIONS OCCUPATIONS	
Power linemen/women	10
Communications equipment installers and repairers	1
Inspectors — electrical power	5
TRANSPORT EQUIPMENT OPERATION OCCUPATIONS	
Air pilots, flight officers, & flight engineers	1
Deck officers	1
Engineer officers, ship	1
OTHER EQUIPMENT OPERATING OCCUPATIONS	
Printing press occupations	1
Printing — engraving occupations	10
Electrical power plant operators	10
Stationary engine operators	1
Water purification — plant operators	10
Pump & pipeline equipment operators	10
Broadcasting equipment operators	10
Audio video	3

10
OBTAINING EMPLOYMENT APPROVAL

As mentioned in chapter 9, the requirement for approved employment applies to both the independent applicant and the assisted relative but *not* to the family class members or the 116 job categories currently in Table #4. As I have stated previously, immigration to Canada is tied directly to the needs of Canada's labor market. Since Canada has been experiencing moderate unemployment for the past four years or so, the flow of immigration to Canada has been increased by government action since 1986.

The major step in this process is the law requiring that each applicant in the independent and assisted categories be approved by the employment division of the Employment and Immigration Commission. While in theory, failure to have such approval only means receiving fewer points, in fact and in practice, failure to have such approval will result in your rejection for immigration to Canada *unless your job is listed in Table #4.*

a. EXCEPTIONS TO THE RULE

The only exceptions to the above rule are people in the 116 job categories (see Table #4), entrepreneurs, investors, self-employed people, and people destined to family businesses. The entrepreneur, family business, and self-employed categories were dealt with in chapter 7. You will recall that those who are self-employed are able to receive 30 additional points if the interviewing immigration officer believes they will settle successfully in Canada. Investors were dealt with in chapter 8.

b. WHAT DOES EMPLOYMENT CANADA DO?

What is required to obtain employment approval and what exactly is it? The employment division of the Employment and Immigration Commission has the task of helping Canadian citizens and permanent residents find employment. It tries to match employers and jobs with people who are looking for work. Employment Canada has been given the additional task of approving or disapproving the job offers made by Canadian employers to prospective immigrants overseas.

This means that Employment Canada is required to look first for qualified Canadians or permanent residents who are available and willing to do the work offered by the Canadian employer to the prospective immigrant overseas. If such people are located by them, then the offer of employment will not be approved. Conversely, if no suitable Canadian or permanent resident is found, then the offer of employment will likely be approved.

c. HOW TO APPLY FOR EMPLOYMENT APPROVAL, AND DIFFICULTIES YOU WILL ENCOUNTER

In order to obtain approval for the job you have been offered, your future employer (who may be a relative of yours) will be required to submit an application to the nearest Canadian Employment Centre (see Sample #7). The prospective employer must complete this form when requesting job clearance for an immigrant or for a non-immigrant who wants a temporary work visa (see chapter 21).

The form, called a Confirmation of Offer of Employment and sometimes referred to by its number, #2151, requires detailed information concerning the job, including wage, vacations, benefits, accommodation, and details of the job and licensing requirements, if any.

The key to obtaining approval is providing a very detailed job description. Obtaining Employment Canada approval means showing the unique requirements of the job and why the person overseas fits the requirements.

This form must be filled out and signed by the employer. The government has made it very difficult to obtain the form by refusing to mail it out and by requiring the employer to come personally to the local employment office to pick it up. In addition, the employer is not allowed to remove the form from the premises but has to sit there and complete it. (This is meant to harass the Canadian employers of prospective immigrants overseas. An employer cannot type the form up, nor is it easy to prepare additions and further explanations if he or she wishes to attach them to Form #2151.)

In my opinion this procedure is aimed at discouraging Canadian employers from hiring overseas. As a prospective immigrant, you would be well advised to tell the person who offers you a job what will have to be done *in advance*. If you do not, your prospective employer might stop the necessary efforts on your behalf when he or she finds out what is required.

The basic problem you will encounter, of course, is that, unless you have very special qualifications, most prospective employers will not wait the nine to twelve months or more necessary for you to be processed (in some countries, such as Hong Kong and India, it will be more than two years).

As indicated, the employer will have to go to Employment Canada and fill out the form there. He or she should take the following information on a separate typed or neatly printed sheet:

(a) All the job benefits

(b) A complete job description giving exact particulars of the job

(c) Any special requirements to do the job including foreign expertise, languages, and the like

(d) Efforts taken to locate suitable Canadians to do the job including copies of newspaper or other advertisements

(e) Efforts to train and promote qualified Canadians already working for the employer and future plans to do so.

Some lawyers will prepare a lengthy submission (20 to 25 pages) for the employer outlining all the above aspects of the job being offered and the attempts to locate suitable Canadians.

After the form has been filed with Employment Canada, that government body will attempt to find qualified and available Canadians or landed immigrants to fill the job. The search will take place first locally and if unsuccessful, provincially, and in some cases even nationally.

Normally, Employment Canada will require that the job offer be circulated by them across Canada for a minimum of eight to twelve weeks. Your prospective employer will be required to place the job order with Employment Canada and interview *all* prospective Canadian and permanent residents who apply for the position that has been offered to you. In addition, your prospective employer will likely be required by the Canadian government to go to the expense of advertising the job offer nationally by way of advertisements in selected Canadian publications. This requirement will be quite expensive

CONFIRMATION OF OFFER OF EMPLOYMENT

NB. THIS DOCUMENT DOES NOT AUTHORIZE THE PROSPECTIVE EMPLOYEE TO ENTER, REMAIN IN OR TAKE EMPLOYMENT IN CANADA SUBJECT TO THE APPROVAL OF AN IMMIGRATION OFFICER AN APPROPRIATE IMMIGRATION DOCUMENT MAY BE ISSUED

NOTA. LE PRÉSENT DOCUMENT N'AUTORISE PAS L'EMPLOYÉ ÉVENTUEL À ENTRER OU À DEMEURER AU CANADA OU À Y OCCUPER UN EMPLOI SOUS RÉSERVE DE L'APPROBATION D'UN AGENT D'IMMIGRATION, UN DOCUMENT APPROPRIÉ RELATIF À L'IMMIGRATION PEUT ÊTRE DÉLIVRÉ

1 IMMIGRATION DOCUMENTS TO BE PROCESSED AT (CIC OR E & I POST CONCERNED) LES DOCUMENTS RELATIFS À L'IMMIGRATION DOIVENT ÊTRE ÉTUDIÉS AUX ENDROITS SUIVANTS (DANS UN CIC OU AU BUREAU COMPÉTENT DE E & I)

A NAME / NOM

I EMPLOYER - EMPLOYEUR

A NAME OF COMPANY OR INDIVIDUAL - NOM DE LA SOCIÉTÉ OU DE L'INTÉRESSÉ: INTERNATIONAL WIDGETS LTD

B RCT NO. - RCI-N° DE L'EMPLOYEUR: ACB 999999

C SIC-CAE

D STREET - RUE: 123 JONES STREET

E CITY - VILLE: WINNIPEG

F. PROVINCE: MANITOBA

G TELEPHONE - TÉLÉPHONE AREA - IND RÉG: 204 123 4567

H POSTAL CODE / CODE POSTAL: Z1P 0G0

II FOREIGN WORKER - TRAVAILLEUR ÉTRANGER

A COMPLETE NAME OF INDIVIDUAL OR GROUP TO WHOM EMPLOYMENT IS OFFERED NOM DE L'INTÉRESSÉ OU DU GROUPE AUQUEL L'EMPLOI EST OFFERT: FREDERICK FOREIGNER

B IF GROUP, HOW MANY? S'IL S'AGIT D'UN GROUPE COMBIEN Y A-T-IL DE MEMBRES?

C STREET - RUE: 15 LONDON STREET

D CITY - VILLE: PLYMOUTH

E COUNTRY - PAYS: UNITED KINGDOM

F. DATE OF BIRTH / DATE DE NAISSANCE: D-J 16 M 06 Y-A 51

G SEX - SEXE: ☒ MALE / HOMME ☐ FEMALE / FEMME

III OFFER OF EMPLOYMENT - OFFRE D'EMPLOI

A JOB TITLE - TITRE DE L'EMPLOI: DIE & TOOL MAKER

B CCDO - CCDP

C LOCATION OF EMPLOYMENT - LIEU DE L'EMPLOI: WINNIPEG, MANITOBA

D NAME OF CEC SERVING THIS LOCATION - NOM DU CEC DESSERVANT CETTE LOCALITÉ: WINNIPEG CENTRAL

E CEC CODE / CODE DU CEC

F JOB DESCRIPTION - DESCRIPTION DES FONCTIONS:

Require a journeyman die and tool maker with a minimum apprenticeship of five years and five years' experience on large lathes and presses.

G JOB REQUIREMENTS (EDUCATION, OFFICIAL LANGUAGE REQUIREMENTS, EXPERIENCE, LICENCES, ETC...) EXIGENCES DE L'EMPLOI (ÉTUDE, EXIGENCES CONCERNANT LES LANGUES OFFICIELLES, EXPÉRIENCE, LICENCES, ETC...):

Must be able to speak English. Must have experience in automotive and heavy equipment (bulldozers) die and tool work. Minimum of 10 years' experience including apprenticeship.

H WAGES AND WORKING CONDITIONS (DETAILS) - SALAIRE ET CONDITIONS DE TRAVAIL (PRÉCISEZ):

Forty hours per week. $10.50 per hour. One-half of medical, hospital, life insurance, and dental plan paid by company. Two weeks' vacation per year, three weeks after four years.

I POSITION - EMPLOI: ☒ PERMANENT

J ☐ TEMPORARY / TEMPORAIRE   IF TEMPORARY: DURATION: SI TEMPORAIRE: DURÉE:

K EMPLOYMENT OFFER OPEN UNTIL / OFFRE VALIDE JUSQU'AU: D-J 15 M 02 Y-A 8-

L TYPE OF FORM / GENRE DE FORMULAIRE: ☒ NEW / NOUVEAU ☐ RENEWAL / RENOUVELLEMENT

ORIGINAL SERIAL NO / N° DE SÉRIE INITIAL

M CERTIFICATION / ATTESTATION

I CERTIFY THAT THE ABOVE INFORMATION IS ACCURATE AND I AFFIRM THAT THE OFFER OF EMPLOYMENT DOES NOT CONFLICT WITH ANY EXISTING COLLECTIVE AGREEMENTS, AND THERE IS NO LABOUR DISPUTE IN PROGRESS AT THIS TIME.

JE CERTIFIE QUE LES RENSEIGNEMENTS CI-DESSUS SONT EXACTS QUE L'OFFRE D'EMPLOI NE VA À L'ENCONTRE D'AUCUNE CONVENTION COLLECTIVE EN VIGUEUR ET QU'IL N'Y A ACTUELLEMENT AUCUN CONFLIT DE TRAVAIL CHEZ L'EMPLOYEUR CONCERNÉ.

SIGNATURE: *John Smith*

TITLE - TITRE: Personnel Manager

DATE: D-J 15 M 11 Y-A 8-

IV CERTIFICATION - ATTESTATION

A ☐ IMMIGRANT

B ☐ TEMPORARY WORKER / TRAVAILLEUR TEMPORAIRE   DURATION OF AUTHORIZED EMPLOYMENT / DURÉE DE L'EMPLOI AUTORISÉ

C I HAVE EXAMINED THIS FOREIGN WORKER REQUEST AND AM OF THE OPINION THAT THE EMPLOYMENT OF THIS FOREIGN WORKER BY THIS EMPLOYER UNDER THE CONDITIONS STATED ABOVE, WILL NOT ADVERSELY AFFECT EMPLOYMENT OPPORTUNITIES FOR CANADIAN CITIZENS OR PERMANENT RESIDENTS IN CANADA

J'AI EXAMINÉ CETTE DEMANDE DE TRAVAILLEUR ÉTRANGER ET JE SUIS D'AVIS QUE L'EMPLOI OFFERT PAR CET EMPLOYEUR SUIVANT LES CONDITIONS PRÉCITÉES NE NUIRA PAS À CELUI DES CITOYENS CANADIENS OU DES RÉSIDENTS PERMANENTS AU CANADA

D CEC NAME - NOM DU CEC

E CODE

F EMPLOYMENT OFFICER'S SIGNATURE / SIGNATURE DE L'AGENT D'EMPLOI   D-J M Y-A

MP 2151 (2-79)

and often mitigates against employers hiring foreign workers.

Do not expect, however, that your prospective Canadian employer can merely refuse to hire the qualified people found or sent by Employment Canada. Refusals to employ such people and insistence on the overseas person being the only person the employer will hire usually result in a refusal by the government to approve the job offer. This is especially so where your future employer is a relative or friend.

As was stated earlier, employment approval is required both for applicants for permanent resident status and for those non-immigrant visitors who are seeking temporary work permits.

Once you have received employment approval, it will be sent overseas to the Canadian consulate or embassy where you applied. Sometimes (but only sometimes) at the discretion of Employment Canada, approval may be sought by the employer prior to your making your application.

Usually, however, employment approval should be sought by your future employer simultaneously with your application, and you should state in a letter with your application that your future employer is seeking approval.

Approval, if you get it, can take from eight weeks to four months; thus, the total average time for immigrating to Canada has been substantially increased since the overseas offices will not begin to process your application until they have received the approved employment clearance form.

Note: Let it be clearly understood that without job approval from Employment Canada it is unlikely that you will be given a visa to come to Canada as an immigrant unless you are on the list of 116 occupations in demand or are an entrepreneur, investor, or destined to a family business.

11
APPLYING TO IMMIGRATE

a. WHERE AND HOW TO APPLY

Applications for permanent residence in Canada can be obtained from Canadian embassies, consulates, or immigration offices overseas or from the Canada Employment and Immigration Commission — Immigration Branch, Ottawa, Ontario, Canada. All applications for independent applicants must be made overseas in these offices. In Appendix 1, you will find a list of most of the cities throughout the world that have either a Canadian embassy or a consulate located there. In Appendix 2 is a list of all of Canada's embassies and consulates that have an immigration section, the countries or counties (states) they are responsible for, and their addresses.

Upon request, most offices will send you the pre-application questionnaire to be completed and, if you pass pre-screening, will forward to you the regular Application Form IMM #8E (see Sample #8).

Most offices, when they send you an application form, will request that you complete it and send it along with your supporting documentation to them. After assessing the documentation, they will ask you in for an interview. Some offices — usually those in areas with problems such as Iran, Syria, Lebanon, and parts of Central America — will have different procedures.

Whatever procedure is followed at the office where you apply, follow their instructions carefully, and be sure to bring all the documents that are applicable to your situation. In addition to the documents listed in section b., you must bring your passport or other travel documents to the interview.

Following your interview and assessment, you will be notified, usually in writing, if you have been rejected or accepted. If accepted, you can move on to the next step, which is the medical and security clearance (see chapter 13).

Generally, if you are in a high-demand employment category, the whole procedure will be completed in eight to ten months. Regular applications can often take about twice this time. The waiting period will vary, however, depending on the number of people applying at the particular time and the embassy or consulate at which you are applying. Check with your local immigration office for a more definite estimate.

If you have been rejected, you will not be told why, other than that you have not satisfied the "norms of assessment," that is, you have not obtained enough points or you have not complied with the approved employment requirements (see chapter 10). If you are rejected, you should try to determine from the immigration authorities what areas under the point system you could improve upon in order to obtain the necessary points and make an application at a future date.

If you are a family class member and are rejected, your sponsor in Canada may have the right of appeal to the Immigration and Refugee Board in Canada (see chapter 25). In such a case, your sponsor should contact a Canadian lawyer familiar with immigration law.

SAMPLE #8
APPLICATION FOR PERMANENT RESIDENCE

◆ Employment and   **Emploi et**
Immigration Canada   **Immigration Canada**

APPLICATION FOR PERMANENT RESIDENCE
IN CANADA

● FOR OFFICE USE ONLY ●
OFFICE FILE NUMBER (OR IMM 1341 CASE LABEL)

1   MY SURNAME (FAMILY NAME) IS:
FRIENDLY   MY FIRST NAME IS: JOHN   MY MIDDLE NAME IS: MURRAY

2   OTHER NAMES I HAVE USED ARE: (INCLUDE MAIDEN NAME IF APPLICABLE)
None

3   SEX   [X] MALE   [ ] FEMALE

4   MY DATE AND PLACE OF BIRTH (SHOW CITY AND COUNTRY) ARE:
DAY 11   MONTH April   YEAR 1951   Bristol, England

5   I AM A CITIZEN OF
United Kingdom

6   MY PRESENT ADDRESS IS:
18 Sommerset Drive
Liverpool, England

MY TELEPHONE NUMBER IS: ▶

7   MY MAILING ADDRESS IS:
[ ] SAME AS IN QUESTION 6 OR:
Same as above

8   I HAVE RESIDED IN COUNTRY OF PRESENT RESIDENCE
[X] SINCE BIRTH   [ ] FOR _____ MONTHS

9   MY PRESENT MARITAL STATUS   (IF MORE THAN ONE APPLIES, PLEASE INDICATE EG. DIVORCED BUT NOW ENGAGED)
[ ] UNMARRIED (NEVER MARRIED)   [ ] ANNULLED   [ ] ENGAGED   [X] MARRIED   [ ] WIDOWED   [ ] SEPARATED   [ ] DIVORCED

10   DATE AND PLACE OF MARRIAGE
DAY 1   MONTH March   YEAR 1975   Newcastle, England

11   I HAVE BEEN MARRIED MORE THAN ONCE
[ ] YES   [X] NO   IF "YES" STATE NUMBER OF TIMES ▶

12   MY PRESENT OCCUPATION IS:
Die Setter

13   MY INTENDED OCCUPATION IN CANADA IS:
Die Setter

14   I DO NOT INTEND TO WORK IN CANADA N/A [ ]

15   I ATTACH A COPY OF A JOB OFFER [X] YES   [ ] NO

16   WORK HISTORY: DURING THE PAST TEN YEARS I HAVE WORKED FOR THE FOLLOWING EMPLOYERS

DATES FROM (MONTH - YEAR)	TO (MONTH - YEAR)	NAME AND LOCATION OF INSTITUTION	SPECIFY YOUR OCCUPATION	GROSS MONTHLY EARNINGS
Feb 1969	Present	Wm. H. Howard Ltd., Bristol, England	Die Setter	$2200.00

17   THE FOLLOWING PERSON OR EMPLOYER IN CANADA HAS OFFERED TO ASSIST ME AFTER MY ARRIVAL (NAME AND ADDRESS)
John Doe
1 Cameron Drive
Calgary, Alberta   Z1P 0G0

18   RELATIONSHIP TO ME OF PERSON NAMED IN 17
Employer and friend

19   DESTINATION IN CANADA
NAME OF CITY / TOWN   Calgary   PROVINCE   Alberta

20   THE NAME AND ADDRESS OF MY CLOSEST RELATIVE OUTSIDE CANADA IS:
Mrs. Daphne Friendly
25 Cambridge Street
Bristol, England

RELATIONSHIP TO ME OF PERSON NAMED ABOVE   Mother

21   THE NAME AND ADDRESS OF MY CLOSEST RELATIVE (IF ANY) IN CANADA IS:
NONE

RELATIONSHIP TO ME OF PERSON NAMED ABOVE

22   INDICATE YOUR ABILITY IN CANADA'S OFFICIAL LANGUAGES ▶

	ENGLISH			FRENCH		
SPEAK	[X] WELL	[ ] WITH DIFFICULTY	[ ] NOT AT ALL	SPEAK [ ] WELL	[ ] WITH DIFFICULTY	[X] NOT AT ALL
READ	[X] WELL	[ ] WITH DIFFICULTY	[ ] NOT AT ALL	READ [ ] WELL	[ ] WITH DIFFICULTY	[X] NOT AT ALL
WRITE	[X] WELL	[ ] WITH DIFFICULTY	[ ] NOT AT ALL	WRITE [ ] WELL	[ ] WITH DIFFICULTY	[X] NOT AT ALL

IMM. 0008E(05-87)   This form has been established by the Minister of Employment and Immigration

Canada

23		
WHAT IS YOUR NATIVE LANGUAGE? English	24 EDUCATION - I HAVE SUCCESSFULLY COMPLETED	

24				
	8	YEARS OF ELEMENTARY PRIMARY SCHOOL		YEARS OF SECONDARY HIGH SCHOOL
		YEARS OF UNIVERSITY / COLLEGE	**3**	YEARS OF FORMAL APPRENTICESHIP / TRAINING

25 DETAILS OF MY EDUCATION ARE AS FOLLOWS

DATES FROM MONTH - YEAR	TO MONTH - YEAR	NAME AND LOCATION OF INSTITUTION (INCLUDING APPRENTICESHIP)	TYPE OF INSTITUTION	TYPE AND DATE OF CERTIFICATE OR DIPLOMA ISSUED
Sept 57	Jun 65	Bristol Primary School, Bristol	Primary School	Leaving 06/65
Jan 66	Jan 69	Apprentice		

26 IF I AM PERMITTED TO GO TO CANADA I WILL

PERSONAL BELONGINGS

A ARRIVE WITH THE FOLLOWING ASSETS	MONEY (STATE AMOUNT)	OTHER (SPECIFY)
- IN MY POSSESSION	$15,000	$25,500.00
- ALREADY IN CANADA		

B LEAVE BEHIND TO TRANSFER AT A LATER DATE	TRANSFERABLE PENSION $150.00 MONTHLY	MONEY (STATE AMOUNT) NIL	PROPERTY (VALUE) NIL

C LEAVE BEHIND LEGAL OBLIGATIONS OR DEBTS OWING TO: (NAME OF PERSON(S) OR ORGANIZATION(S)
NIL

TOTAL DEBTS (STATE AMOUNT) NIL

27 PERSONAL DETAILS OF MY SPOUSE (ITEM A) AND ALL MY CHILDREN UNDER AGE 21

	FAMILY NAME	FIRST NAME	SECOND NAME	TOWN COUNTRY AND DATE OF BIRTH	RELATIONSHIP TO ME	CITIZENSHIP	TO ACCOMPANY ME TO CANADA
A	FRIENDLY	Sara	Louise	Newcastle	Wife	U.K.	[X] YES [ ] NO
B	FRIENDLY	Michael	John	Liverpool	Son	U.K.	[X] YES [ ] NO
C	FRIENDLY	Mary	Daughter	Liverpool	Daughter	U.K.	[X] YES [ ] NO
D							[ ] YES [ ] NO
E							[ ] YES [ ] NO
F							[ ] YES [ ] NO
G							[ ] YES [ ] NO
H							[ ] YES [ ] NO
I							[ ] YES [ ] NO
J							[ ] YES [ ] NO

28

	DATE OF BIRTH DAY MO YEAR	CITY, TOWN AND COUNTRY OF BIRTH	PRESENT ADDRESS IN FULL (IF DECEASED GIVE DATE)
FATHER'S FULL NAME David Friendly	01 11 21	Newcastle, England	25 Cambridge St. Bristol, U.K.
MOTHER'S FULL NAME BEFORE MARRIAGE Daphne Wells	12 04 21	Edinburgh, Scotland	25 Cambridge St. Bristol, U.K.

29 DURING THE PAST 10 YEARS I HAVE LIVED AT THE FOLLOWING ADDRESSES

DATES FROM MONTH - YEAR	TO MONTH - YEAR	STREET AND NUMBER	CITY OR TOWN	COUNTRY
Mar 73	Mar 75	88 Erskine Court	Bristol	England
Mar 75	Nov 81	3131 Queensway Avenue	Bristol	England
Nov 81	Present	18 Somerset Drive	Liverpool	England

30 SINCE MY 18TH BIRTHDAY, I WAS (OR STILL AM) A MEMBER OF, OR ASSOCIATED WITH THE FOLLOWING POLITICAL, SOCIAL, YOUTH, STUDENT OR VOCATIONAL ORGANIZATIONS (INCLUDING TRADE UNIONS AND PROFESSIONAL ASSOCIATIONS)

DATES FROM MONTH - YEAR	TO MONTH - YEAR	NAME AND ADDRESS OF ORGANIZATION	TYPE OF ORGANIZATION	POSITION HELD (IF ANY)
01 71	Present	Die Setters International Alliance	Trade Union	Member

31 HAVE YOU OR HAS ANY ONE OF THE PERSONS IN QUESTION **27** EVER: (ANSWER "YES" OR "NO")

A	HAD OR BEEN TREATED FOR ANY PHYSICAL OR MENTAL DISORDERS?	NO	F	BEEN REFUSED ADMISSION TO, OR ORDERED TO LEAVE CANADA OR ANY OTHER COUNTRY? — NO
B	SUFFERED FROM ANY COMMUNICABLE OR CHRONIC DISEASES?	NO	G	APPLIED PREVIOUSLY FOR AND/OR BEEN REFUSED A VISA TO CANADA OR ANY OTHER COUNTRY? — NO
C	BEEN CONVICTED OF OR CURRENTLY CHARGED WITH ANY CRIME OR OFFENCE IN ANY COUNTRY?	NO	H	APPLIED PREVIOUSLY FOR A CANADIAN SOCIAL INSURANCE NUMBER? — NO
D	APPLIED PREVIOUSLY FOR ADMISSION TO CANADA?	NO	I	RESIDED IN ANOTHER COUNTRY, OTHER THAN AS A TOURIST? — NO
E	VISITED CANADA?	NO		

IF THE ANSWER TO ANY OF THE ABOVE IS "YES", ATTACH A SEPARATE SHEET. IN THE CASE OF 'E' ABOVE, SPECIFY LOCATIONS IN CANADA, DATES AND PURPOSE OF VISIT.

32 PASSPORT DETAILS FOR MYSELF (PRINCIPAL APPLICANT) AND FOR PERSONS LISTED IN QUESTION **27**

	FIRST NAME	PASSPORT NUMBER	COUNTRY	DATE OF ISSUE	DATE OF EXPIRY	IDENTITY CARD NO
	PRINCIPAL APPLICANT	XY 999555	United Kingdom	June 1, 198-	June 1, 199-	N/A
A.	Sara	AC 189991	United Kingdom	May 3, 198-	May 3, 199-	N/A
B.	Michael	WX 299229	United Kingdom	July 4, 198-	July 4, 199-	N/A
C.	Mary	AC 189991	United Kingdom	May 3, 198-	May 3, 199-	N/A
D.						
E.						
F.						
G.						
H.						
I.						
J.						

SAMPLE #8 — Continued

33 I WISH TO LEAVE FOR CANADA WHEN PROCESSING OF THIS APPLICATION IS COMPLETED ☐ OR

IN THE MONTH OF_____ 19_____

34 AUTHORITY TO DISCLOSE PERSONAL INFORMATION AND SOLEMN DECLARATION

I, __John Murray Friendly__, hereby authorize all governmental authorities, including the Department of Defence, all

police, judicial and state authorities in __United Kingdom__ to release to the Canadian Immigration authorities all records and information that they may possess on my behalf concerning any investigations, arrests, charges, trials, convictions and sentences. I understand that this information will be used to assist in evaluating my suitability for admission to Canada, or any other reason, pursuant to Canadian Immigration Legislation.

I understand that, having applied for permanent residence in Canada, I (and my family) may be required to undergo a medical examination, and I therefore consent to the release of all particulars concerning the medical condition of myself (and my family if applicable), as may be relevant to my admission to Canada, to the following:

       Immigration and Visa Officers; authorities of Health & Welfare Canada and the province of my destination; my prospective employer in Canada; my relatives in Canada; the Immigration Appeal Board and other judicial bodies.

I also understand and agree that

- any false statements or concealment of a material fact may result in my permanent exclusion from Canada, and even though I should be admitted to Canada for permanent residence, a fraudulent entry on this application could be grounds for my prosecution and / or removal from Canada; and
- should my answers to questions 9, 27 and 31 change at any time prior to my departure for Canada, I must report such change and delay my departure until I have been informed in writing, by the office dealing with my application, that I may proceed to Canada.

I further declare that

- I understand all the foregoing statements, having asked for and obtained an explanation on every point which was not clear to me; and
- the information I have given in this application is truthful, complete and correct, and I make this solemn declaration conscientiously believing it to be true and knowing that it is of the same force and effect as if made under oath.

Declared before me at_____ this _____ day of _____ 19_____

_____   _____
SIGNATURE OF THE OFFICER OF THE GOVERNMENT OF CANADA   SIGNATURE OF THE APPLICANT

35 INTERPRETER DECLARATION

I,_____, do solemnly declare that I have faithfully and accurately interpreted in the

_____language the content of this application and any related forms as duly completed with

respect to _____, as well as the content of item 34 (Authority to Disclose Personal Information and Solemn Declaration), to the person concerned. I have been informed by the person concerned, and I do verily believe, that he / she completely understands the nature and effect of these forms, and I make this solemn declaration conscientiously believing it to be true and knowing that it is of the same force and effect as if made under oath.

_____   _____
(SIGNATURE OF INTERPRETER)   (DATE)

36 TWO INDIVIDUAL PASSPORT SIZE PHOTOGRAPHS OF YOURSELF AND OF EACH DEPENDANT ACCOMPANYING YOU TO CANADA MUST BE ATTACHED IN THIS SPACE.

b. PRE-SCREENING

Most of Canada's immigration offices abroad now use a pre-application questionnaire to pre-screen applicants. This form is very important since most applicants *do not* get past this pre-screening process and merely receive a rejection letter.

This pre-screening process is usually carried out by a local employee of the embassy or consulate and you may never receive an application form or be reviewed by one of the senior immigration officials abroad. Therefore, you must give all possible details on this pre-application form. *Remember,* if there is not enough room, attach a separate sheet with details. Include a copy of any job offer in writing with this pre-application form.

You should include with your application form *certified copies of documentation* which will aid in the processing of your application. (Failure to include these documents will only delay the processing of your application.) These include the following:

(a) All school certificates, diplomas, and degrees

(b) Transcripts of school marks

(c) All trade certificates of apprenticeship records

(d) Memberships in professional institutes or bodies

(e) Your marriage certificate

(f) Your birth certificate

(g) Letters of reference from past employers

(h) Character references from people such as your priest, minister, or rabbi

(i) Offers of employment in Canada (see chapter 9)

(j) Certified divorce certificate or separation papers if applicable

(k) Original police certificate of character from the police of your homeland and any place where you have lived for more than six months in the past ten years

(l) Proof of assets—bank books, stocks, bonds, deeds for property, etc.

(m) Your passport

All the above documents, except the police certificate, should be certified copies since they will not be returned to you. Keep the originals and take them with you to the interview.

c. COMPLETING THE APPLICATION FORM

The application for permanent residence in Canada is known as Form IMM #8E and is four pages long (see Sample #8).

If the prospective immigrant to Canada is married, the form should be completed by the head of the family and details of the occupation and training of a working spouse should be given on a separate attached sheet of paper. As was stated in chapter 6 concerning independent applicants, the head of the family need not necessarily be the husband. The head of the family should be the spouse whose occupation is most needed in Canada such as a registered nurse.

There are 36 questions in the application form, and all of them must be completed. If a particular question does not apply to you (e.g., where it asks the names of your spouse and children and you are single), simply fill in the words "not applicable."

Remember, a great number of people will have to read this form, so, if possible, use a typewriter when completing it. The psychological effect of a neat, typewritten, well-prepared and completed application form cannot be over-emphasized.

Remember also that you will be required to declare that the information given in the application form is true and that such a declaration is equivalent to an oath. If at a future time it is discovered that you deliberately lied on the application form, you could lose your immigrant status in

Canada and be deported to your homeland.

The following explanations of some of the questions on the form (see Sample #8) indicate the information the Canadian authorities are often seeking:

Question 1:

Your family name means your last name or surname. If you come from a country which does not use Latin characters, such as Japan, China, or India, all of your names should be written both in Latin characters phonetically and in the characters of your homeland.

Question 2:

If you are a married woman, you should put your maiden name here; for example, a woman whose married name is Joan Elizabeth Smith but whose maiden name was Brown would put "Joan Elizabeth Brown" in Box #2.

If you have used any other names during your lifetime, these should also be included in Box #2. This could happen in the case of an adopted child or a person who had legally changed his or her name. If there is not enough space in Box #2, put the information on a separate sheet and attach it to the application.

Question 3:

You should put an "X" in the box that applies to you.

Question 5:

Your citizenship should be the country in which you are currently a citizen and not your place of birth unless they are the same. If you are a stateless person, write the word "stateless."

Question 6:

Your present address should be the place where you normally live and not the place where you might currently be on a temporary basis. For example, a graduate student from Zambia might be studying in the United States and applying for immigra-

tion to Canada. The permanent address would be the Zambian address. The mailing address (see Question 7) would be in the United States. You should give a complete address. See below for instructions.

Question 7:

Your mailing address should be your current place of residence and should include the street name, street number, apartment number (if any), the village, town, or city name, the province or state, and the country where you live. Spell all names out in full and avoid abbreviations.

Question 8:

The question applies to the place where you normally live.

Question 9:

"Unmarried" means never married in any form of ceremony recognized anywhere in the world where the ceremony took place. If divorced or separated, copies of these documents (certified) will be required.

Question 11:

If you have been previously married, you must indicate that by putting an "X" in the appropriate box. If you have never been married before, you must indicate that also. Proof of a legal divorce recognized in Canada will be required if previously married. This might entail providing a legal opinion from a lawyer that the prior divorce is valid and recognized in Canada.

Question 12:

Your present occupation should be the job that you are currently working at and should be a complete description of what you do. For example, if you are a mechanic working on both automobile and diesel trucks, you should say "Automobile and Diesel Engine Mechanic" and not just the word "mechanic."

Question 13:

For your intended occupation in Canada, you should list all the jobs that you are currently qualified to perform and in which you have experience. Often there is not enough space in Box 13. Use a separate piece of paper if necessary.

Question 14:

You should put an "X" in this box only if you do not intend to work in Canada at any time — that is, if you are going to be retired and live with your family or on your savings.

Question 15:

If you have a job offer in writing, you should bring the offer or photocopies of it to the interview and you should put an "X" in the box. The letter of employment should state the kind of work you will do and the rate of pay you will receive. (See chapter 10 for a fuller discussion of jobs.)

Question 16:

List all your employers. Give *your* occupation, not that of your employer. Do not use vague terms, such as supervisor or mechanic. Be specific: "clerical supervisor," "automobile mechanic," "diesel truck mechanic," or "small engine mechanic." If there is not enough space, list your responsibilities and a full description of your various job experiences on a separate sheet.

Note: Be sure to give dates by month and year accurately.

Question 17:

This box should list a person who will help you in getting to know Canada when you arrive here. If possible, list a relative in the same city or area of Canada where you are going or your prospective employer. If you have no relatives in Canada, then list a friend.

Question 19:

If you do not know your destination in Canada, then leave this section blank for the time being; it can be filled in when you decide. However, it could be to your advantage to choose to go to an area of Canada such as the Prairies or northern Ontario, rather than one of the large urban centres, such as Toronto, Hamilton, London, Montreal, or Vancouver, since the Canadian government is discouraging immigration to overpopulated areas.

Question 20:

This should list your closest relative anywhere in the world other than Canada. It might be a parent or an aunt or uncle. Give the complete name and full address of this person and the relationship of the person.

Question 21:

List here your closest relative in Canada and give his or her relationship to you. Close relatives should include parents, grandparents, brothers, sisters, brothers-in-law, sisters-in-law, aunts, and uncles. More distant relatives would include nieces and nephews and cousins. If you have no such relatives, say so.

Question 22:

You should put an "X" in the box to indicate the degree of efficiency with which you read, write, and speak English and French. As mentioned, you will likely be tested on your abilities.

Question 23:

If you speak more than one native language or dialect, I suggest listing all of them here even though the question asks merely for one.

Questions 24 and 25:

You should write in the box the number of years you went to elementary school. Elementary school means primary school or preparatory school. In most countries, this is usually five, six, seven, or eight years. You must indicate the numbers or grades successfully completed and not the number of years you went to school. Next enter in the appropriate box the number of years *successfully* completed in secondary school or high school and college or university. Any formal apprenticeship training (usually for trades such as mechanic, electrician, plumber, welder, die and tool machinist, etc.) should be shown in the appropriate box. Remember, you will be required to prove what you state with the submission of certificates and diplomas. In Question 25, you should list all schools you attended, their names, addresses, and when you went to them. (See chapter 9 for more specific explanations of education and training.) You must also include all places where you took your apprenticeships, if any.

Note: Be sure to give all dates by month and year accurately.

Question 26:

Question 26 has three parts: (a), (b), and (c). Part (a) asks you to put down the amount of cash in Canadian dollars that you will bring with you to Canada or that is already in Canada and the value of other assets you will bring to Canada. The last category will include the value of any personal belongings, stocks and bonds, automobiles, jewellery, art works, and the like. This figure for other assets should be a realistic amount in Canadian dollars. Do not underestimate or overestimate the value of your belongings. Part (b) asks you to put down the cash you are leaving behind you in your homeland for transfer later, the value of any property you own overseas, any other assets you may have overseas, and the value of any pension that your country of residence will allow you to transfer to Canada. Part (c) requires you to list all debts you may have. These include loans of money from institutions such as banks or companies, loans from individuals, mortgages on land or on personal belongings, money owed to the government for taxes or other reasons, and so on.

If there is not enough room to complete Question 26, put additional information on another sheet of paper and include it with the application. Remember, you only have to put totals in each of the sections in Question 26.

Question 27:

In Question 27 you must list your spouse and all of your children. If you are single and have children, they must be listed in Box 27. Only children under 21 years of age need be listed in this section. While single unmarried children between the ages of 18 and 21 without children of their own will be included as dependants, they must complete their own application forms. Such a child (between 18 and 21 and never married) should attempt to show that he or she is dependent upon you for support and maintenance, that is, to show that he or she is, in fact, your dependant. This is necessary or otherwise such a child might be assessed as an independent applicant and most such children could never qualify in the independent category. Never-married children between 18 and 21 must be shown in your original application but can be sponsored by you after you have obtained your landed immigrant status. Remember that these children must be under 21 years old on the date when you apply for them. Recent changes in the definition of family class now includes never-married children over 21 who must come with you when you apply.

Question 28:

Give answers to the best of your knowledge concerning your parents. If some information is not known, give an explanation on a separate sheet of paper. For example, you might write, "Father left mother 10 years ago and not heard from since."

Question 29:

List all the addresses at which you have lived for the previous 10 years — in full. If at all possible, do not leave any gaps in time. If there is not enough space, use a separate sheet. These addresses are places of permanent residence and not places you have stayed during vacations or trips of relatively short duration for a temporary purpose.

Question 30:

You must list here any such organization of which you have been a member since your eighteenth birthday. This includes trade unions. Remember, if you are a student, often you are automatically a member of some local and national student union.

Question 31:

These questions apply both to the applicant, his or her spouse, and all the children included in the application. In 31(a) regarding physical disabilities, remember that if you wear eyeglasses, you should answer yes and say: "I wear eyeglasses." In 31(c) a crime or offence does not mean parking tickets for automobiles or driving offences, other than those contained in the Criminal Code of Canada. Those include dangerous driving, drunk driving, criminal negligence in the operation of a vehicle, to mention several. If you previously applied for a Canadian social insurance number, you must answer yes to 31(h) and put the number in the margin if you received such a number.

Question 32:

Unless you are stateless or a refugee, to immigrate to Canada you must possess a valid current passport. Enter its number and the original date of issue and last date of expiry here. In addition to passports, some countries issue identity cards. The number of such a card should be put in the last column. This information must be provided for you and *all* members of your family.

Question 34:

You must fill in your name and sign the application. It is a medical and security release allowing the government to discuss your medical situation, if you have a problem, with provincial authorities, your employer, or your relatives. While I do not like this section, it must be signed. See chapter 13 concerning medical clearance.

d. IMMIGRATION RECORD AND VISA

If you are successful, you will receive an immigrant visa to Canada called a Canadian Immigration Record and Visa (see Sample #9).

This visa will be given to you in a sealed envelope with the instructions to present it to the immigration officer upon your arrival in Canada. Do not forget to ask for this officer when you arrive by saying, "I am immigrating to Canada and wish to see an immigration officer." DO NOT FORGET THE ENVELOPE WITH THE VISA.

CANADIAN IMMIGRATION RECORD AND VISA – *FICHE D'IMMIGRATION CANADA ET VISA*

DO NOT USE RÉSERVÉ | DO NOT USE - RÉSERVÉ

3 1

MODE OF TRAVEL – *MODE DE TRANSPORT*
Air Canada Plane

SURNAME GIVEN NAMES – *NOM DE FAMILLE PRÉNOMS*
FRIENDLY JOHN MURRAY

BIRTH DATE / DATE DE NAISSANCE
1 1 0 4 1 9 4 1 Bristol,

PLACE OF BIRTH – *LIEU DE NAISSANCE*

COUNTRY OF BIRTH – *PAYS DE NAISSANCE*
England 0 0 0

CITIZEN OF - *CITOYEN DE*
England 0 0 0

SEX – *SEXE*
1- M/H
2- F/F

MARITAL STATUS – *ÉTAT MATRIMONIAL*
1- SINGLE – CÉLIBATAIRE
2- MARRIED – MARIÉ(E)
3- WIDOWED – VEUF/VEUVE(VE)
4- DIVORCED – DIVORCÉ(E)
5- SEPARATED – SÉPARÉ(E)   2

HAVE YOU BEEN CONVICTED OF A CRIME OR AN OFFENCE, REFUSED ADMISSION TO OR REQUIRED TO LEAVE CANADA
AVEZ-VOUS ÉTÉ DÉCLARÉ(E) COUPABLE D'UN CRIME OU D'UNE INFRACTION ESSUYÉ UN REFUS CONCERNANT VOTRE ADMISSION AU CANADA OU ÉTÉ PRIÉ DE QUITTER LE CANADA
YES OR NO / OUI OU NON   No
INITIALS – INITIALES   JMF.

ACCOMPANYING FAMILY MEMBERS – *MEMBRES DE LA FAMILLE QUI VOUS ACCOMPAGNENT*

NAME – *NOM* | AGE | RELATIONSHIP – *LIEN DE PARENTÉ*
Friendly, Sara Louise | 36 | Wife
Friendly, Michael John | 14 | Son
Friendly, Mary Louise | 12 | Daughter

NAME ADDRESS RELATIONSHIP OF CLOSEST RELATIVE OUTSIDE OF CANADA
NOM ET ADRESSE DU PLUS PROCHE PARENT À L'EXTÉRIEUR DU CANADA ET LIEN DE PARENTÉ AVEC CELUI-CI
Mrs. Daphne Friendly (Mother)
25 Cambridge St.
Bristol, England

I CERTIFY THAT MY ANSWERS TO THESE QUESTIONS ARE TRUE AND CORRECT
JE CERTIFIE QUE MES RÉPONSES À CES QUESTIONS SONT EXACTES ET CONFORMES À LA VÉRITÉ

COUNTRY OF LAST PERMANENT RESIDENCE
PAYS DE DERNIÈRE RÉSIDENCE PERMANENTE
England 0 0 0

SOURCE AREA – *EN PROVENANCE DE*
Bristol

NATIONAL *RESSORTISSANT*
1- YES - OUI
2- NO - NON   1

IMMIG / CATEGORY *CATÉGORIE D'IMM.*

FAMILY STATUS *SITUATION PAR RAPPORT À LA FAMILLE*
1- PRINCIPAL APPLICANT / APPLICANT PRINCIPAL
2- SPOUSE - ÉPOUSE
3- DEPENDANT – DÉPENDANT   1

PASSPORT NO – *Nº DU PASSEPORT*
XY 999555

COUNTRY OF ISSUE – *PAYS DE DÉLIVRANCE*
United Kingdom

EXPIRY DATE – *DATE D'EXPIRATION*
June 1, 198-

PASSAGE PAID BY OR TRANS WARRANT NUMBER
PASSAGE PAYÉ PAR OU NUMÉRO DU BON DE TRANSPORT
Self

CANADIAN LANGUAGE CAPABILITY
CONNAISSANCE DES LANGUES OFFICIELLES DU CANADA
- ENGLISH – ANGLAIS
2- FRENCH – FRANÇAIS
- ENG & FR – FR ET ANGL
4- NONE - AUCUNE   1

NATIVE LANGUAGE – *LANGUE MATERNELLE*
English   5 5 5

EDUC QUALIF *DIPLÔMES*
Eleven

YEARS OF SCHOOLING *ANNÉES D'ÉTUDES*
1 1

INTENDED OCCUPATION – *EMPLOI ENVISAGÉ*
Stonemason/Carpenter

YEARS OF EXPERIENCE – *ANNÉES D'EXPÉRIENCE*
Twenty-three   2 3

J.C. NUMBER / Nº

P C P
C P

FULL NAME AND ADDRESS OF PERSON WILLING TO ASSIST / DESTINATION
NOM ET ADRESSE AU LONG DE LA PERSONNE OFFRANT SON AIDE / DESTINATION
John Doe
1 Cameron Dr.
Calgary, Alberta

AMOUNT OF MONEY TO BE TRANSFERRED TO CANADA
SOMME D'ARGENT À TRANSFÉRER AU CANADA EN DOLLARS CANADIENS
CDN $. 0 0

REGULATIONS – *RÈGLEMENT*

PRIORITY – *PRIORITÉ*

EMPLOYMENT STATUS – *SITUATION D'ACTIVITÉ*
1- DEO – PD
2- OVC - OEMCE
3- ARE / NO EMP 2151 - E R - AUCUN EMP 2151
4- ARE / VALID EMP 2151 - E R / VALIDE EMP 2151

SPECIAL PROGRAM – *MOUVEMENT SPÉCIAL*

OF. OF ISS – *BUREAU DE DÉLIVRANCE*

POST AREA CODE
CODE RÉGIONAL DU BUREAU

DATE OF ISSUE / DATE DE DÉLIVRANCE
1 0 0 2 8 0

DATE OF EXPIRY - *DATE D'EXPIRATION*
1 0 0 5 8 0

SIGNATURE OF VISA OFFICER *SIGNATURE DE L'AGENT D'IMMIGRATION*

DATE OF ... MED
1 5 0 5 8 0

MEDICAL NO AND CATEGORY – *Nº DE LA FICHE ET DE LA CAT MÉD*
XYZ 99559900-05

ACCOMPANYING PRINCIPAL APPLICANT *ACCOMPAGNANT LE REQUÉRANT PRINCIPAL*
0 - N/A S/O   1 - YES OUI   2 - NO NON

APPLICATION SERIAL NO – *Nº DE SÉRIE DE LA DEMANDE*

MONEY IN POSSESSION *ARGENT LIQUIDE*
CDN $ 7 5 0 0 . 0 0

IMMIGRANT – *IMMIGRANT*
- LANDED - AYANT OBTENU LE DROIT D'ÉTABLISSEMENT
- ARRIVED - ARRIVÉ

ON LE
0 3 0 3 8 0

SIGNATURE OF IMMIGRATION OFFICER - *SIGNATURE DE L'AGENT D'IMMIGRATION*

CONDITIONS – *CONDITIONS*
Must Travel to Calgary, Alberta.

NAME OF OFFICE AND CODE NO – *NOM ET CODE NUMÉRIQUE DU BUREAU*
Toronto International Airport

REMARKS – *OBSERVATIONS*

ERROR - *ERREUR* | TYPE - *GENRE* | RELATIONSHIP *LIEN DE PARENTÉ* | YEAR / INTL INT *ANNÉE D'ENTRÉE INIT* | ORIG INT CATEGORY *CAT À L'ENTRÉE INIT* | TRANS CO *TRANSPORTEUR* | LONG STUDY *ÉTUDE LONGITUDINALE*
1- YES OUI
2- NO NON

R 1000 112 771

THIS FORM HAS BEEN ESTABLISHED BY THE MINISTER OF EMPLOYMENT AND IMMIGRATION
FORMULAIRE ÉTABLI PAR LE MINISTRE DE L'EMPLOI ET DE L'IMMIGRATION

HEADQUARTERS
ADMINISTRATION CENTRALE   1

12
WHO CANNOT COME: THE PROHIBITED CLASSES

When you have successfully received sufficient points to be eligible to come to Canada as an independent or assisted immigrant, or if you are a family class member and your sponsor has completed the application for you, you will be required to pass a security check.

This chapter outlines the classes of people who will be automatically rejected as immigrants to Canada; chapter 13 deals with the nature of security and medical clearances.

Section 19 of the Immigration Act lists the following individuals and classes of people who will be *refused* admission to Canada:

(a) Persons suffering from any disease, disorder, disability, or other health impairment that might be or become a public danger or place an excessive demand on our health or social services (see chapter 13)

(b) Persons who are unwilling or unable to support themselves thereby becoming a burden to the Canadian taxpayer

(c) Persons who have been convicted of an offence that corresponds to any federal offence in Canada punishable by a maximum of more than 10 years in jail unless they can prove they have rehabilitated themselves and 5 years have passed since completion of sentence

(d) Persons who it is believed will commit one or more serious crimes or will engage in organized criminal activity

(e) Persons who did or might engage in espionage or subversion of our government

(f) Persons who did or it is believed will engage in terrorist activities

(g) Persons who it is believed in the opinion of an adjudicator are not genuine visitors or immigrants

(h) Persons who there are reasonable grounds to believe have committed war crimes or crimes against humanity

(i) Persons who are inadmissible and do not have the consent of the Ministry of Immigration to enter into Canada.

The above sections apply to anyone attempting to enter Canada other than a Canadian citizen. Thus it applies to visitors, arriving immigrants, and to *permanent residents* who have left Canada even for a short visit to the U.S.A. and are now attempting to return.

It should be noted that for all practical purposes the section dealing with jail for a period of more than 10 years applies primarily to permanent residents attempting to return to Canada, since later sections (see below) deal with far lesser offences as they apply to visitors and immigrants to Canada.

Immigrants to Canada and visitors will be refused entry at the border into Canada or when they apply overseas for a visa (THIS DOES NOT APPLY TO PERMANENT RESIDENTS) if they fall into one of the following four categories:

(a) Persons who have been convicted of an offence that corresponds to any federal offence in Canada punishable by indictment for which a maximum term of imprisonment of *less than* 10 years has been imposed

(b) Persons who have been convicted of two or more offences that correspond to any federal offence in Canada punishable by summary conviction

(c) All members of the family of a person not admissible to Canada on one of the above reasons

(d) Any person who cannot or does not comply with any requirement or conditions under the Immigration Act that apply to him or her.

You can see that there are a lot of reasons why a person will not be allowed to come to Canada.

I have often been asked to explain an "offence punishable by indictment" and an "offence punishable by summary conviction." Simply put, indictable offences are more serious offences in Canada and include murder, manslaughter, rape, robbery, breaking and entering, theft over $200, arson, indecent assault, escape from custody, sales of a narcotic (including marijuana), fraud, kidnapping, and forgery, to mention but a few.

Summary conviction offences are less serious crimes and include theft under $200, common (simple) assault, inmate of a brothel or gambling house, causing a disturbance, possession of a narcotic, impaired (drunk) driving, soliciting for prostitution, damage to private property under $50, to mention but a few.

Under the current law, an immigrant or visitor to Canada who comes within sections (a) or (b) above, that is, punishable by way of summary conviction, is able by in-

dictment for less than 10 years in jail, or two or more offences punishable by way of summary conviction, is able to obtain a cancellation of the prohibition.

A person who has been convicted of such a crime may be allowed to immigrate to Canada if, in the case of a person over 21 years old when convicted of the crime, at least 5 years have passed without further trouble and the prospective immigrant has been successfully rehabilitated. In the case of a prospective immigrant who was under 21 years of age when convicted, at least 2 years must have passed without trouble, and the prospective immigrant must have been successfully rehabilitated.

The period of time for rehabilitation begins to run following the completion of any time in jail or parole or probation. In order to satisfy the Minister of Immigration that you have rehabilitated yourself, you will have to submit proof of no further problems with the police, a good employment record, reference letters from people in the community, and similar documents. Following a complete check by the Royal Canadian Mounted Police (RCMP), you will be granted a waiver from the prohibition of entering Canada.

Chapters 23 and 24 deal with the situation of how anyone, whether visitor, applicant for permanent resident status, or permanent resident who is already inside Canada may lose his or her status and be removed, excluded, or deported from Canada. Each of these terms refers to a different method of removing people from Canada and returning them to where they came from.

If a prospective immigrant does not fall into one of these prohibited classes of people, all that remains are the security and medical clearances.

13
SECURITY AND MEDICAL CLEARANCES

a. SECURITY

In order to determine whether or not you fall into one or more of the prohibited classes outlined in chapter 12, the immigration department will conduct a security check with the police authorities in your homeland and in all countries in which you have been a resident.

This security check will request information concerning your background, particularly regarding past arrests (and/or convictions) for criminal offences. In all probability, information concerning the possibility of your being a security risk to Canada will also be sought.

Often you will be required to complete a Supplementary Information form for the security clearance. Sample forms, typical of those used, are illustrated here for Korea (IMM #1052) and Japan (IMM #1077). These forms must be completed in English or French *and* in your native language (see Samples #10 and #11).

This security report is not, and will not be, made available to you or to any lawyer or other person representing you. Thus, if you receive a negative report, there is almost no way you can question and attack the evidence, if any, upon which an adverse security report is made.

The length of time the security report takes will vary greatly, depending on the number of cities and countries you have lived in during the previous 10 years. Also, it will be easier and quicker to obtain police reports from North American and western European countries than from countries in the Far East, South and Central America, and Africa. A final security clearance can take from six to twelve months depending on the circumstances.

In unusual and rare circumstances the security clearance may take longer than 12 months and as much as 18 months or more. Some of these countries currently include India, South Africa, Thailand, Pakistan, and other southeast Asian countries.

You should also obtain a police certificate in advance from each city or town you have lived in more than six months during the past ten years stating you do not have a criminal record. While this will not necessarily speed up the security approval, which involves contacts with the national police of the places where you have lived, it usually helps and is now a requirement in almost all cases.

b. MEDICAL

While your security report is being prepared, you will be asked to have a complete medical examination to determine if you are healthy and not a member of the prohibited classes for medical reasons.

You will be required to take a specific medical examination either from a Canadian doctor working for the government or from a local doctor appointed by the Canadian government for the purpose of conducting immigration medical examinations. In either case, the medical form established by the Canadian government must be completed by the doctor and all the tests in it must be conducted, including:

(a) A chest x-ray negative, not more than one month old, at least 35cm by 43cm (14 inches by 17 inches). The plates and an analysis of the plates (by a professional radiologist) must be sent to:

The Chief
Immigration Medical Service
Department of National Health
    and Welfare
Ottawa, Ontario
K1A 0K9 Canada

or to one of several overseas Canadian government medical stations. You *must* send your medicals to the particular office that is provided in your medical instructions.

(b) A blood test, including a test for venereal disease

(c) A stool examination for people immigrating from countries where parasites are a problem

(d) A urinalysis

Sample #12 is a copy of the medical report (known as Form IMS #1017) which must be completed by the doctor examining you. It must have a photograph of you attached by a staple (not glued). You should fill in questions 1 to 10. The remainder of the form will be completed by the doctor.

If you have a minor medical problem that will not prevent your immigration to Canada but which is discovered in the medical, you may be required to be treated before you go to Canada and sign an undertaking (see Sample #13) to that effect. This form is your agreement to be monitored in Canada and to report to the provincial health authorities so they can make sure there is no recurrence of your illness. If you pass the medical and security clearances, you will receive your visa to come to Canada as a permanent resident.

The major problem will occur if you do not pass your medical examination. In the past, there was a specific list of diseases such as tuberculosis, cholera, smallpox, and trachoma that prevented entry into Canada on medical grounds. Since Canada has medical and hospital services completely paid for by the government, many of the provinces complained that many people, especially elderly "family class members," were being brought to Canada by their relatives to obtain free medical and hospital care. As a result of this concern, each province has the right to review and reject potential immigrants who might place an excessive burden on the medical services of Canada. This consultation takes place with two doctors employed by the federal government in the Ministry of Health and Welfare.

One of the prohibited groups includes people who are a danger to public health and safety *and* people who, in the opinion of two government medical doctors, suffer from any disease or disorder or impairment that "would cause, or might reasonably be expected to cause, excessive demands on health or social services."

Recently there was a case of a woman who had breast cancer and had been declared cured, but was refused admission on the grounds that she was a cancer risk who *might* require extensive treatment in the future. Similarly, an applicant with a kidney problem was also refused. In the case of the woman with cancer, she was eventually allowed to immigrate after five years had passed since her operation.

While there is as yet no formal appeal from a refusal on medical grounds, an appeal is possible to the Federal Court of Appeal on a medical refusal that is not justified (such as the woman with cancer) if you have sufficient medical opinions to prove that the person is cured (see chapter 26 for appeals to the Federal Court) or that the decision is frivolous and not grounded in accepted medical diagnosis and prognosis.

KOREA
CORÉE
한국

NOTE TO APPLICANT – *AVIS AU REQUÉRANT*	Office – *Bureau*
• This form must be completed in either English or French AND in Hangul. • *Ce formulaire doit être rempli en français ou en anglais ET en han-geul.* • 신청자에 대한 주의사항 : 이 용지는 영어나 불어중 하나와 반드시 한글로도	File – *N° de réf.*
	Date

	English or French *Français ou anglais*	Hangul – *Han-geul* – 한글
1. Surname – *Nom* 성 (姓)		
2. Given Names – *Prénoms* 이름		
3. Sex – *Sexe* – 성 (性)	☐ Male *Homme* ☐ Female *Femme*	☐ 남 ☐ 여
4. Date and Place of Birth *Date et lieu de naissance* 생년월일 및 출생지		
5. Full Address in Korea *Adresse au long en Corée* 한국내 주소 (상세하게)		
6. Name of Householder and Permanent Address *Nom et adresse permanente du chef de famille* 호주성명 및 본적		
7. Passport No. – *N° du passeport* 여권번호		
8. Military Service No. – *N° matricule militaire* 병역번호		
9. Employment – *Emploi* 직장		
10. Name and Date and Place of Birth of Spouse *Nom, date et lieu de naissance du conjoint* 배우자의 성명, 생년월일 및 출생지		
11. Present Address of Spouse *Adresse actuelle du conjoint* 배우자의 현주소		
12. Name and Date and Place of Birth of Father *Nom, date et lieu de naissance du père* 부친성명, 생년월일 및 출생지		
13. Name and Date and Place of Birth of Mother *Nom, date et lieu de naissance de la mère* 모친성명, 생년월일 및 출생지		
14. Permanent Address of Parents *Adresse actuelle des parents* 부모의 본적		
15. Name of Father-in-law *Nom du beau-père* 장인 (또는 시부)의 성명		
16. Name of Mother-in-law *Nom de la belle-mère* 장모 (또는 시모)의 성명		

Signature of Applicant – *Signature du requérant* – 신청자의 서명 ▶

74

SAMPLE #11
SUPPLEMENTARY INFORMATION FORM
FOR SECURITY PURPOSES — JAPAN

Employment and Immigration Canada

SUPPLEMENTARY INFORMATION FORM

JAFON

日本

Office	
File	
Date	

NOTE TO APPLICANT
● This form must be completed in either English or French AND Japanese.

● 申請者への注意: この用紙は英語又は仏語及び日本語で記入しなければならない.

	English or French	Japanese — 日本語,
1. Name in Full 姓名		
2. Other Names (including maiden name) 他の名前 (旧姓を含む)		
3. Sex — 性別	☐ Male ☐ Female	☐ 男子 ☐ 女子
4. Date and Place of Birth 生年月日及び出生地		
5. Permanent Domicile (Honseki) 本籍		
6. Present Address in Full 現住所 (完全に記入っこと)		
7. Addresses during past ten years — with months and years 過去10年間の住所 (年月を記入っこと)		
8. EDUCATION: Senior high schools and universities attended — including months and years 学歴: 通学した高等学校及び大学 (年月を記入っこと)		
9. Present Employment 現在の職業		
10. Employment during past ten years — including months and years 過去10年間の職歴 (年月を記入っこと)		

Signature of Applicant — 申請者の署名 ▶

IMM. 1077 (5-79)

75

NOTE: The medical examiner should record any abnormality found or any disease suspected as applicants are subject to a complete medical examination at the Canadian port of arrival and if some condition is found which is not recorded on this form the applicant may be subjected to delay, serious inconvenience, or deportation.

THIS EXAMINATION DOES NOT CONSTITUTE IMMIGRATION MEDICAL CLEARANCE

PRELIMINARY MEDICAL EXAMINATION
IMMIGRATION MEDICAL SERVICE—MEDICAL SERVICES
DEPARTMENT OF NATIONAL HEALTH AND WELFARE

CANADA

THIS SECTION TO BE COMPLETED BY INITIATING OFFICER

IMMIGRANT	NON-IMMIGRANT	OTHER	APPROVING PORT FILE NO.	APPROVING PORT
☐ SPONSORED ☒ UNSPONSORED	☐ VISITOR ☐ STUDENT			London, England
IF STUDENT, STATE PROGRAM OR PLAN, IF APPLICABLE			VISA OFFICE FILE NO.	VISA OFFICE London, England

PARTICULARS OF APPLICANT *(Print in block letters)*

1. NAME (LAST OR FAMILY NAME) / (FIRST NAME) / (MIDDLE NAMES)

FRIENDLY   JOHN   MURRAY

I.M.S. SERIAL NO.

ATTACH PASSPORT SIZE PHOTOGRAPH (NOT REQUIRED FOR INFANTS UNDER 18 MONTHS)

2. HOME ADDRESS IN FULL

18 Somerset Drive, Liverpool, England

3. SEX	4. BIRTH (DAY, MONTH, YEAR)	PLACE AND COUNTRY OF BIRTH
☒ MALE ☐ FEMALE		Bristol, England

5. CITIZEN OF
United Kingdom

7. PRESENT OCCUPATION
Stonemason

(STAPLE—DO NOT GLUE)

6. MARITAL STATUS

SINGLE	MARRIED	WIDOWED	DIVORCED	SEPARATED
	X			

INTENDED OCCUPATION
Stonemason/Carpenter

8. PASSPORT NO.	9. NO. OF PERSONS IN FAMILY MEDICALLY EXAMINED AND COMING TO CANADA	10. IF ITEM 9 APPLIES, STATE FULL NAME OF HEAD OF FAMILY
XY 999555	4	N/A

EXAMINING PHYSICIAN TO COMPLETE THIS SECTION BY INFORMATION OBTAINED FROM APPLICANT

11. HAS APPLICANT BEEN EXAMINED BEFORE FOR EMIGRATION TO CANADA?   ☐ YES ☐ NO   IF YES, WHEN AND WHERE

12. HAS APPLICANT EVER RECEIVED OR IS NOW RECEIVING A DISABILITY PENSION?   ☐ YES ☐ NO   IF YES, FOR WHAT REASON

13. HAS APPLICANT EVER SUFFERED FROM OR RECEIVED TREATMENT FOR PLEURISY OR TUBERCULOSIS OF ANY KIND OR ATTENDED A SANATORIUM OR TUBERCULOSIS CLINIC, EITHER AS AN IN-PATIENT OR AS AN OUT-PATIENT?   ☐ YES ☐ NO

14. HAS APPLICANT EVER SUFFERED FROM OR RECEIVED TREATMENT IN A MENTAL INSTITUTE OR OTHERWISE FOR A MENTAL OR NERVOUS DISORDER?   ☐ YES ☐ NO

15. HAS APPLICANT EVER BEEN TREATED IN HOSPITAL?   ☐ YES ☐ NO   IF YES, LIST NAMES OF HOSPITALS, CONDITIONS TREATED AND DATES

16. HA APPLICANT EVER HAD OR IS NOW SUFFERING FROM ANY OF THE FOLLOWING?

	YES	NO		YES	NO		YES	NO		YES	NO
(1) TRACHOMA	☐	☐	(7) HAEMORRHOIDS	☐	☐	(13) STOMACH TROUBLE	☐	☐	(19) FAINTING SPELLS	☐	☐
(2) OTHER EYE TROUBLE	☐	☐	(8) RUPTURE	☐	☐	(14) DIABETES, MELLITUS OR OTHER GLANDULAR DISORDERS	☐	☐	(20) FITS OR SEIZURES	☐	☐
(3) NOSE OR THROAT TROUBLE	☐	☐	(9) KIDNEY OR BLADDER TROUBLE	☐	☐	(15) RHEUMATISM OR JOINT TROUBLE	☐	☐	(21) NERVOUS DISORDERS	☐	☐
(4) EAR TROUBLE OR DEAFNESS	☐	☐	(10) VENEREAL DISEASE	☐	☐	(16) LUNG DISEASE OR CHRONIC COUGH	☐	☐	(22) INTESTINAL PARASITES	☐	☐
(5) HEAD INJURIES	☐	☐	(11) VARICOSE VEINS	☐	☐	(17) HEART DISEASE	☐	☐	(23) TROPICAL DISEASES	☐	☐
(6) BACK INJURIES	☐	☐	(12) SKIN DISEASES	☐	☐	(18) RHEUMATIC FEVER	☐	☐	(24) OPERATIONS	☐	☐

ELABORATE ON POSITIVE FINDINGS

SIGNATURE OF APPLICANT	DATE, PLACE OF EXAMINATION	SIGNATURE OF EXAMINING PHYSICIAN

I.M.S. 1017 (4-67)
7540-21-029-1408

See other side ⟶

PHYSICAL EXAMINATION OF APPLICANT

17. HEIGHT	18. WEIGHT	19. EYE ABNORMAL- ITIES:	RIGHT		LEFT	

20. HEARING (CONVERSATIONAL VOICE)	VISUAL ACUITY:	WITHOUT GLASSES RIGHT EYE 20/ OR 6/	LEFT EYE 20/ OR 6/	WITH GLASSES RIGHT EYE 20/ OR 6/	LEFT EYE 20/ OR 6/
RIGHT EAR FEET					
LEFT EAR FEET	21 EAR DRUMS	RIGHT		LEFT	

22. HEAD AND NECK	23. SPINE	24. LUNGS

25. HEART	26. PULSE	27. BLOOD PRESSURE SYSTOLIC DIASTOLIC	REPEAT IF ABNORMAL

28. ABDOMEN	29. HERNIA	30. GENITO-URINARY

31. IS APPLICANT PREGNANT?	32. RECTUM

33. UPPER
EXTREM- ITIES: LOWER

34. SKIN	35. LYMPHATIC SYSTEM	36. SURGICAL SCARS

PSYCHIATRIC AND NEUROLOGICAL FINDINGS

37. DETAILS OF NEUROLOGICAL ABNORMALITIES

38. DETAILS OF PSYCHIATRIC ABNORMALITIES

39. MENTAL DEVELOPMENT

☐ NORMAL   ☐ DULL NORMAL   ☐ BELOW NORMAL

40.
X-RAY FILMS NOT SMALLER THAN 14″ x 17″ OR 30 x 40 CENTIMETERS
TO BE ATTACHED ALONG WITH RADIOLOGIST'S REPORT   X-RAY FILM NO. ▶

LABORATORY FINDINGS (ATTACH REPORTS)

41. ROUTINE BLOOD SEROLOGICAL TEST FOR SYPHILIS (APPLICANTS 15 YRS. OF AGE OR UNDER ARE EXEMPT)	42. STOOL EXAM. IF INDICATED (PARASITES)

43. URINALYSIS:	(A) SPECIFIC GRAVITY	(B) ALBUMEN	(C) SUGAR	(D) MICROSCOPIC

ELABORATE ON POSITIVE FINDINGS:

CONCLUSIONS OR DIAGNOSIS:

PROGNOSIS:

SIGNATURE OF EXAMINING PHYSICIAN

NAME OF EXAMINING PHYSICIAN (PRINT IN BLOCK LETTERS)

ADDRESS: NUMBER, STREET, PLACE, COUNTRY (PRINT)

Employment and Immigration Canada   Emploi et Immigration Canada

UNDERTAKING — _ENGAGEMENT_

Office — _Bureau_	Visa No. — _Visa nᵒ_	Med. Ref. No. — _Réf. serv. méd._
London, England	ZZZ 10000-0	XYZ 99559900-05

Name — _Nom_	First Names — _Prénoms_	Name of Spouse _Nom du conjoint_
FRIENDLY	SARA LOUISE	JOHN MURRAY FRIENDLY

Canadian Address — _Adresse au Canada_	CIC — _C.I.C._
100 Jones Ave., Calgary, Alberta	Calgary West

- I understand that the Provincial Health Authorities at my destination in Canada may wish to monitor my health after I arrive there. I agree to them doing so and I hereby undertake to immediately report my address, and any change of address, to the Provincial Health Authorities or to the nearest Canadian Immigration Centre.

- _Je, soussigné, comprends que les autorités médicales de la province où je me rends peuvent désirer contrôler mon état de santé après mon arrivée au Canada. J'accepte cette éventualité et je m'engage, par les présentes, à faire connaître immédiatement mon adresse et tout changement d'adresse ultérieur aux autorités médicales de la province ou au Centre d'Immigration Canada le plus près de mon domicile._

"GOOD HEALTH IS EVERYONES BUSINESS.
PLEASE DO YOUR PART."   _"PROTÉGEZ VOTRE SANTÉ"_

Signature of Applicant — _Signature du requérant_	Date	Officer's Signature — _Signature de l'agent_
Sara Louise Friendly	Dec. 15. 198—	

IMM- 535 (5-78)

ORIGINAL — APPLICANT _REQUÉRANT_	BLUE COPY — MED. SERVICES OTTAWA _COPIE BLEU — SERV. MÉD., OTTAWA_	PINK COPY — MED. SERVICES OTTAWA _COPIE ROSE — SERV. MÉD., OTTAWA_

14
APPLICATIONS FROM INSIDE CANADA

a. THE GENERAL RULE

No person who wishes to immigrate to Canada and obtain permanent resident status is allowed to make an application from inside Canada. Any person who attempts to apply from inside Canada will be told to leave the country, and if you fail to comply with that order, you will be deported or removed from Canada. You *must* apply to immigrate to Canada in your homeland or in your country of permanent residence.

This policy is outlined in section 9(1) of the Immigration Act. Immigrants are required to be in possession of an immigrant visa issued outside of Canada.

The same section also applied to all visitors — they, too, require a visa to visit Canada — with the exception of visitors from certain countries listed in the regulations. At the end of chapter 20 you will find a list of those countries from which visitors do not require a visa.

b. EXCEPTIONS

1. Family class — humanitarian and compassionate considerations

One of the exceptions to the above rule affects the family class members — the spouses, minor unmarried children, parents, and grandparents of Canadian citizens and permanent residents. Even in these situations, the Immigration Department must seek special government approval in each case, by way of a special law called an order-in-council, to waive the sections of the Immigration Act and regulations that require all applications to be made outside of Canada. This permission alone can take between six and nine months to obtain. In the meantime, your dependant will usually be allowed to remain in Canada until processing has been completed under special permission given by the Minister of Employment and Immigration or as a visitor. Following the obtaining of that permission, the file will be processed in the ordinary manner, taking perhaps another six to nine months.

In my opinion, and that of the Canadian Bar Association — Immigration Section, the only approach consistent with the legislation is to permit any foreign spouse who is in Canada with valid visitor status to adjust his or her status to that of permanent resident, provided that the Canadian sponsor can meet sponsorship requirements, and subject to section 19 admissibility, that is, the spouse is not in one of the prohibited categories.

As a result of six years of active lobbying by the Canadian Bar Association — Immigration Section and its predecessor the Association of Immigration Lawyers, the Minister of Employment and Immigration announced early in 1985 that Canadian citizens or permanent residents may apply for permanent resident status for their spouses while visitors in Canada.

There is a requirement that it be a *bona fide* marriage, that is, a real marriage and not one contracted solely for the purposes of immigrating to Canada.

Once you are granted an interview, you should provide all the usual documentation including a letter from your employer, proof of citizenship or permanent resident status, proof of savings and, most important, proof of the *bona fide* marriage, such as wedding invitations, photographs of the engagement party or wedding ceremony, tickets and hotel bills for the honeymoon, and the like.

Provided that these requirements are satisfied, the application will be processed in Canada.

With respect to other family class members (other than spouses), in my opinion there is no useful purpose in returning such people to their country of origin to await processing. In the case of parents over the age of 60 or parents of Canadian citizens, returning to the country of origin often causes hardship. It prolongs the separation of the family; in cases where no close family members reside in the home country, loneliness is an important factor; and where there are medical concerns, the Canadian children fear for the parents' welfare. In many cases, the parents have come to Canada to reside under the care and protection of the offspring in order to avoid racial discrimination or other difficulties that caused them to fear for their safety.

Then, too, parents are often dependent on their Canadian children for support and have no means of earning a living in the country of origin. In such cases, the children have to send money overseas to maintain their parents (which doesn't help the present Canadian balance of payments problem) and this plus the cost of returning parents to distant countries to await processing works a financial hardship on the Canadian citizen or permanent resident. This is often compounded by the fact that the grandparents are looking after the children while both parents work. On departure of the grandparents, the children are forced into day care or one of the parents has to give up employment.

Finally, there are certain benefits that accrue by virtue of the processing of family class applications in Canada. The processing can take place in a leisurely and orderly fashion and pressure on the family is resolved by their unification in Canada while pending approval. The Immigration Commission appears to have the resources in Canada to adequately handle the volume. In addition, the processing of some applications inland relieves some of the pressures on the overworked offices abroad. Most important, the landing of family class members inland demonstrates to recent immigrants and to the Canadian immigrant community that the commission will take a positive and humane approach to their family problems, which is good public relations for the commission.

It is almost impossible to explain to a family the rationale behind forcing elderly people or young children to travel long distances and wait in isolation for a considerable length of time to obtain a visa that they know will be issued in due course. Sending them home creates an impression among the immigrant community that the Immigration Commission is unduly technical and overly bureaucratic.

The approach I recommend calls for a complete reversal of the current trend so that the regular adjustment of status in Canada for people who meet all the requirements for immigrant admission as family class members would be allowed. It could be conveniently achieved by passing a regulation to create a class of people not subject to the requirement of obtaining an immigrant visa outside of Canada. This would surely create a more equitable situation, more in line with the intent of the legislation.

Unfortunately, all of the above represents only my personal opinion and that of the Canadian Bar Association — Immigration Section. Therefore, *remember* that the policy of the government to allow sponsored dependants to remain in Canada while being processed is merely a policy; it is not the law of Canada. In fact, the law says just the opposite, and the policy can be changed or altered at any time as seen with the new policy concerning spouses, or applied differently to people in exactly the same situation.

I believe that the law will be enforced and that those family class relatives who can afford to return home for processing or who do not have strong humanitarian and compassionate grounds for remaining in Canada while they are processed will be pressured, asked, and sometimes required to leave Canada for processing.

Note: Unless the applicant for humanitarian and compassionate consideration is "in status," that is, legally here in Canada and not a person whose visiting time has expired, he or she will be required to leave Canada to apply outside of this country. If there are very strong humanitarian grounds, such as serious illness, a minister's permit *may* be issued.

So, you must be aware that your relative, other than a spouse, or other individual will likely have to return home during the period that the application is being processed as described in chapter 4.

Sample #14 shows the notice that you will likely receive when immigration officials require further information about your sponsorship or wish to discuss situations such as an application for an adjustment of status for someone already in Canada.

2. Non-family class — humanitarian and compassionate considerations

Under very unusual and special circumstances, there is a possibility under section 115(2) of the Immigration Act for the Minister of Immigration to allow independent applicants who have no family in Canada to remain in this country and apply for permanent resident status in this country.

This procedure has evolved as a result of court decisions about the right of an individual to apply to the Minister of Immigration for such special consideration.

These applications must be submitted while an individual is currently "in status" in Canada (see above).

It is my opinion that the procedures used to review individuals applying for special consideration as a result of recent court decisions will be changed by legislation limiting such applications only to individuals who fall within the family class and, perhaps, assisted relatives. I highly recommend against any person coming to Canada as a visitor and making such an application with the hope of being allowed to remain inside Canada and obtain permanent resident status in this country. I have included this section in the book because a great deal of misinformation has been circulating among various immigrant and ethnic communities within Canada saying that a person can stay in this country and apply. This is *not* true.

Such a situation will be looked at in the case of independent applications and reviewed only where they either have very close relatives here in Canada or have lived themselves in Canada for a long period of time — a minimum of five years and preferably at least ten years, and have, in fact, become residents of Canada if not in law then in practice.

In making such an application to the government of Canada, you would be required to submit the following documentation:

(a) Application for permanent residence

(b) Affidavit of the individual petitioning the government to be allowed to remain in this country on humanitarian and compassionate grounds

SAMPLE #14
CALL IN NOTICE

<u>**CALL IN NOTICE**</u>

SUBJECT:	Sponsorship of your parents

Date of Interview	Time	Send	Bring	The following indicated below:
November 27, 199-	10:00 am			

TO:

Office Location

Canada Immigration Centre
(Toronto Central)
443 University Avenue
5th Floor
Toronto, Ontario
M5G 2H6

When calling present this letter for file identification

Completed application for permanent residence	_____
Passport and travel documents	_____
Certificate of Canadian Citizenship	XX
Canadian Immigration Identification Record	_____
Evidence of income and savings	XX
Letter from previous and/or present employer indicating nature of employment, salary, and length of time employed	_____
Have your husband/wife accompany you	_____
Other:	_____

The services rendered by Canadian
Immigration officers and interpreters
are without cost

Date	Canada Immigration

(c) Affidavits in support from relatives and friends in Canada

(d) Letters from prospective employers

(e) Letters from friends and relatives

(f) Family tree

(g) Police certificates and supporting documentation

At the present time, over 90% of these so-called long-term *de facto* residents of Canada who have been here illegally, "underground," are being refused adjustment of status if they turn themselves in and are being removed from Canada.

3. Foreign domestic workers or program-nannies

The only other exception is a special program for foreign domestics or "nannies" established by the Minister of Immigration in 1981. It allows individuals who have been working as either domestics or nannies in Canada for a two-year period to apply for permanent resident status from within the country.

These individuals will be required to be processed by a special government decree called an order-in-council.

Individuals who are either working in Canada as domestics or who apply to work in Canada as domestics from overseas WILL BE REQUIRED TO DECLARE THEIR INTENTION TO APPLY FOR PERMANENT RESIDENCE AT THE SAME TIME THAT THEY APPLY FOR THEIR EMPLOYMENT AUTHORIZATION TO COME TO CANADA AS A NANNY OR A DOMESTIC.

Since this program has been in effect, most of the domestics who were in Canada at the time it began have now been handled under its provisions; therefore, in the future, this program will be restricted to individuals who are applying to come to Canada on temporary employment authorizations as domestics.

As stated above, it is necessary for you to state your desire to be included in the foreign domestic worker program. This intention will be included on your employment authorization issued overseas prior to coming to Canada. If this intention is not shown on the visa that you receive overseas, you will not be able to apply for the program once in Canada.

When interviewed overseas as a potential domestic worker, you will be assessed by the interviewing officer on your education, experience and aptitude for learning, and any previous experience or formal training that you have had as a domestic and, in the case of caring for children, as a nanny. At the present time, a prospective nanny will have to prove either one year's paid work as a nanny prior to coming to Canada or prove that she or he has taken a course as a nanny — which courses to my knowledge are only available in some western European countries.

To be put on this special program, you must indicate that you have initiative and be able to describe the kinds of courses that you wish to take while in Canada to upgrade yourself. Remember, the officer will be looking at your ability to establish yourself in Canada after you have completed your term as a nanny or domestic.

The interviewing officer will consider whether you are motivated, adaptable, resourceful, possess communication skills, show initiative, and have positive attitudes about working in Canada and upgrading your skills. All these factors will be used in determining whether to put you on this special program.

In addition, you will be asked to provide details of your family composition. The fact that you are married and/or have dependants may be used in your favor to show reliable work habits, or potentially against you in that you might be considered unable to earn sufficient money in the future to support your children.

When you arrive in Canada as a foreign domestic, you will be asked to contact the local Canada Employment Centre for counselling and assessment of your training and skill upgrading needs. Employment Canada counsellors will tell you about the various training programs that are available and will assist you in the selection of appropriate training courses.

If these courses are given through educational institutions, you will also be sent to the nearest Canada Immigration Centre for the purpose of obtaining authorization to attend school.

Prior to the completion of your first year in Canada, you will be assessed by an immigration officer concerning your progress. The Immigration Office will continue to monitor your progress over the period of the first two years in Canada.

At the completion of the first two years in Canada, a decision will be made about whether you have upgraded your skills sufficiently to become self-sufficient in this country. If there is a positive determination in your case, your permit to work in Canada as a domestic or in any other job for which you have received an employment offer will be approved for a further year while processing of your permanent resident papers is begun.

Some of the factors that determine whether or not you will receive a favorable decision on the part of the immigration officers include the following:

(a) Have you been working continuously for a period of at least two years?

(b) Have you taken steps to improve your education or language skills?

(c) Have you taken steps to upgrade your occupational skills or learn new ones?

(d) If you wish to continue to remain in the domestic work field, could you earn an adequate income to ensure self-sufficiency?

(e) If you want to leave domestic work, what is the level of income that you could earn in a new area?

(f) Will the possible reunification of close family with you in Canada create financial hardships on you?

(g) Have you adapted to the Canadian lifestyle, established contacts in the community, and made friends?

If the determination is made that you have not established yourself successfully in Canada, you will be informed that you will not be considered for this special program. A FINAL ONE-YEAR EXTENSION OF YOUR EMPLOYMENT PERMIT WILL BE GRANTED AND THEN YOU WILL BE REQUIRED TO LEAVE CANADA.

As you can see from the above, the opportunity for foreign domestic workers or nannies to remain in this country is a special and exceptional program that has resulted from political pressure on the government of Canada by various women's groups in this country in support of this one, particular class of individuals.

Your employer in Canada will be required to enter into a contract with the local Canada Employment Centre outlining the details of your domestic employment in this country. The salary, room and board allowance, and duties of a domestic worker in Canada will be outlined in this contract. Sample #15 is an example of the domestic contract required in the Ontario Region of the Immigration Department.

In my opinion, while this program is not liked by most government officials, the government will continue it for the near future although it is likely to be reviewed on a regular basis.

EMPLOYER/EMPLOYEE AGREEMENT

 Employment and Emploi et
Immigration Canada Immigration Canada

**EMPLOYER/EMPLOYEE AGREEMENT
HOUSEHOLD DOMESTIC WORK
ONTARIO REGION**

OFFER OF EMPLOYMENT AS A DOMESTIC MADE BY:

MARY   SULLIVAN
(Employer Name)   PLEASE PRINT CLEARLY

123   MAIN   STREET TORONTO   MIA IAI
(Address)   (Postal Code)

123-4567
(Telephone)

TO:

SUSAN SALTER
(Employee Name)   PLEASE PRINT CLEARLY

55 SPENCER ROAD   TORONTO   M2C 3G2
(Address)   (Postal Code)

By affixing their signature to this document, both parties agree to the terms and conditions of employment, as outlined below.

_____   NOV 20/9-
(Employer Signature)   Date

_____   _____
(Employee Signature)   Date

Distribution

(a)   After signed by Employer:

   – 1 copy to be given to Employer by CEC
   – 1 copy to be retained by CEC
   – Original is forwarded to post abroad by CEC:

(b)   After signed by Foreign Worker:

   – 1 copy to be given to Foreign Worker by Visa Officer
   – 1 copy to be, retained on Foreign Post File

Canadian representative abroad

TEMPEMP6079LMP0189B
ONT 1978   Français au verso

JOB DUTIES

A. **Cooking**

Entire responsibility for meals   □ _____

Partial responsibility for meals   ☑ _____

No cooking   □ _____

Dishes and clean-up   □ _____

B. **Child Care**

Details of children to be cared for are as follows:

First/Last Name of Child	Age	Gender	Relationship to Employer	Hours/Week Attending School
MARCIA SULLIVAN	16 MONS.	F	DAUGHTER	NIL

Is employee required to escort children to school, medical appointments, lessons, etc?   Yes □   No ☑

If yes, describe briefly: _____

If employee required to supervise children's homework?   Yes □   No ☑

If yes, describe briefly: _____

Are any particular child rearing techniques to be carried out by the employee?   Yes ☑   No □

If yes, describe briefly: READING & SPEAKING ENGLISH, PLAYING GAMES, ETC.

C. **Housekeeping**

Is the employee responsible for all aspects of maintenance such as:

- Laundry   ✓ ONLY CHILD'S
- Dusting   ✓
- Washing Floors   _____
  - walls   _____
  - windows   _____
  - dishes   _____
- Grocery Shopping   _____
- Making beds   ✓ ONLY CHILD'S
- Recording and controlling household expenses _____
- Other (please specify) WASHING CHILD'S CLOTHES

List major appliances to be used by the employee: WASHER AND DRYER.

_____

Description of the dwelling which employee is to maintain (i.e. number of rooms, any special conditions, etc.)

NOT REQUIRED TO MAINTAIN HOME EXCEPT OWN ROOM AND BATH.

D. **Miscellaneous**

Is the employee required to travel with the employer?   Yes ☑   No □

Is the employee required to have or obtain a driver's license?   Yes □   No ☑

Is the employee required to care for pets?   Yes ☑   No □

Specify: SMALL DOG

WORKING CONDITIONS

I. WAGES

Employer agrees to pay said employee a minimum sum of $ _5.00_ per _HOUR_

*NB: These employees are entitled to Ontario's Hourly Minimum Wage. The employee must also be paid one and one-half their regular hourly rate of pay for each hour worked beyond 44 hours a week.

II. ROOM AND BOARD

Cost of room and board provided to employee shall be $ _63.00_ per _WEEK_

*NB: The cost of room and board must not exceed the maximum amount as specified by the Ontario Ministry of Labour.

III. ACCOMODATION

Private room: yes _✓_

Other (please specify) _____

IV. EMPLOYER/EMPLOYEE DEDUCTIONS

Employer is required to make all appropriate employer/employee deductions and contributions for (1) Canada Pension Plan, (2) Unemployment Insurance, (3) Revenue Canada and (4) OHIP. Please refer to the local offices of Revenue Canada and OHIP for current premium rates.

V. JOB DURATION shall be as follows: ☑ temporary   number of months _12_

VI. HOURS OF WORK shall be as follows:

_8.75_ hours per day. Work day starts at _flexible_ and ends at _flexible_.
_5_ days per week. _MIN. 40 hrs/wk – MAX 44 hrs/wk_

VII. TIME OFF shall be as follows: _2 days per week_

*NB: A domestic employee is considered to be working if required to be on the premises. Ontario Ministry of Labour Regulations require every householder to give to a live-in domestic two free periods each week – one of 36 consecutive hours and one of twelve consecutive hours – free from the performance of any duties and without any deduction from the regular wages of the domestic. These two periods may be combined to give 48 consecutive hours off each week. If, with the consent of the domestic, duties are performed during the free periods mentioned , the equivalent amount of time off must be added to one of the next four periods of free time or the hourly wage agreed upon must be paid for the hours worked. If time off is not granted, the employer must pay not less than one and one-half their regular rate of pay for each hour worked during the free period.

VIII. VACATION WITH PAY shall be as follows: _2 weeks or 4% of gross_

The employer must give the employee at least two weeks vacation for each year of employment, and the pay for that vacation must not be less than 4% of the employee's gross earnings. Gross earnings include the value of room and board. The vacation may be one two-week period or two one-week periods. If the employee continues to "live in" during the vacation, the employer may make a deduction from the vacation pay for room and board. If the employee does not live in during the vacation, the employer may not make a charge for room and board. Regardless of the reason for termination, where employment terminates before the completion of a working year, the employee must receive at least 4% of any earnings on which the employee has not previously received vacation pay.

IX. PUBLIC HOLIDAYS shall be as follows: _9 as listed_

After three months of employment, including employment prior to 1 January 1981, domestic workers are entitled to seven paid statutory holidays each year. These are: New Year's Day, Good Friday, Victoria day, Dominion Day, Labour Day, Thanksgiving Day and Christmas Day. The employer may, with the agreement of the domestic, substitute another working day for the holiday, however, this substitute day shall not be later than the next annual vacation of the domestic. If the holiday falls on a non-working day or in a vacation period, the employer shall designate a working day as the holiday or, with the agreement of the domestic, pay the domestic an additional day's pay during the pay period in which the holiday falls.

↳ Boxing Day / Easter Monday

X.   TRAINING

If the domestic so chooses, time off (minimum 3 consecutive hours weekly over and above the 48 hours referred to above) will be provided for purposes of attending training and employer will be required to pay cost of said training up to a maximum of $20.00 monthly.

*NB: Prior to commencing any sort of outside training, a domestic must be in possession of a valid Student Authorization from the local Canada Immigration Centre.

XI.   WORKERS COMPENSATION

Employers must register domestic workers with the Ontario Workers Compensation Board. They are required to prepay coverage for one year costing $3.09 for every $100.00 of the worker's gross salary.

PROTECTION FOR EMPLOYER/EMPLOYEE

EMPLOYER

1.   The employment of the domestic worker is for the care of the employer's dependant children.

2.   Failure to honour the terms of this contract by the employer may result in the denial of future requests.

3.   Should this domestic worker be unable to perform his/her job duties please contact the local Canada Employment Centre to discuss hiring a replacement.

DOMESTIC WORKER

1.   A domestic worker who loses his/her job should report immediately to a local Canada Immigration Centre:

If, in the opinion of the Immigration Officer, he/she has lost said job through no fault of his/her own, he/she may be eligible for assistance from the local Canada Employment Centre in finding a new job.

2.   All domestic workers are covered by the general enforcement provisions of the Employment Standards Act of the Province of Ontario, with respect to the collection of wages, equal pay, equal benefits, pregnancy leave and termination pay.

Employees who believe they are not receiving these minimum standards may file a complaint with the Employment Standards Branch of the Ontario Ministry of Labour. If, upon investigation, the Officer finds that the employer is not complying with the Regulations, he may compute the wage arrears for a two-year period to a maximum of $4,000.00. The employer may be asked to pay the arrears directly to the employee, or pay the arrears plus a 10% penalty to the Director of the Employment Standards Branch, in trust. Where the money is paid to the Director, the employer has the opportunity to ask for a review of the assessment by a referee. Failure to comply with the Regulation could also result in prosecution.

The Employment Standards Act also prohibits an employer from taking any reprisals against an employee who seeks the enforcement of the Act and Regulations.

To be completed by the CEC:

A.   This form has been received and approved by:

CEC	Canada Employment Centre	D	M	Y
ADDRESS	2221 Yonge Street	0 1	0 1	9 0
	Toronto, Ontario M4S 3B8	RESPONSIBILITY CENTRE CODE		

B.   The appropriate CCDO Code for this employment is: (Indicated by X)

☐ 6142-110   Housekeeper   ☐ 6147-110   Babysitter
☐ 6142-126   Companion   ☐ 6147-114   Childrens Nurse, Private Household
☐ 6142-130   Servant/Domestic   ☐ 6147-130   Parents Helper

15
IMMIGRATING TO QUEBEC

In 1976, the Parti Quebecois lead by René Levesque came to power as the government in the Province of Quebec. For 10 years, until they lost the 1986 election to the Liberals, the Parti Quebecois, with an avowed separatist policy, ruled the province.

One of the first issues the Parti Quebecois raised with the federal government was that of immigration. Quebec wanted to set the rules, interview, and decide upon immigrants to their province independently from the procedures previously carried out by the federal government's Immigration Department.

Quebec had a strong constitutional basis for its request. Section 95, a little-known section of the British North America Act, 1867, the statute of the British Parliament that created Canada, provides that in the areas of immigration and agriculture each of the provinces can make laws affecting that particular province. Such laws, the section goes on to say, are valid so long as they are "not repugnant to" (in serious contradiction to) a law of the federal government. Since the cost to a province of opening and maintaining immigration offices around the world would be very high, in the past the provinces had stayed out of the field of immigration law and left the rules for and the choosing of immigrants up to the federal government.

All of this changed in 1976 when Quebec declared that it wanted to establish its own immigration policy and rules and control who would be able to immigrate to Quebec. The Parti Quebecois government entered into negotiations with the Government of Canada which resulted in an agreement governing permanent and temporary immigration to Quebec being signed on February 20, 1978.

This agreement with Quebec clearly sets forth a general policy that immigration to Quebec must contribute to Quebec's cultural and social heritage, taking into account Quebec's French character. As a result, Quebec has established its own rules, point system, and job demand list for immigration to that province. Also, Quebec conducts its own interviews with prospective immigrants and determines whether to accept or reject them.

What is left for the federal government is to conduct and pass on medical and security/criminal checks (see chapter 13). Apart from this, the federal government no longer makes decisions about the selection of immigrants to Quebec. If Quebec accepts you for immigration, they will issue you a "Certificat de Selection du Quebec" which must be accepted by the federal government subject to medical and security/criminal clearances. On the other hand, the actual immigrant visa (see Sample #9) is still issued by the federal government, which means that you will likely have to deal with two sets of offices and forms when immigrating to Quebec. This may be inconvenient but it is not onerous and many people find Quebec easier and faster to deal with — especially if they are fluent in the French language.

The Quebec/Canada Agreement provides a point system for an assessment of a person destined for Quebec. If you fail to qualify for Quebec, but receive more than 30 points, the application will be referred to a Canadian visa office so that you may be assessed to see if you qualify to immigrate somewhere else in Canada. For example, let us say that auto mechanics have 1 point for demand in Quebec, but 10 points under the federal rules. Such an individual may be rejected by Quebec, but accepted by the Government of Canada.

The Province of Quebec's point system is similar to but different from the one outlined in chapter 9. The major differences are in the points for occupational demand, specific vocational preparation (SVP), language, and personal suitability/ adaptability. The Quebec point system with the maximum points available in each category is shown in Table #5.

As can be seen from this table, Quebec puts much greater emphasis on the ability to speak French fluently (15 points) and adaptability to Quebec (22 points).

Appendix #3 gives a list of Quebec Immigration Offices abroad, their addresses, and the countries which they cover.

As stated above, Quebec has its own list of occupations in demand. This list, unlike the federal one, is not a published, public document. I have tried to obtain a copy of this list but have been unsuccessful.

TABLE #5
POINT SYSTEM FOR QUEBEC

1.	Education	11 points
2.	Occupational Demand/Employment	15 points (if approved)
		0 - 10 points (based on Quebec list)
3.	Specific Vocational Preparation (SVP)	10 points
	- less than 6 months	2
	- 6 to 12 months	4
	- 1 to 2 years	6
	- 2 to 4 years	8
	- 4 years or more	10
4.	Experience (not including training or apprenticeship)	10 points

Years	
½	1
1	2
1½	3
2	4
2½	5
3	6
3½	7
4	8
4½	9
5 or more	10

In experience there is no tie-in to SVP as there is in the federal point system. Therefore, a person with a low SVP can still obtain 10 points for experience if they have 5 or more years in their occupation.

5.	Age	10 points
	up to 35	10
	36	9
	37	6
	38	4
	39	2
	40	1

TABLE #5 — Continued

6.	Language	French - 15 points
		English - 2 points
French		
	Understand	6
	Speak	5
	Read	3
	Write	1
English		
	Understand	1
	Write	1
7.	Adaptability to Quebec	22 points
	Personal Qualities	15
	Motivation	5
	Knowledge of Quebec (at least one visit of 2 weeks in preceding 5 years)	2
8.	Relatives in Quebec	5 points
	In settlement area	5
	Elsewhere in Quebec	2

TOTAL   100 points

Bonus Points

1.	Spouse who speaks French fluently	4 points
2.	Spouse with an occupation in average demand in Quebec	4 points
3.	Children under 12	7 points
	1 child	1 point
	2 children	2 points
	3 children	4 points

16
DRAFT DODGERS AND DESERTERS

The fact that you are a draft dodger or deserter from the armed services of your country does not prohibit you from applying to become an immigrant to Canada.

Draft dodging and desertion are not considered criminal offences in Canada unless they occur during wartime and you are deserting the armed forces of one of Canada's allies. Thus, for example, Americans evading military service in the United States during the Vietnam conflict could immigrate to Canada, and their status with the military authorities in the United States was of no concern to the Canadian authorities.

Remember, however, that your application must comply in all respects with the criteria outlined earlier in this book; a breach of any of the immigration rules or regulations could lead to your being rejected as an immigrant (except in cases outlined in chapter 14).

In addition, since applicants cannot apply from inside Canada, the difficulty of applying from one's homeland while evading the local draft is difficult. While Canadian officials in the embassy or consulate in your homeland may not directly inform your country of your application, the fact that a security check is made will possibly tip off your own country about your plans to immigrate to Canada. Therefore, in reality, you will probably have to apply from a third country where you will be able to remain while your application is being processed. This will not be easy.

17

REFUGEES — THE NEW SYSTEM

a. GENERAL

Canada's record with respect to refugees has been one of the best in the world since 1950. As a relatively small country, we have taken a large share of the world's refugees — from Hungary in 1957, from Czechoslovakia in 1968, from Uganda, and now southeast Asia. In addition, over the years we have taken in many individual cases of refugees. Although Canada's overall record is enviable, the procedure for becoming a refugee in Canada in the situation of individual cases is long, much longer than in the United States, France, or England, and in the case of certain countries our record is not good.

Canada is a signator of the United Nations Convention for Refugees (1951), and unlike other nations we generally live up to this obligation. Under the terms of that Convention, refugees are defined as follows:

> Owing to well-founded fears of being persecuted for reasons of race, religion, nationality, membership of a particular social group or political opinion, is outside the country of his, or her, nationality and is unable, or owing to such fears, is unwilling to avail himself, or herself, of the protection of that country; or who not having a nationality and being outside the country of his or her, former habitual residence, is unable or owing to such fears, is unwilling to return to it.

This definition has been included in Canada's Immigration Act in section 2(1), and Canada's obligation to take in refugees has been included in section 3(g) of the act.

While the above definition seems very wide, Canada is, in fact, reluctant to accept refugees from countries other than where the most extreme forms of persecution take place. Thus, in order to be a refugee, you must be able to prove either a past history of persecution including jailings, torture, and the like, without due process of law or the probability (not possibility) that such actions would occur.

Canada will usually accept refugees from most communist countries, though not all, and has in the past accepted refugees from Uganda and Chile (though in the latter case, somewhat reluctantly and only after political pressure in Canada by various social, political, and religious organizations).

In the case of countries that are "right-of-centre" oriented or are allies of Canada or of Canada's allies, it is unlikely that refugee status would be granted by Canada. Such countries include Greece, Turkey, and many South American and Central American countries such as Brazil, Bolivia, and Peru.

In any case, if you or a relative of yours is in a position to make a claim for refugee status, you should consult a lawyer — if possible, one who confines a significant portion of his or her practice to the field of immigration law. The immigration of refugees to Canada is a complex legal problem. A lawyer is, for all practical purposes, a necessity in a case such as this. Remember, you may not be a refugee just because you think you are; you are a refugee if you fall within the above definition and conform to past precedents concerning refugees.

Canada's extremely complex refugee system could result in a refugee claimant going through a seven-step procedure that could take well over five years without the claimant ever once appearing before the person actually deciding the case. (It could all be done on the basis of transcripts of testimony at hearings.) A court challenge to this process was launched in 1983.

In April, 1985 the Supreme Court of Canada in the famous *Singh* decision ruled that all refugee claimants were entitled to a full oral hearing before the Immigration Appeal Board (now the Immigration and Refugee Board). The government, realizing it could not give oral hearings to all 63 000 refugee claimants then in the system, set up an Administrative Review Programme (ADR) to clear up the backlog.

Unfortunately, while this process was unfolding, several incidents involving the movement of alleged refugees occurred, including the arrival of a large number of Turkish and Brazilian claimants and one boatload (approximately 175) of Sikh refugee claimants from Germany. The backlash from the Canadian government resulted in the introduction of two pieces of legislation — Bills C-55 and C-84. In my opinion, as expressed to a committee of the Parliament of Canada, these bills create a much more efficient system but take away from our past 40-year commitment to refugees and do not provide the protection and rights of appeal that Canada has been noted for in the past.

b. INDIVIDUAL CLAIMS TO REFUGEE STATUS

In order to make a claim for refugee status, you must do so at an immigration office or at a point of entry into Canada upon your arrival here. It is best if such a claim can be made inland with your lawyer in attendance. If you make your claim at a border entry point (such as an airport, dock, or land crossing) you should say you wish to be referred immediately to the local Law Society or Legal Aid in order to obtain a lawyer. When you speak to that organization, explain that you are claiming refugee status and insist upon being referred to a lawyer who is knowledgeable in the field of immigration law. As I said above, refugee cases are complex and require someone with prior experience.

Persons who are already in Canada must make their refugee claim to an immigration officer at an immigration office. You will be referred to a senior immigration officer who will interview you. The purpose of this interview is first to determine if you have broken any immigration laws (see chapters 12 and 23) and if you have (for example, overstayed your visitor's status, worked illegally, entered Canada with false documents, etc.), your case will go into the regular immigration enforcement stream and you will make your refugee claim at your immigration inquiry (see below).

If you are not in breach of any laws, your refugee claim will be referred to a hearing before an immigration adjudicator and a member of the Convention Refugee Determination Division (CRDD) of the Immigration and Refugee Board (IRB). This hearing will determine whether you are eligible to make a refugee claim and, if you are eligible, will determine whether there is a "Credible Basis" for your claim.

In either case you will end up before a two-member hearing panel composed of an immigration adjudicator from the immigration department and a member of IRB, an independent board not part of the immigration department. We will deal with the hearing process in detail later.

At your initial interview, the immigration officer will want to hear why you are claiming to be a refugee. He or she will also want a great deal of biographical information.

You will be asked to complete a nine-page Personal Information Form for People Claiming Convention Refugee Status (PIF) (see Sample #16). If at all possible, you or your lawyer should prepare this document *prior* to going to the immigration department. *Your reasons for your refugee claim, which should appear in paragraph 33 of the PIF, will become crucial to your case.* First, these reasons may be sufficient to have the government case presenting officer (CPO) (the government's legal representative — the prosecutor) concede the "credible basis" to your claim before the adjudicator and IRB member at your first hearing. This means you would go directly to your full hearing before the IRB. Second, your PIF will be used throughout the proceedings and can be used to cross-examine you — this means it can be used to show not only consistency in your refugee claim but also to show inconsistencies and discrepancies in your story. *It is crucial that this form be properly prepared.*

c. THE INQUIRY/HEARING

The next stage will be the opening of an inquiry before an adjudicator. This is described in chapter 24. The government will be represented by a case presenting officer (CPO). At this stage, the inquiry will proceed to the point where a determination is made that *other than* for your claim to refugee status you would be subject to deportation from Canada. This will be done usually on the basis that you came to Canada as a visitor and now intend to stay and wish to be an immigrant and you do not have an immigration visa as required by law. Usually this issue can be admitted to by you or your lawyer.

The next stage will be to determine whether or not you are eligible to claim refugee status in Canada. *You must make your intention to claim refugee status no later* *than at this point in time, before any evidence is taken. If you fail to do so you will be prohibited from making your claim later on. It is sufficient if you made your claim to the initial immigration officer who interviewed you provided he or she has given you written proof of your claim.*

The issues of eligibility to make a refugee claim are very complex. They are summarized briefly in chapter 18 and are the same in both situations. Once the issues of admissibility and eligibility have been determined, the primary issue comes into play — do you have a "credible basis" for your refugee claim? The first two steps are handled by the immigration adjudicator alone. For the third step, the CRDD member of the IRB joins the adjudicator to make the decision. You need only convince one of the two of them in order to succeed at this step.

What constitutes "credible basis"? Since the new laws only came into being on January 1, 1989, there have not as yet been very many decisions from the superior courts to the IRB. This is in a sense a mini-trial. You are subject to being called as a witness and can be examined by your own lawyer and cross-examined by the CPO. The decision concerning credible basis can be made on evidence deemed to be credible (believable) or trustworthy in all the circumstances. This may be your own oral testimony, documentary evidence about yourself, your family, or friends, or general documentary evidence about conditions in your country. As stated earlier, the CPO can concede (agree that you have) credible basis. Often this will be based on what you have said in your personal information form and on your counsel's negotiations with the CPO prior to the hearing.

It is not yet clear what is enough evidence to prove "credible basis." Must you tip the balance at least 51% in your favor or is it sufficient to merely prove a possibility of success? I believe the latter should be the test; however, I think that somewhere in between these two standards is where the cases are at the present time.

Remember, you only have to convince one of the two to proceed to the next hearing. If you are found to have a credible basis, you will be sent to a full hearing before two members of the IRB. The IRB member who sat on your credible basis hearing is not allowed to sit on your full hearing before the IRB. This hearing will take place in about four to seven months and will be dealt with in the next section.

Unfortunately if both the adjudicator and the IRB member turn down your credible basis claim, then you have virtually no right of appeal and you will be removed from Canada usually within three or four days.

d. CONVENTION REFUGEE DETERMINATION DIVISION

Persons found to be eligible to make a refugee claim and to have a credible basis for the claim are referred on for a full hearing before the CRDD. Two members normally sit at the hearing. You may request or consent to one member hearing the claim. However, *under no circumstances should you choose one member to hear your case unless the refugee hearing officer indicates in writing that your case will be conceded.*

In practice, the minister is not represented at hearings. However, the CRDD has refugee hearing officers (RHOs) who assist in the hearings on behalf of the board members. The RHO is supposed to have an examination/investigation function, not a cross-examination/adversarial function. To date there appear to be few problems with the RHOs, but care should be taken to ensure that an RHO does not take on an adversarial role. If your lawyer is concerned that the RHO is acting as a prosecutor, he or she should make an objection on the record.

As can be seen from the above discussion, you clearly need a competent lawyer knowledgeable in immigration law at this hearing. You are required to prove that you are a convention refugee as defined at the beginning of this chapter at least on a balance of probability — that is, at least 51% your way.

Evidence at the hearing is any evidence that may be considered to be credible or trustworthy. The rules of evidence do not apply. Testimony of the claimant, witnesses, and documentary evidence may be presented. Medical evidence in the form of medical reports, such as those done on the Amnesty International Protocol, may be helpful where there has been past physical injury from persecution.

If you lose your case there is virtually no right of appeal and you will likely be removed from Canada within several days — at most a week or two if you are lucky.

e. GROUP SPONSORSHIP OF REFUGEES

The Immigration Act also provides for the group sponsorship of refugees. Under this program, a group of not fewer than five Canadians or a corporation may be allowed to sponsor the immigration to Canada of a person who has been determined to be a refugee by an immigration officer abroad. This group sponsorship plan has been used very effectively with the large refugee population in southeast Asia (known as the boat people).

Under the group sponsorship, the 5 or more sponsors (up to as many as 25) must have a total annual income of approximately $100 000 and have on hand about $1 000 for each immigrant refugee being sponsored. The $100 000 figure is a guideline; the amount could be somewhat less for an enthusiastic and well-organized group.

Samples #17, #18, #19, and #20 show the information package and sponsorship applications prepared by the Canadian government. You should read them carefully if you wish to sponsor a refugee. These forms indicate very clearly the level and degree of support that you and your group will be required to undertake for a period of one year.

f. DESIGNATED CLASSES

In addition to the refugee cases outlined in this chapter, the government of Canada has also created designated classes of both large and small movements of people to Canada. The government is prepared to accept that individuals moving under specific circumstances from these countries to Canada will be allowed to immigrate to Canada if they are outside their country of origin and not in Canada without having to go through the procedures outlined above. The designated class regulations are currently in force for the following countries:

INDOCHINESE

Democratic Kampuchea

People's Democratic Republic of Laos

The Socialist Republic of Vietnam

SELF-EXILED PERSONS

Albania

Bulgaria

Czechoslovakia

German Democratic Republic (East Germany)

Hungary

Poland

Romania

Haiti

U.S.S.R.

LATIN AMERICANS

Argentina

Chile

Uruguay

Guatemala

El Salvador

Given the developments in eastern Europe during the last six months of 1989 and the first few months of 1990, there are likely to be changes in the designated class regulations over the next year or so. How can Poland, Hungary, East Germany, and other eastern European countries with democratically elected non-communist governments remain on this list? Only time and the next edition of this book will tell.

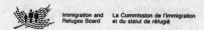

Immigration and Refugee Board
La Commission de l'immigration et du statut de réfugié

**PERSONAL INFORMATION FORM
FOR PEOPLE CLAIMING CONVENTION REFUGEE STATUS**

Instructions

The purpose of this form is to inform the Immigration and Refugee Board about your claim to Convention refugee status.

The confidentiality of information contained in this document is protected by Federal legislation. The Board must have your written consent before disclosing to the public any of the personal information you have provided.

This form must be completed in English or in French. If you require the services of an interpreter, ensure that the interpreter signs the declaration on page 9.

When you have completed this form, return a copy of it to the Immigration office where your hearing is to be held and take the original and another copy to the adjudicator at your hearing. Keep a copy for your own records.

Answer all questions, marking "N/A" for those that do not apply to you. If there is insufficient space provided to answer questions fully, use the back of the pages.

Give exact details where requested. Please **print clearly.**

IDENTIFICATION:

1. Family Name	Given Names	2. Male [ ] Female [ ]

3. Give any other name(s) you have used (include family name at birth if different from 1.):

4. Date of Birth: (Day) (Month) (Year)	5. Place and Country of Birth:
6. Citizenship at Birth:	7. Present Citizenship:
8. Nationality, Ethnic Group or Tribe	9. Religion:

10. If you have no country of citizenship, please name your country of habitual residence:

11. Other country or countries of citizenship:

12. In which country or countries do you fear persecution?:

13. Present Marital Status:

Married or common law spouse [ ]
Divorced or Separated [ ]
Widowed [ ]
Never Married [ ]

CRDD rev. 22.06.89

Canada

2

14. Complete the following information about your married or common law spouse, any children, your parents, brothers, and sisters:

Complete Name	Relationship	Birth-date DD / MM / YY			Citizenship	Place and Country of Residence

SKILLS AND EDUCATION:

15. State the number of years of formal education/training you have had: _____ years

Give the following information:

(From) Month / Year	(To) Month / Year	Name of School Place and Country	Level obtained and/or Degree

16. Work history:

(From) Month / Year	(To) Month / Year	Name of Company/Employer Place and Country	Type of Work

3

RESIDENCE:

17. List the places and countries where you have resided for the last (10) years, beginning with your last residence:

(From) Month / Year	(To) Month / Year	Place and Country	Status in Country*

*examples: student, temporary worker, permanent resident, citizen, or other status given by the country.

PASSPORT, TRAVEL AND/OR IDENTITY DOCUMENTS:

18. Did you apply for a passport?   Yes [ ]   No [ ]

If **no**, why not? _____

_____

If **yes**, were you issued a passport?   Yes [ ]   No [ ]

If **yes**, give the following information: Date of Issue: _____

Expiry Date: _____

Country of Issue: _____

Where was it issued?: _____

19. Did you need an exit visa/permit to leave your country of citizenship or habitual residence?   Yes [ ]   No [ ]

If **yes**, were you issued a visa?   Yes [ ]   No [ ]

If **yes**, give the following information: Date of Issue: _____

Expiry Date: _____

20. Did you apply for a Canadian visa to travel to Canada?   Yes [ ]   No [ ]

If **no**, why not? _____

_____

If **yes**, were you issued a visa?   Yes [ ]   No [ ]

If **yes**, give the following information: Date of Issue: _____

Expiry Date: _____

Where was it issued?: _____

4

21. List any other documents, **genuine or false,** used to travel from your country of citizenship or habitual residence to Canada:

Document Type	Document Number	Issued by	Date of Issue DD / MM / YY	Date of Expiry DD / MM / YY	Where is the document now?

Indicate with an asterisk (*) any of these documents which were false or not issued in your name.

TRAVEL TO CANADA:

22. List the exact route of your journey to Canada, starting with departure from your country of citizenship or of habitual residence and ending with your departure for Canada:

Country	Methods of Transportation	Date of Departure DD / MM / YY

23. Place and date of arrival in Canada

_____   _____ _____ _____
                                (Day)   (Month) (Year)

24. When, where and to which official in Canada did you first state your intention to make a refugee claim?

Where: _____   When: _____ _____ _____
                                    (Day) (Month) (Year)

To Whom: _____

25. Have you been to Canada before?   Yes [ ]
                                                           No [ ]

If **yes,** give details as follows:

(From) Month / Year	(To) Month / Year	Purpose

5

26. Prior to your present journey to Canada, have you travelled outside your country of citizenship or habitual residence within the last five years?

Yes [ ]
No [ ]

If yes, give details: _____

_____

_____

_____

MILITARY SERVICE:

27. Is military or other service compulsory in your country of citizenship or habitual residence?

Yes [ ]
No [ ]

Draft Age: _____

Length of service required: _____

Were you required to serve?

Yes [ ]
No [ ]

If yes, did you serve?

Yes [ ]
No [ ]

If yes, did you complete your service?

Yes [ ]
No [ ]

Dates of Service: From: _____ _____ _____ To: _____ _____ _____
                        (Day) (Month) (Year)   (Day) (Month) (Year)

If you did not serve or did not complete your service, why not?

_____

_____

_____

POLICE RECORD:

28. Are you, or were you, wanted by the police or military or any other authorities in any country?

Yes [ ]
No [ ]

29. Have you ever committed or been convicted of any crime or offence?

Yes [ ]
No [ ]

If you answered yes to questions 28 and/or 29, please explain:

_____

_____

_____

6

PREVIOUS REQUESTS FOR CONVENTION REFUGEE STATUS:

30. Have you previously requested refugee status...

In Canada? Yes [ ] No [ ]

At a Canadian office abroad? Yes [ ] No [ ]

In any other country or countries? Yes [ ] No [ ]

If you answered yes to any of the above, complete the following:

Date DD/MM/YY	Where and of whom?	Result

31. Have you been recognized as a refugee by the United Nations High Commissioner for Refugees? Yes [ ] No [ ]

If you answered yes, indicate the country in which this recognition was given: _____

Do you have a document confirming this recognition? Yes [ ] No [ ]

If yes, give the following information: Date of Issue: _____

Document Number: _____

32. Have any of your relatives previously requested refugee status...

In Canada? Yes [ ] No [ ]

At a Canadian office abroad? Yes [ ] No [ ]

In any other country or countries? Yes [ ] No [ ]

If you answered yes to any of the above, complete the following:

Name and Relationship	Date DD/MM/YY	Where and of whom	Result

7

CURRENT CLAIM TO CONVENTION REFUGEE STATUS:

33. Your claim to a well-founded fear of persecution must be related to one or more of the five (5) grounds cited in the definition of a Convention refugee as contained in the United Nations Convention Relating to the Status of Refugees and Canada's Immigration Act.

    Check which ground or grounds apply to your claim.

    RACE   [ ]

    RELIGION   [ ]

    NATIONALITY   [ ]

    POLITICAL OPINION   [ ]

    MEMBERSHIP IN A PARTICULAR SOCIAL GROUP   [ ]

    Please set out, in point form and in chronological order, the incidents which have caused you to have a fear of persecution and explain *why* these incidents have caused you to have such fear:

    _____
    _____
    _____
    _____
    _____
    _____
    _____
    _____
    _____
    _____
    _____
    _____
    _____
    _____
    _____
    _____
    _____
    _____
    _____
    _____
    _____
    _____
    _____
    _____
    _____
    _____
    _____
    _____

8

_____
_____
_____
_____
_____
_____
_____
_____
_____
_____
_____
_____
_____
_____
_____
_____
_____
_____
_____
_____
_____
_____
_____
_____
_____
_____
_____
_____
_____
_____
_____
_____
_____
_____
_____
_____

If more space is required, use the reverse side of these pages.

9

POINTS OF CONTACT IN CANADA:

34. Address & telephone no. where you are staying in Canada:

_____
(No. & Street, Room or Floor, Apt. #)

_____
(City, Province, Postal Code)

Telephone: Area Code [   ] Telephone number [   ]

You must tell the Board of any change in this address for the purpose of receiving any documents regarding your claim.

35. Name, address & phone no. of counsel authorized to represent you:

_____   _____
(Name)   (Firm)

_____
(No. & Street, Room or Floor, Apt. #)

_____
(City, Province, Postal Code)

Telephone: Area Code [   ] Telephone number [   ]

If there is any change in counsel authorized to represent you, you should tell the Board as soon as possible.

36. Do you require the services of an interpreter for any proceedings before
the Refugee Division?   Yes [   ]
                                                                              No [   ]

Language to be interpreted: _____

CLAIMANT DECLARATION:

I declare that the information contained herein is true and correct to the best of my knowledge and belief.

_____   _____
(Date)   (Claimant's Signature)

INTERPRETER DECLARATION:

I _____ , hereby certify that I have translated the complete contents of these nine (9) pages and all attached documents to the claimant from the English to the _____ language. He/she has assured me that he/she fully understands the contents of these pages and all attached documents as translated.

_____   _____
(Date)   (Interpreter's Signature)

Each year the Canadian government agrees to accept a certain number of the world's persecuted and displaced people for resettlement in this country.

Apart from those accepted under this annual refugee resettlement plan, there are always many others in need of our help who are equally capable of becoming self-supporting members of our society if they can be assured of the friendship and support of concerned Canadians.

Canadian groups and organizations who are prepared to act as sponsors, supplying the more personalized settlement services needed by displaced and persecuted people, will have a direct influence on the total number of refugees that can come to Canada. This is because refugees assisted in this way are admitted over and above those planned for in the government's annual refugee resettlement plan.

WHO CAN BE SPONSORED

The Refugee Sponsorship Program applies to two groups of people:

Convention Refugees - those having a well-founded fear of persecution on the grounds of race, religion, nationality, political opinion, or membership in a particular social group, and

Special Designated Classes - those displaced by emergency situations, and others for whom the Canadian public feels a special humanitarian concern.

The program includes only those refugees who are still abroad. The means by which refugees already in Canada may be assisted are discussed on page nine of this brochure.

WHO CAN SPONSOR

Canadians can enter into sponsorship agreements with the Canada Employment and Immigration Commission (CEIC) in either of two different ways:

- Local groups of at least five Canadian citizens or permanent residents (landed immigrants), 18 years of age or older, and local legally incorporated organizations may sign individual agreements at Canada Immigration Centres in their own communities, or

- National organizations with a humanitarian tradition may sign a comprehensive agreement with the Minister covering all their member groups across the country.

HOW SPONSORSHIP WORKS

Sponsoring groups or organizations offer to assist a refugee or refugee family for one year starting from the date of their arrival in the community.

Sponsors may specify the number of people and the ethnic groups they wish to help. It is also possible to name a particular family, but sponsoring groups should remember that locating specific refugees is sometimes difficult and may take longer.

Whether participating on their own or under a national agreement with their parent organization, sponsors agree to provide certain services, which the federal government will supplement, as follows:

SPONSORING GROUP SERVICES

Material Assistance - furnished accommodation and household effects, food, clothing and incidental expenses for one year.

Housing may be in the residence of one of the sponsors or elsewhere, but it must be adequate to accommodate the number of people in the refugee family.

Usually refugees are able to support themselves before the end of their first year in Canada, in which case sponsoring groups will not have to provide as much material assistance as in the initial months. However, if refugees start to work and are laid off before the end of the first year, groups will resume their responsibilities for the remainder of the period.

Sponsoring refugees cannot claim welfare support during their first twelve months in Canada.

Health Care. Refugees are eligible for coverage under provincial hospital and medical insurance plans as soon as they arrive in Canada, but it is up to the sponsoring group to ensure that they register immediately and that the necessary premiums are paid during the first twelve months. In provinces where there is a waiting period for coverage, sponsors are required to arrange private insurance or pay health care costs until the provincial plan comes into effect.

General Orientation and Moral Support. The welcome for refugee families will start when sponsors meet them on arrival in the community and explain the role the group will be playing in helping them get established.

Sponsors will assist refugees to adjust to their new surroundings, advising them of the various community and government services available to them, helping the working family members find employment, introducing them to Canadian shopping habits, transportation and entertainment, as well as schools for their children.

FEDERAL GOVERNMENT SERVICES

The Canada Employment and Immigration Commission (CEIC) will supplement the services provided by sponsors, in the following ways:

Transportation Loans - interest-free loans for transportation from overseas to final destination in Canada, to be repaid by refugees when they become self-supporting.

Temporary Medical Assistance - emergency hospital, medical and dental care in the interval between admission to Canada and arrival at final destination.

Employment Services - job counselling and placement services from the Canada Employment Centre (CEC) in the community.

Language Training Courses - the CEC may also arrange full-time language courses for refugees entering the labour force, if their lack of English or French prevents placement in employment. Sponsors continue to provide material assistance for the duration of the course.

Occupational Training - refugees may be enrolled in full-time courses, if required and available, to upgrade job skills. Trainees are provided with living allowances to be supplemented by the sponsoring group.

HOW SPONSORS CAN PREPARE

Groups and organizations should plan to have on hand at least $1200 for each refugee they sponsor. Refugees usually become self-supporting within four to six months of their arrival in Canada. However, it may take longer for some individuals, and sponsors should have the capacity for generating additional funds if necessary. Of course, sponsoring groups that can supply material assistance and support services from the resources of their own membership will reduce their financial outlay accordingly.

Members of the sponsoring group must be prepared to devote their time on a regular basis to help refugees learn about Canada and get settled in their new community. They have undergone a traumatic experience and will need time to adjust and learn a completely new way of life. Sponsors should locate interpreters who speak the refugees' language, find a family doctor and arrange other essential services. Also, resource groups in the community such as ethnic and immigrant service associations, as well as other local sponsors, can provide useful guidance in easing the cultural transition of refugees when they first arrive in Canada.

The Canada Employment and Immigration Commission will maintain its interest in the resettlement of sponsored refugees and will, from time to time, contact sponsors concerning their progress. In the meantime, if groups encounter difficulties, they can call upon the expertise of officers at the Canada Employment Centre or the Canada Immigration Centre in their community.

AGREEMENTS WITH LOCAL GROUPS

Local groups or organizations, not covered by a national agreement with a parent body, may enter into individual sponsorship agreements with the CEIC at their nearest Canada Immigration Centre (CIC).

When groups apply at the CIC they will be asked to supply information on the make-up, size and history of their group, its financial resources and the number of members available to provide counselling or other social assistance for refugees.

Sponsors should be prepared to show proof of citizenship or residence, and evidence of length of employment, salary and other resources available to the group. In addition, the group should have a plan outlining the members who will be responsible for meeting the refugees, helping them find work and housing, and so on.

To be approved as sponsors, groups must be able to demonstrate
thay they are able to arrange for the reception and settlement of refugees
and that they have sufficient funds and expertise to provide the required
lodging, care and maintenance. Adult members of the same family may act
as sponsors but they must have proof of adequate resources and be able to
carry out their sponsorship responsibilities; otherwise it may be advisable
to increase the number of sponsors in the group.

AGREEMENTS WITH NATIONAL ORGANIZATIONS

Any recognized national organization with a history of involvement
in social assistance programs may sign a formal Letter of Agreement with the
Minister of Employment and Immigration, assuming responsibility for refugee
sponsorships undertaken by its constituent groups. Under such arrangements
the legal responsibility lies with the parent body but the actual support
and services are provided by its membership in local communities.

Such agreements make it possible for large national
organizations to undertake multiple refugee sponsorships with a minimum of
time and paperwork because evaluation procedures will not be required for each
group.

Constituent Group Involvement

When a national organization signs a sponsorship agreement, copies
will be sent to all Canada Immigration Centres across the country. Then,
sponsoring groups of the national organization can approach their local CIC,
present a letter of approval from the parent body, and sign the necessary
sponsorship documents.

SPONSORSHIP PROCEDURES

Eligible groups will be required to complete a form providing the
basic information necessary for matching the group with a refugee family.
When suitable refugees have been identified, information about the family
will be provided to the sponsors through the CIC where they made their
initial application. This information will include the number of people in
the family, their ages, what languages they speak, and some basic facts about
their educational and working backgrounds.

112

The sponsoring group will then decide whether they are willing to assist the refugee family. Although every effort will be made to select the requested refugees, this may not always be possible and sponsors should be prepared to be flexible when deciding if they will accept a particular family. When sponsors agree to accept certain refugees, their group representatives will sign a form naming the sponsored individuals and outlining the assistance to be provided.

When the sponsored refugees meet medical and background requirements abroad, the CIC will advise the group of their travel arrangements.

Time Involved

The time needed to identify and transport sponsored refugees to Canada varies depending on the situation in the country where the refugees are and whether immigration officers must travel to remote camps to interview them.

From the time the sponsorship application is submitted it usually takes between one and three months for refugees to be processed and brought to Canada. For this reason, sponsors should not make final commitments for accommodation or employment until advised by the CIC that the refugee family is destined to their group. However, when they are so advised, sponsors should be prepared to act as soon as the family arrives in their community.

YOUR COMMITMENT TO SPONSOR

Refugees are people in trouble and making a commitment to help them is a serious responsibility that should not be taken lightly. Most refugees become self-reliant and financially independent within four to six months of their arrival in Canada. But long after this, even after your legal commitment has expired, the refugees you have sponsored will continue to need your friendship and moral support to successfully adapt to new surroundings and a different culture, In fact, the amount and quality of your assistance can mean the difference between their success and failure in building a new life for themselves in Canada.

<u>QUESTIONS SPONSORS FREQUENTLY ASK</u>

<u>How can interested Canadians who are not part of a sponsoring group help refugees?</u>

They can -

. get in touch with other interested individuals, community or church groups, and form a sponsoring group. More than one group may wish to join together for the purpose of sponsoring;

. contact the local immigrant aid organization, appropriate ethnic group, or Canada Employment Centre, and volunteer to help refugees who have just arrived in Canada; or

. contact the local Canada Immigration Centre regarding substantial offers of material assistance such as accommodation, job offers, furniture in good condition, so that they can benefit refugees soon to arrive in Canada.

<u>What is the sponsoring group's legal responsibility for a sponsored refugee?</u>

The group undertakes to provide material assistance and moral support to the refugees they sponsor for a one year period. In the unlikely event that the refugee contracts excessive debts, or is sued or arrested, the group will not be held responsible.

<u>WHO TO CONTACT</u>

For further information concerning the sponsorship of refugees contact your nearest Canada Immigration Centre.

Cet exposé est aussi disponible en français sous le titre "Parrainage des réfugiés".

SAMPLE #18
TYPICAL EXPLANATION LETTER CONCERNING REFUGEES

Dear Sir/Madam:

Thank you for your letter of November 27, 198- concerning group sponsorship of Convention refugees pursuant to section 7 of the Immigration Regulations. The following narrative describes our recent processing procedures in this area. I trust the information will be of assistance to you.

A group of not less than five individuals (all 18 years of age or over, Canadian citizens or permanent residents) or a legally incorporated Canadian organization, may undertake to provide support to a named or unnamed Convention refugee or designated humanitarian case. Should such a group wish to initiate this type of undertaking, their representatives should contact the nearest Canada Immigration Centre in order to provide the following details:

(a) the name of the organization;

(b) the type of group or organization, e.g., local chapter or national organization; religious or ethnic group, immigrant aid society, private company;

(c) size of its membership; (for groups not legally incorporated, the following information is requested about those members (from 5 to 25 in number) who are interested in participating in the sponsorship: name, date of birth, occupation, length of residence in Canada and status — Canadian citizen or permanent resident);

(d) the length of its existence;

(e) its financial resources;

(f) the number of volunteer workers who would be available to assist the immigrant in finding employment, etc.; and

(g) previous experience in aiding refugees, displaced persons, ordinary immigrants.

In order to formalize the information mentioned above, representatives of the group or organization will be asked to complete form IMM 1266. (Sample attached.) Bearing in mind the requirements as set out in section 7 of the Immigration Regulations, the Director General, Immigration, for Ontario Region, is responsible for deciding whether or not the group or organization may undertake to provide assistance to one or more individuals or families. Based on the form IMM 266, the Director General will also make a determination as to how many commitments the group or organization will be entitled to undertake at a given time. If a group is not legally incorporated and has more than the minimum of 5 members, it will be decided how many members must formally undertake to support the Convention refugee or designated humanitarian cases. It is anticipated that not more than 25 members would be asked to sign the IMM 1266. In arriving at any decision in this matter, we anticipate that the Director General may, from time to time, consult with provincial authorities as well as our own settlement officers.

Should it be decided that the group or organization has the necessary resources and expertise to fulfill such an undertaking of support, the responsible Canada Immigration Centre will ask at least two representatives of the group or organization to complete form IMM 1267. (Sample attached.) This form is basically an indication of the willingness of the group or organization to assist either a particular individual Convention refugee or designated humanitarian case or a member of a specified affinity group. It will normally be considered to be in effect for two years unless the group or organization specifies a shorter time period.

When a specific Convention refugee or designated humanitarian case is named on this form, the local Canada Immigration Centre will forward it to the responsible post abroad. Our overseas office will then attempt to contact the individual named.

When no specific individual has been named by the group or organization, the post (or posts) abroad which have been identified as having some degree of contact with a particular affinity group will institute processing by attempting to identify and interview candidates from the group whose background and skills match the requirements of the "sponsoring" organization as closely as possible.

Once a named individual or suitable affinity group member has been identified and processed, our overseas post will forward full particulars regarding the applicants to the local Canada Immigration Centre handling the case. Our local office will then contact the "sponsoring" group or organization with a view to discussing the applicant's occupational profile, labour market skills, and language abilities. These discussions should determine, having due regard for the applicant's circumstances and background, whether the "sponsoring" group or organization is both willing and able to provide the support or additional assistance judged to be necessary for the individual's settlement in Canada.

Should the person seeking to come to Canada meet the eligibility criteria, our overseas visa officer, in determining whether the individual would be able to establish himself successfully in Canada within a reasonable period of time, will take into consideration the government assistance available to Convention refugees or members of special movements as well as the specific help which would be offered by the prospective sponsoring group or organization. In general, the latter will consist of:

      (a)   the arrangement of initial accommodation;

      (b)   provision of food and clothing for the initial adjustment period before the immigrant is placed in continuing employment in Canada;

      (c)   provision of general reception and resettlement assistance including:

         (i) meeting the family upon arrival in the community;

         (ii) orientation to life in Canada and counselling;

         (iii) assistance in seeking employment.

Should the applicant be acceptable to the "sponsoring" group or organization, the final step in the assistance program will occur with the completion of the formal "Undertaking of Support" as embodied in our form IMM 1268 (copy attached). This undertaking will formalize the understandings and agreements reached in earlier discussions by specifying the extent of the assistance to be provided and the form it will take. An Immigration Officer, at the responsible Canada Immigration Centre, will witness the Undertaking and insure that the representatives of the group or organization fully understand the responsibilities they are assuming. Unless otherwise specified by the Canada Immigration Centre, the form IMM 1268 will remain valid for a period of one year.

When informed that an IMM 1268 has been signed, the post abroad will continue to process the application. The applicant will be fully informed about the sponsorship: the name of the organization, its geographical location and the assistance it has offered. If, for any reason, the applicant is unwilling to accept the support of the Canadian organization or to be destined to that particular location, he will be assessed as either a Convention refugee or a humanitarian case without benefit of "sponsorship." The responsible Canada Immigration Centre will keep the Canadian organization or group informed of developments relating to the progress of any persons whom they've "sponsored."

If, for any reason, the "sponsoring" group or organization were unwilling or unable to sign the IMM 1268, the earlier IMM 1267 would be considered invalid. This situation, however, would not prevent the group or organization from submitting another IMM 1267 for our consideration. If the earlier IMM 1267 had been completed on behalf of a specified affinity group, the local Canadian Immigration Centre will meet with the group to develop a more precise description of the type of applicant (age, occupation, family composition, etc.) that they would be willing to accept. From such a dialogue a new IMM 1267 might be prepared.

Should you have any further questions regarding processing, please do not hesitate to contact us.

Yours very truly

Manager
Canada Immigration Centre
(Toronto Central)
480 University Avenue
Toronto, Ontario
M5G 1V2

SAMPLE #19
APPLICATION TO SPONSOR A REFUGEE

Employment and Immigration Canada   Emploi et Immigration Canada

APPLICATION TO SPONSOR A REFUGEE OR MEMBER OF A DESIGNATED CLASS

DEMANDE EN VUE DE PARRAINER UN RÉFUGIÉ OU UN MEMBRE D'UNE CATÉGORIE DÉSIGNÉE

OFFICE USE ONLY / RÉSERVÉ À L'ADMINISTRATION	CIC	File No. – N° de référence
☐ Approved – Approuvée ☐ Rejected – Rejetée	CIC Officer – Agent du CIC Signature	Date

SPONSORSHIP BY / PARRAINAGE PAR ▶ ☐ LEGALLY INCORPORATED ORGANIZATION / UN ORGANISME LÉGALEMENT CONSTITUÉ   ☒ PRIVATE GROUP / UN GROUPE DE PARTICULIERS

Name of organization or group – Nom de l'organisme ou groupe

ABC Church Brotherhood

Telephone No. – N° de téléphone: **2 34 5678**

Mailing address – Adresse postale: **234 Helpful Street**

City – Ville: **Anytown**

Province: **B.C.**

Postal Code / Code postal: **V 2 L3 P3**

Length of existence of organization or group – Depuis combien de temps l'organisme ou le groupe existe-t-il?

Since 1964

Reason for formation – Pourquoi a-t-il été mis sur pied

Funds to be available upon arrival of sponsored persons / Quel montant sera disponible à l'arrivée des personnes parrainées	Funds to be transferred/raised at a later date / Quels montants seront virés ou recueillis plus tard	Anticipated monthly expenses (food, rent, incidentals, etc) / Dépenses mensuelles prévues (nourriture, logement, menues dépenses, etc.)
$ 5000	$ 3000	$1200

Experience in assisting in the resettlement of refugees, displaced persons, or other immigrants / Le groupe a-t-il déjà aidé des réfugiés, des personnes déplacées ou d'autres immigrants à se réétablir

None, but we have organized an accommodation referral centre for single mothers and it has been running successfully for 13 years.

IF THIS APPLICATION IS BEING MADE ON BEHALF OF A SPECIFIC PERSON OR FAMILY, PLEASE SPECIFY / SI LA DEMANDE EST PRÉSENTÉE EN FAVEUR D'UNE PERSONNE OU D'UNE FAMILLE EN PARTICULIER, VEUILLEZ PRÉCISER

Name of head of family – Nom du chef de famille	Number in family / Nombre de membres de la famille	Nationality – Nationalité
YUNG LUK WEI	2	Vietnamese

IF THIS APPLICATION IS NOT BEING MADE ON BEHALF OF A SPECIFIC PERSON OR FAMILY, PLEASE INDICATE THE PARTICULARS OF THE PERSON OR FAMILY YOU ARE INTERESTED IN SPONSORING / SI LA DEMANDE N'EST PAS PRÉSENTÉE EN FAVEUR D'UNE PERSONNE OU D'UNE FAMILLE EN PARTICULIER, VEUILLEZ INDIQUER LE GENRE DE PERSONNE OU DE FAMILLE QUE VOUS AIMERIEZ PARRAINER

Number in family / Nombre de membres de la famille ▶	Nationality – Nationalité	Other – Autres

A. FOR LEGALLY INCORPORATED ORGANIZATIONS – POUR LES ORGANISMES LÉGALEMENT CONSTITUÉS

Name – Nom	Signature	Position – Fonction
1.		
2.		

IMM. 1266 (9-87)

Canada

• SEE REVERSE – VOIR AU VERSO

118

SAMPLE #19 — Continued

B. FOR PRIVATE GROUPS ONLY – *RÉSERVÉ AUX GROUPES DE PARTICULIERS*

Name – *Nom*	Signature	Address – *Adresse*	Telephone No. *Nº de téléphone*	(✓) Canadian citizen *Citoyen canadien* Permanent resident *Résident permanent*
1.				
2.				
3.				
4.				
5.				
6.				
7.				
8.				
9.				
10.				
11.				
12.				
13.				
14.				
15.				
16.				
17.				
18.				
19.				
20.				
21.				
22.				
23.				
24.				
25.				

Employment and Immigration Canada — **Emploi et Immigration Canada**

UNDERTAKING OF SUPPORT FOR A REFUGEE OR MEMBER OF A CLASS DESIGNATED UNDER 6(2) OF THE IMMIGRATION ACT, 1976
ENGAGEMENT D'AIDE EN FAVEUR D'UN RÉFUGIÉ OU D'UN MEMBRE D'UNE CATÉGORIE DÉSIGNÉE AUX TERMES DU PARAGRAPHE 6(2) DE LA LOI SUR L'IMMIGRATION DE 1976

SERIAL NO. – N° DE SÉRIE
A07112

CIC

File No. – N° de référence

Visa Office – Bureau des visas

File No. – N° de référence

UNDERTAKING BY / ENGAGEMENT PAR
☐ LEGALLY INCORPORATED ORGANIZATION / UN ORGANISME LÉGALEMENT CONSTITUÉ
☐ PRIVATE GROUP / UN GROUPE DE PARTICULIERS

Name of sponsoring organization or group – Nom de l'organisme répondant ou groupe
ABC CHurch Brotherhood

Telephone No. / N° de téléphone
2 3 4 5 6 7 8

Mailing address – Adresse postale
234 Helpful Street

City – Ville
Anytown

Province
B.C.

Postal Code / Code postal
V2 L 3P 3

PERSONS COVERED BY UNDERTAKING – PERSONNES VISÉES PAR L'ENGAGEMENT

Surname – Nom de famille	Given names – Prénom(s)	Relationship – Lien de parenté	Date of Birth / Date de naissance
YUNG	Luk Wei	Husband	10-2-54
YUNG	Mei Ing	Wife	7-6-56

Complete mailing address of the above-named immigrant(s) – Adresse postale complète des immigrants susnommés

c/- Refugee Centre #1, Hong Kong

NAMES AND ADDRESSES OF ANY RELATIVES OF THE ABOVE-NAMED LIVING IN CANADA
NOM ET ADRESSE DE TOUT PARENT DES PERSONNES SUSNOMMÉES VIVANT AU CANADA

	Name – Nom	Address – Adresse
1.		
2.		

In consideration of approval being given by the Minister of State (Immigration) for the admission to Canada of the above-named refugee(s) or member(s) of a designated class

1. We undertake:
   (a) to provide or assist in providing reasonably required adequate lodging to the above-named immigrant(s) during the period of resettlement in Canada.
   (b) to provide reasonably required adequate food, clothing and incidental living needs to the above-named immigrant(s) during the period of resettlement in Canada.
   (c) to provide general reception and resettlement assistance including:
      (i) meeting the immigrant(s) on arrival in the community
      (ii) orientation to life in Canada and counselling
      (iii) assistance in seeking employment
   (d) to provide financial assistance to the above-named immigrants so that such person(s) shall not require financial maintenance support from any federal or provincial assistance program prescribed by regulation under the Immigration Act, 1976.

2. We also understand and agree:
   (a) that the Minister of State (Immigration) may assign his interest in this undertaking to Her Majesty in right of any province in which the above-named immigrant(s) reside or resided during the period of resettlement in Canada.
   (b) that where payments made to the above-named Refugee(s) or Member(s) of a designated class from any federal, or provincial assistance program described by regulation under the Immigration Act, 1976 are for services which were guaranteed in 1 (a) (b) (c), such payments shall be deemed to be a breach of this undertaking.
   (c) that Her Majesty in right of Canada or in right of any province so assigned may take action in any court of competent jurisdiction to recover such payments as a debt to Her Majesty.
   (d) that the period of resettlement for which this undertaking is given shall be for a period of one year from the date of admission of the above-named immigrant(s) to Canada.

3. It is further agreed and understood by all persons signing as members of the group known as **ABC Church Brotherhood** that we shall be personally and severally liable for all obligations named hereunder.

In witness whereof we offer our hands and seals

this **7th** day of **March** 19 **9-**

Compte tenu de l'approbation donnée par le Ministre d'État à l'Immigration concernant l'admission au Canada des réfugiés ou membres d'une catégorie désignée susnommés,

1. Nous nous engageons :
   a) à fournir ou à contribuer à fournir un logement dont pourront avoir raisonnablement besoin les immigrants susnommés au cours de la période de réétablissement au Canada;
   b) à fournir une aide dont pourraient raisonnablement avoir besoin les immigrants susnommés pour la nourriture, le vêtement et d'autres menus besoins au cours de la période de réétablissement au Canada;
   c) à nous occuper de l'accueil général et à fournir une aide au réétablissement, y compris
      i) les accueillir à l'arrivée dans la collectivité;
      ii) les renseigner sur la vie au Canada et à les conseiller à ce sujet;
      iii) les aider à trouver un emploi;
   d) à accorder une aide financière aux immigrants susnommés afin qu'ils n'aient pas besoin de demander une telle aide en vertu de tout programme d'aide fédéral ou provincial prescrit par voie de règlement aux termes de la Loi sur l'immigration de 1976.

2. En outre nous convenons et acceptons :
   a) que le Ministre d'État à l'Immigration puisse céder ses droits découlant du présent engagement à Sa Majesté la Reine du chef de toute province où résident ou ont résidé les immigrants susnommés au cours de la période de réétablissement au Canada;
   b) que, lorsque les sommes versées aux réfugiés ou membres d'une catégorie désignée susnommés en vertu de tout programme d'aide fédéral ou provincial prescrit par voie de règlement en application de la Loi sur l'immigration de 1976 le sont pour les services garantis aux termes des 1 a), b) et c) ci-dessus, le versement desdites sommes soit considéré comme une rupture du présent engagement;
   c) que Sa Majesté du chef du Canada ou du chef de toute province à qui un tel droit a été cédé puisse engager devant tout tribunal compétent des poursuites afin de recouvrer les montants versés qui constituent une dette envers Sa Majesté.
   d) qu'aux fins du présent engagement la période de réétablissement soit d'une durée d'un an à compter de la date d'admission au Canada des immigrants susnommés.

3. Il est en outre entendu et convenu que tous les soussignés, membres du groupe connu sous le nom de, _____ reconnaissent être solidairement débiteurs de toutes les obligations ci-dessus.

En foi de quoi nous avons signé et scellé de notre main le présent document, ce _____ jour de _____ 19 ____

IMM. 1268 (9-87)

OVER – VERSO

Canada

WHITE / BLANCHE : SPONSOR – RÉPONDANT   CANARY / CANARI: CIC

A. FOR LEGALLY INCORPORATED ORGANIZATIONS ONLY – *RÉSERVÉ AUX ORGANISMES LÉGALEMENT CONSTITUÉS*

1.	Signature of Witness – *Signature du témoin* ▷		
	Name of Representative *Nom du représentant*	Signature	Position – *Fonction*
2.	Signature of Witness – *Signature du témoin* ▷		
	Name of Representative *Nom du représentant*	Signature	Position – *Fonction*

B. FOR PRIVATE GROUPS ONLY – *RÉSERVÉ AUX GROUPES DE PARTICULIERS*

	Signature of Witness *Signature du témoin*	Signature of Group Member *Signature du membre du groupe*	Name of Member *Nom du membre*
1.			John Smith
2.			Janice Smith
3.			Murray Allen
4.			Jane Hume
5.			George Hume
6.			Albert David
7.			Gary Lawrence
8.			
9.			
10.			
11.			
12.			
13.			
14.			
15.			
16.			
17.			
18.			
19.			
20.			
21.			
22.			
23.			
24.			
25.			

18

REFUGEE BACKLOG CLEARANCE PROGRAM

The problems involving refugees to Canada as outlined in chapter 17 were greatly magnified by the inability of the federal government to make decisions and enact new legislation quickly. When the Supreme Court of Canada decided in the *Singh* case that all refugee claimants in Canada were entitled to a full oral hearing before the Immigration Appeal Board (now the Immigration and Refugee Board), the government decided that it was impossible to do this for the 63 000 who were now entitled to a full trial.

To remedy this situation, the federal government held an Administrative Review (ADR) of all those people who were refugee claimants in Canada prior to May 21, 1986. As long as they had no criminal or security problems either before coming to Canada or while here and provided they passed their medicals, they were allowed to stay and become permanent residents of Canada if they could show that while here they were or were likely to become successfully established in Canada. Basically, this meant you had to show that you had not been on welfare after being given permission to work, that you had a job, that you had become involved in community activities, and so on.

While, on the whole, the ADR program was effective, its main problem was that the government did not have its new refugee legislation prepared and ready to go at the same time. The new refugee laws did not go into effect until January 1, 1989 — *two years, seven months, and ten days after the end of ADR.*

The results of this delay were horrendous. Tens of thousands of people poured into Canada during this time claiming refugee status and hoping that another ADR or amnesty would be declared for those who were in Canada before the new refugee laws went into effect. By January 1, 1989, over 125 000 new refugee claimants were in this new and growing backlog. At best, it would take 10 to 15 years to give them all full trials as guaranteed by the *Singh* decision, a fact that did not escape most of the people who came to Canada between May 22, 1986 and January 1, 1989.

These new backlog refugee claimants came not only from refugee-producing areas such as the African Horn, Iran, Iraq, Lebanon, parts of Central and South America, but also from countries such as Portugal, Turkey, Brazil, islands in the Caribbean, and elsewhere where there was no basis for a refugee claim based on persecution for political, religious, racial, ethnic, or other similar reason. They came because times in their home countries were tough and they believed a better life could be made in Canada.

The response of the federal government and of the Minister of Employment and Immigration was not to declare an amnesty or a new ADR, but to put each and every refugee claimant in this backlog through a "credible basis" hearing as outlined in chapter 17. This means that all 125 000 backlog cases will go through the procedures outlined below. The government has appointed an additional 100 judges for the Refugee Division of the IRB and 100 new adjudicators, and has made available offices, support staff, court clerks, translators, courtrooms, etc., to handle this backlog clearance. The government has budgeted $180 million to handle the trials and hopes to have its work completed by January 1, 1992.

As you will see from the figures presented below, this is wishful thinking, a pipe dream. They will be lucky to complete it all in less than four or five years at a cost of $350 to $400 million.

Under the refugee backlog clearance program, you must have made a refugee claim in Canada or at a port of entry on or before January 1, 1989. If you did, you would be eligible for the program provided you were *not* —

(a) a previous successful refugee claimant prior to January 1, 1989,

(b) a person previously ordered removed (i.e., deported) from Canada but the order has not as yet been carried out,

(c) a person previously issued a Departure Notice but the order has not as yet been carried out,

(d) a person previously refused under the old ADR program (1986),

(e) a person who failed to appear in the past for an immigration examination, hearing, or inquiry,

(f) a person who has a criminal record, or

(g) a person who has, after December 27, 1989, left Canada for more than seven days.

Under the refugee clearance program, there is, in simple terms, a three-step procedure with various alternatives along the way. The first step is a Humanitarian and Compassionate (H & C) hearing. This hearing is held before an immigration officer and is to determine only two issues:

(a) Whether you are a member of an official delegation, athletic team, cultural group, or other famous person who, by seeking to stay in Canada, so embarrasses your government as to leave you open to severe punishment if you were to return home

(b) Whether you are a member of the family class — that is, do you have a spouse, adult child, adult grandchild, or parent in Canada who is a Canadian citizen or permanent resident of Canada

If you fall into either of the above two situations, you will succeed on your H & C review and be processed for permanent residence. Of course, in the second situation, your Canadian relative will have to sign an Undertaking of Assistance on your behalf. For this H & C review you might receive a Call In Notice (see Sample #21) setting up the date for your appointment. It will be necessary to complete the Immigration Form for Humanitarian and Compassionate Review (see Sample #22). (This form does not have a number.)

If you do not qualify for H & C, you will be told immediately and then offered an opportunity to leave Canada voluntarily. This means that you will be given usually three to six weeks to clean up your affairs and leave Canada. If you choose this route, you will be given a letter from the government guaranteeing you an interview at a Canadian visa office so that you may apply to immigrate to Canada in the proper manner like everyone else. *This does not mean you are guaranteed an immigrant visa. It only means you are guaranteed an interview.* You must still comply with the point system and everything else outlined in chapters 4, 6, 9, 10, 11, 12, and 13.

In reality, the only persons who appear to be choosing to voluntarily leave Canada and taking the guaranteed interview letter are those who have high points on the occupational demand list (see Table #4) or those who are able to obtain an approved job offer (see Sample #7) prior to leaving Canada (see chapter 10).

If you do not receive H & C and choose not to leave Canada voluntarily, you will be sent to an immigration inquiry which will determine three things:

(a) Are the allegations against you correct?

(b) Are you eligible to be in the backlog?

(c) Do you have a credible basis for your claim to be a refugee?

The allegations against you will likely be that you came to Canada without a passport or without an immigrant visa intending to be an immigrant, etc. Usually these allegations are true and can be admitted to. Eligibility is outlined above. If you fall into one of the seven categories *not* eligible, that is the end of your hearing and you will be removed from the backlog program. Last, you will have your credible basis hearing. It will be the same as the one outlined in chapter 17 for refugee claimants under the new rules.

In some cases, the government will concede (admit) that you have a credible basis and that will be the end of the hearing. You will be processed for permanent residence *without any further hearings*. This decision will often be based on your nine-page personal information form (see Sample #16 and the discussion of it in chapter 17) which should be completed and filed at this time. If the government does not concede, you will have a full trial as outlined in chapter 17. If you win, you will be processed for permanent residence. *If you are found not to have a credible basis, there is no further appeal and you will be deported from Canada.*

There is, however, a final humanitarian and compassionate review to determine whether under all the circumstances of your case it is felt you should not be removed from Canada. It appears this will be used only if there is some life-threatening situation in your home country such as a civil war. Do not put your hopes on this review.

In the period from May/June, 1989 to December 31, 1989 approximately 5 300 cases were completed with the following results:

11%	allowed to stay on H & C grounds (most were family class situations)
22%	took voluntary departure
65%	found to have credible basis
2%	rejected and deported

You must understand that during the first phase of the program most of the cases have come from countries that produce many refugees. In the future, there will be many more rejections and deportations. More important, by January 31, 1990, the government had handled only 6 500 out of 125 000 cases. It will take many years to clean up this backlog.

Note: The government finally enacted the regulations permitting the backlog program to exist. These regulations came into effect at on December 27, 1989.

In March, 1990, the Federal Court of Appeal ruled that the first stage Humanitarian and Compassionate review was unfair and the government's restriction to family class members and famous people unduly fettered the discretion and decision-making powers of ordinary immigration officers. Subsequently, the Minister of Immigration issued new guidelines for H & C consideration and everyone in the backlog will now be considered pursuant to these guidelines.

The new guidelines are virtually identical to those for "long-term illegal *de facto* residents of Canada" making applications for permanent residence inside the country as outlined in chapter 14, section **b.**

In my opinion, these guidelines are far too restrictive for backlog applicants and they will be the subject of another court challenge in the near future.

Employment and　　Emploi et
Immigration Canada　Immigration Canada　　　　　　　Our file:

Ontario Region　　　Région de l'Ontario

CALL-IN NOTICE - HUMANITARIAN AND COMPASSIONATE REVIEW

Dear

This letter refers to your immigration status in Canada.

You are requested to attend an interview on _____
at 123 Edward Street, Suite 500, Toronto. An immigration officer will
review your case to determine whether sufficient humanitarian and
compassionate reasons exist to process an application for permanent
residence on your behalf from within Canada.

You will find attached to this letter a description of the criteria
used by immigration officers to make this assessment. The criteria
which apply to this initial review are at paragraphs 1 and 2 of the
attached page.

If you feel that your case deserves consideration in light of these
criteria, you are invited to prepare the reasons in writing and submit
them to the immigration officer when you come to the interview.

If this initial review is unsuccessful you will have the option of
departing Canada voluntarily or being scheduled for an oral hearing.
Attached are details of voluntary departure.

Should you not elect the voluntary departure option you will be
subsequently convoked for an oral hearing to determine whether or not
a credible basis exists for your claim to refugee status.

Failure to establish a credible basis will result in your being convoked
for an inquiry.

Should you succeed in establishing a credible basis you will be eligible
to apply for permanent residence in Canada or to proceed to a full
hearing before the Immigration and Refugee Board.

If your spouse or children are in Canada please bring them with you.
Due to limited space at this office, please do not have other relatives
or friends accompany you.

Yours sincerely,

Signature

Immigration Officer

Canada

SAMPLE #22
INFORMATION FORM (IMMIGRATION)

INFORMATION FORM
(IMMIGRATION)

Surname	Given Name	
Refugee	John	☒ Male
Middle Name	Other Names	
Amos	N/A	☐ Female

Date and Place of Birth: Y 4 | M 30 | D 04 — Tehran, Iran Nationality: Iranian

Present address: 123 Anystreet, Toronto, Ontario

FAMILY STATUS

| sngle ☐ | Eng. ☐ | Mar. ☒ | Div. ☐ | Date and Place of Marriage: Y 70 M 01 D 01 — Tehran, Iran | No. of Children: 3 |

Name of Spouse: Smith, Jane   Neé   Date and Place of Birth: Y 50 M 01 D 01 — Tehran, Iran

Present Address: 123 Anystreet, Toronto, Ontario

Father's Family & First Name: Refugee, James — Date and Place of Birth: Y 20 M 02 D 02 — MASHAD, IRAN

Mother's Family & First Name: JONES, Susan — Date and Place of Birth: Y 21 M 04 D 04 — Tehran, Iran

Father's Present Address: 12/C Tehran Ave., Mashad, Iran

Passport Number: 123456 | Place of Issue: Iran | Date of Issue: Y 80 M 05 D 05 | Date of Expiry: Y 90 M 05 D 05

ADDRESSES FOR THE PAST TEN (10) YEARS

FROM M	FROM Y	TO M	TO Y	STREET AND NO.	CITY	COUNTRY
JAN	1979	APR	1986	12/C Tehran Ave.	Mashad	Iran
APR	1986	PRESENT		123 Anystreet	Toronto	Canada

OFFICIAL USE ONLY

126

DETAILS OF EDUCATION   P-2

DATE				NAMES AND LOCATION OF INSTITUTE	TYPE OF INSTITUTE	TYPE OF DIPLOMA OR CERTIFICATE
FROM		TO				
M	Y	M	Y			
Sep	50	June	56	Tehran Elemen.	Primary	N/A
Sep	56	June	61	Mashad High School	High School	Diploma
Sep	61	Jun	66	University of Iran	University	M Sc Architecture

FORMER AND PRESENT EMPLOYERS FOR THE PAST TEN YEARS

DATE				NAME AND ADDRESS OF EMPLOYER	OCCUPATION
FROM		TO			
M	Y	M	Y		
Jan	1967	Apr	1986	Iran Architecture Inc.	Architect
APR	1986	June	1987	Unemployed - Awaiting status in Canada	
July	1986	Present		Toronto Architecture Ltd.	Architect

MEMBER OF OR ASSOCIATED WITH THE FOLLOWING MILITARY, POLITICAL, SOCIAL, YOUTH, STUDENT AND VOCATIONAL ORGANIZATIONS.

DATE				NAME AND ADDRESS OF ORGANIZATION	TYPE OF ORGANIZATION	POSITION HELD
FROM		TO				
M	Y	M	Y			
				N/A		

YES	NO			
	✓	Have you been convicted of or currently charged with any crime or offence?		
	✓	Resided in another country?	If "yes", where?	

LIST THE PERSON(S) WHO OFFERED TO ASSIST YOU IN CANADA?

NAME	ADDRESS	RELATIONSHIP
	N/A	

I certify that the information I have given is truthful, complete and correct.

__April 28, 199-__
DATE

__John Refugee__
SIGNATURE

19
CUSTOMS: WHAT CAN YOU BRING TO CANADA?

I am often asked what personal possessions immigrants to Canada may bring with them. This area of the law is covered by the Customs and Excise Division of Revenue Canada and is not under the Immigration Act. Tariff Item 9807-00-00 deals with "settlers' effects" regulations.

Under this law, any settler in Canada may bring once, and *once only*, settlers' effects consisting of all his or her household and personal effects imported to Canada for personal use and not for use in a business, manufacturing, or contracting operation.

You may only bring your goods into Canada on one occasion. Thus, if you were a student in Canada or on a work authorization for more than 36 months, or a permanent resident in the past and brought settlers' effects to this country then and subsequently left, you will *not* be allowed to bring settlers' effects in again if you return a second time as a permanent resident.

One man recently returned to Canada as a permanent resident having been on a work permit here between 1966 and 1970. At that time, he brought settlers' effects to Canada and removed them when he returned to the United States in 1970. He was not allowed to claim a second time and was required to pay duty on the goods he had not owned for six months.

A person in Canada for a temporary purpose of less than 36 months (work permit) or a student is not entitled to the settlers' effects provisions. Such a person will be allowed to bring in personal belongings, including an automobile, under a temporary six- to twelve-month permit (which can be renewed) and may be required to post a bond ensuring the removal of the items following the completion of his or her temporary stay in Canada.

Under the settlers' effects provisions, an immigrant or anyone else coming to Canada for a lawful temporary purpose may bring into Canada duty-free all household and personal effects including automobiles and recreational vehicles that were "owned and in his possession and use" before arrival in Canada.

This means that before you arrive as a permanent resident you must own, possess, and have used the item you want to bring with you. In the case of an automobile, this means it must be in your name (title), have license plates, and have been driven some distance in order to comply with the use requirement.

Automobiles and other motor vehicles built after 1971 brought in as settlers' effects must comply with automobile pollution standards in Canada.

If you are coming to Canada a second time, having had settlers' effects before, you are considered to be a returning resident (*under the Customs laws only*) and you must have owned, been in the possession of, and used the item abroad for *at least six months before* you return in order to bring it in duty free. The only exception to the requirement that goods be used prior to their entry under this item are the gifts received by a bride prior to entry into Canada and her trousseau.

When you are preparing your list of goods, you should make two lists: one of goods that are with you and one of goods to follow in the future, for example, on a ship. The list should be very detailed and complete, listing model and serial numbers of all items that have them and proper descriptions and valuations of jewellery. Clothing should be listed by description such as six men's suits (two gray, one brown, two blue, one charcoal). These lists should be prepared in duplicate and should be presented to Customs when you first arrive even if most of your belongings are following you later on.

A recent change in Customs law on March 16, 1989, states that persons who are in Canada as temporary residents and thereafter obtain permanent residence status subsequent to arrival in Canada *without resuming residence in their country of former domicile* will be allowed to bring to Canada *only* those goods owned, used, and possessed *prior to the date they filed their application for permanent residence in Canada.*

This section was enacted in order to prevent temporary workers in Canada who were processing their permanent residence applications at a Canadian consulate in the United States from buying large items in the United States such as cars, computers, stereos, appliances, etc. just prior to receiving their permanent residence status.

Sporting rifles and shotguns owned prior to January 1, 1979, do not require a permit for Canada. All pistols, revolvers, and semi-automatic firearms must be presented to Customs and will not be released without the proper police permit. Automatic firearms are prohibited as is a long list of weapons, such as spring-knives and nanchuka sticks, under our Criminal Code. If you have such firearms or weapons, consult a Canadian lawyer before bringing them here or you could be in serious trouble.

The importation of plants, animals, meat products, and the like are governed by other regulations, and you should consult Customs in advance.

If you are coming from a country that has currency restrictions, you can have up to three years to import items purchased in your homeland with blocked funds — goods such as jewellery, etc.

Note: These blocked funds must be deposited in a bank in your homeland prior to coming to Canada. You will have to prove in detail that you had this blocked money prior to coming to Canada. You should consult a lawyer concerning blocked funds situations. The following are some of the countries with blocked funds.

Argentina
Austria
Belgium
Brazil
Czechoslovakia
Denmark
East Germany
Eire
Finland
France
Germany
Greece
Korea
Poland
India
Israel
Italy
Malaysia
Netherlands
Norway
Pakistan
Philippines
South Africa
Sri Lanka
Sweden
United Arab Republic (Egypt)
Yugoslavia

20
VISITORS TO CANADA: TOURISTS, STUDENTS, BUSINESS PEOPLE, AND ARTISTS

a. GENERAL

Section 9 of the Immigration Act makes provisions for the entrance into Canada of visitors. As you will recall, the difference between immigrants and visitors was discussed in chapter 3. A visitor is a person who desires to enter Canada for a relatively short period of time and who does not intend to become a permanent resident of Canada. Such persons include tourists, business people, students, artists, and members of ships' crews.

Visitors to Canada must have a visa to enter this country. This visa may be obtained at any Canadian consulate or embassy with an immigration section (see Appendix 2).

You should note, however, that if you do not apply from your country of ordinary residence, you may have to wait as much as a month or two to obtain the visa if it is necessary to make inquiries about you in your homeland.

Section g. of this chapter provides a long list of those countries whose citizens are *not* required to obtain visas if they are coming as visitors other than to work or go to school.

Despite the list you should obtain a visa if you are a tourist from any country other than the United States, England, Australia, New Zealand, and the countries of the European Economic Community (the Common Market). I say this even though it may be difficult to obtain such a visa. Often you will be told, "You don't need one."

Your reply should be, "I do not wish to have any problems upon my arrival in Canada to visit my (relatives, friends, parents...) so I would like a visa."

You should note, as explained more fully in chapter 25, that if you are in possession of a visitor's visa when you arrive in Canada and are refused entry, you will have a right of appeal to the Immigration and Refugee Board. Without such a visa, you do not have this right.

All students and all persons wishing to work in Canada on a temporary basis must obtain permission to attend school or work *before* coming to Canada (see exemptions in chapter 21 for those who can apply to work from inside Canada). This permission is obtained outside of Canada at one of the embassies or consulates with an immigration section. The requirements for a visitor to obtain either student authorization or an employment authorization is explained more fully below and in chapter 21.

In the case of a person (usually in a communist country) who wishes to visit relatives in Canada, the Canadian relative will be asked to complete a Confirmation of Proposed Visit (see Sample #23). The Canadian relative will be required to attend an interview at a local immigration office, after the prospective visitor has sought to obtain a visa in his or her homeland and has been interviewed at a Canadian embassy.

If you are called to such an interview because a relative has applied for a visa, you should bring with you your passport,

Canadian citizenship card, or landed immigrant card or record, bank book, letter from your employer stating salary and description of your job and how long you have had it. If you are married, your spouse should go with you.

It is not always necessary for your relatives to go first to the embassy. You can go with the above documents first to your closest immigration office and say you wish to sponsor *a visit* of your relatives from abroad. In this case, following approval, a letter will be sent to your relatives inviting them to the embassy for an interview.

Occasionally a security report from the Royal Canadian Mounted Police (RCMP) will be requested concerning both you and the visiting relative from abroad you wish to bring here. In such a case, a private visitor report will be sent to the RCMP for their comment and report. This report is secret and not available to either you or your relative.

Given the recent developments in eastern Europe, many of these requirements either no longer exist or will be cancelled in the near future. Check with your local immigration office for up-to-date procedures for particular eastern European countries.

When applying for a visitor's visa to come to Canada, everyone who is applying from countries that require visas must complete an Application for Temporary Entry (see Sample #24).

All applicants for student authorization from any country are required to complete the form shown in Sample #25 and provide photos. A medical examination is also required (see chapter 13).

Visitors who are seeking employment authorization must complete the form shown in Sample #26 and provide photos. A medical exam is required if you are coming to work in Canada for more than three months or if you are going to work in the food or hospitality industry or in a hospi-

tal. The only exception to the three-month rule is for citizens or permanent residents of the U.S. and most western European countries. In these cases a medical exam will be required only if the employment period is for more than one year. The hospital and food industry requirements apply to everyone and there is no one-year waiver for *anyone* with employment approval in these industries.

Sample #27 is a sample visitor's visa.

Note: If you are allowed entry as a visitor into Canada without a specific time limit to your visa, you are by law deemed to have been allowed entry into Canada as a visitor for three months from your date of arrival.

b. STUDENTS

Students from foreign countries who wish to come to Canada to study must enrol at an institution of education approved by the government. Such institutions include all recognized universities and colleges, most private secondary schools, and many private schools teaching technical and secretarial skills. If you wish to determine whether or not a particular institution is approved, you should write to:

Employment and Immigration
    Commission
Immigration Division
Ottawa, Ontario
K1A 0J9

If you are a student, contact the nearest Canadian embassy or consulate in your homeland with —

(a) a letter of acceptance, which you must have, from the Canadian school,

(b) proof of your ability to support yourself while in Canada, approximately $10 000 per year,

(c) proof that you have paid your first year's tuition fees, approximately $6 000, and

SAMPLE #23
CONFIRMATION OF PROPOSED VISIT

Employment and Immigration Canada Emploi et Immigration Canada
CONFIRMATION OF PROPOSED VISIT
CONFIRMATION DU SÉJOUR ÉVENTUEL

CIC ADDRESS — ADRESSE DU CIC	
DATE	FILE NO. — Nº DE RÉFÉRENCE

(COMPLETE ADDRESS OF CANADIAN POST CONCERNED)
(ADRESSE AU LONG DU BUREAU CANADIEN COMPÉTENT)

PART A — DETAILS OF PROPOSED VISITOR   PARTIE A — VISITEUR ÉVENTUEL

SURNAME — NOM DE FAMILLE	GIVEN NAMES — PRÉNOMS	SEX — SEXE
LAWRENCE	GARY DAVID	XXXX M.H ☐ F

DATE, PLACE AND COUNTRY OF BIRTH — *DATE, LIEU ET PAYS DE NAISSANCE*
D-J 31, M 05, Y-A 46 | Moscow, USSR

PRESENT CITIZENSHIP - *CITOYENNETÉ ACTUELLE*
U.S.S.R.

PRESENT OCCUPATION *PROFESSION ACTUELLE*
Medical Doctor

ADDRESS (IF NOT RESIDING IN COUNTRY OF CITIZENSHIP, GIVE DETAILS)
ADRESSE (S'IL NE RÉSIDE PAS DANS LE PAYS DE CITOYENNETÉ, PRÉCISER)

21 ALBANOVICH ST. MOSCOW, U.S.S.R.

PURPOSE AND PROPOSED LENGTH OF VISIT — *OBJET ET DURÉE ENVISAGÉE DU SÉJOUR*
two months

NAMES OF ANY OTHER PERSONS TO BE VISITED IN CANADA
NOM DE TOUTE AUTRE PERSONNE CHEZ QUI SE RENDRA LE VISITEUR AU CANADA
XX N/A OR / S/O OU ▶

PARTICULARS OF PREVIOUS VISITS (IF APPLICABLE)
PRÉCISION SUR LES SÉJOURS ANTÉRIEURS (S'IL Y A LIEU)
☐ N/A OR / S/O OU
One month in December, 1981

PERSONS ACCOMPANYING (INCLUDE RELATIONSHIP)
PERSONNES QUI ACCOMPAGNENT LE VISITEUR (Y COMPRIS LE LIEN DE PARENTÉ)
☐ N/A OR / S/O OU JILLIAN DIANNE LAWRENCE (Wife)

PART B — HOST IN CANADA   PARTIE B — HÔTE AU CANADA

SURNAME — NOM DE FAMILLE	GIVEN NAMES — PRÉNOMS	RELATIONSHIP TO PROPOSED VISITOR — LIEN AVEC LE VISITEUR ÉVENTUEL
BEAN	Jennifer	SISTER

COMPLETE ADDRESS IN CANADA — *ADRESSE COMPLÈTE AU CANADA*
99999 MAIN STREET
TORONTO, CANADA
TÉLÉPHONE 555-1234

STATUS IN CANADA (CHECK ONLY ONE) — *STATUT AU CANADA (NE COCHER (✓) QU'UNE SEULE CASE)*
XXX CANADIAN CITIZEN — *CITOYEN CANADIEN*   ☐ OTHER (SPECIFY) — *AUTRE (PRÉCISER)*
☐ PERMANENT RESIDENT — *RÉSIDENT PERMANENT*

DECLARATION
I UNDERSTAND AND AGREE THAT COMPLETION OF THIS FORM IS NOT A GUARANTEE THAT THE PROPOSED VISITOR WILL BE ISSUED A VISITOR VISA, AND THAT THE PROPOSED VISITOR MUST FIRST DEMONSTRATE, AT A CANADIAN VISA OFFICE OUTSIDE CANADA, THAT HE/SHE COMPLIES WITH THE REQUIREMENTS OF THE IMMIGRATION ACT, 1976 AND REGULATIONS THEREUNDER. I ALSO ACKNOWLEDGE THAT I AM AWARE OF THE RESTRICTIONS IMPOSED ON FUNDS WHICH MAY BE REMOVED FROM THE PROPOSED VISITOR'S CURRENT COUNTRY OF RESIDENCE, AND THAT, IF THE VISIT IS APPROVED, I AM OBLIGED TO PROVIDE ADEQUATE LODGING, FOOD AND INCIDENTAL LIVING NEEDS TO THE VISITOR WHILE HE/SHE IS IN CANADA.

DÉCLARATION
JE COMPRENDS ET CONVIENS QUE LE PRÉSENT FORMULAIRE DÛMENT REMPLI NE CONSTITUE PAS UNE GARANTIE QUE LE VISITEUR ÉVENTUEL OBTIENDRA UN VISA DE VISITEUR ET QUE LEDIT VISITEUR DOIT D'ABORD PROUVER À UN AGENT (BUREAU) CANADIEN DES VISAS À L'ÉTRANGER QU'IL (ELLE) SE SOUMET AUX PRESCRIPTIONS DE LA LOI SUR L'IMMIGRATION DE 1976 ET DU RÈGLEMENT ÉTABLI SOUS SON AUTORITÉ. JE RECONNAIS ÉGALEMENT ÊTRE AU COURANT DES RESTRICTIONS IMPOSÉES QUANT AUX FONDS QUE LE VISITEUR ÉVENTUEL PEUT SORTIR DU PAYS OÙ IL RÉSIDE ACTUELLEMENT. DE PLUS, JE RECONNAIS QUE, SI LE SÉJOUR EST AUTORISÉ, JE SUIS TENU DE SUBVENIR COMME IL CONVIENT AUX BESOINS (ARGENT, NOURRITURE ET FRAIS ACCESSOIRES) DU VISITEUR DURANT SON SÉJOUR AU CANADA.

Jennifer Bean

SIGNATURE OF HOST / SIGNATURE DE L'HÔTE	SIGNATURE OF HOST'S SPOUSE (IF APPLICABLE) / SIGNATURE DU CONJOINT DE L'HÔTE (S'IL Y A LIEU)	SIGNATURE OF CIC MANAGER / SIGNATURE DU DIRECTEUR DE CIC	DATE

PART C — FOR OFFICIAL USE ONLY   PARTIE C — RÉSERVÉ AU BUREAU
THE POST ABROAD WILL COMPLETE THIS SECTION ONLY IN APPROVED CASES ATTACH A COPY OF THE PHOTOGRAPH OF THE VISITOR TO THIS COPY (COPY 1) AND SEND IT IMMEDIATELY TO EXTERNAL AFFAIRS HQ 125 SUSSEX DR., OTTAWA K1A 0G2 ATTN: CSO 683
LE BUREAU À L'ÉTRANGER NE REMPLIRA LA PRÉSENTE PARTIE QUE SI LA DEMANDE A ÉTÉ APPROUVÉE, JOINDRA UN DOUBLE DE LA PHOTO DU VISITEUR À LA PRÉSENTE FEUILLE (FEUILLE 1) ET L'ENVERRA SANS DÉLAI À L'ADMINISTRATION DU MINISTÈRE DES AFFAIRES EXTÉRIEURES, 125, PROMENADE SUSSEX, OTTAWA, K1A 0G2, À L'ATTENTION DE CSO 683

IMM 1346 VISA NUMBER — NUMÉRO DU VISA - IMM 1346	DATE ISSUED — DÉLIVRÉ LE	ANTICIPATED DATE OF ARRIVAL — DATE PRÉVUE DE L'ARRIVÉE

REMARKS:
OBSERVATIONS:

IMM 683 (6-83)

APPLICATION FOR TEMPORARY ENTRY TO CANADA
(VISITOR STATUS)

◼◼ Employment and Immigration Canada Emploi et Immigration Canada	**File** — *Réf.*
	Visa No. — *Visa nº*
APPLICATION FOR **DEMANDE D'AUTORISATION DE**	**No. of Entries** — *Nombre d'entrées*
TEMPORARY ENTRY TO CANADA **SÉJOUR TEMPORAIRE AU CANADA**	**Until** — *Jusqu'au*
(VISITOR STATUS) **(STATUT DE VISITEUR)**	**Length of Stay** — *Durée du séjour*

1. Surname (Family name) *Nom de famille*	First name *Prénom*	Middle name *Autres prénoms*	**Issued on** — *Délivré le*
FRIENDLY	BRUCE	NORMAN	**Officer** — *Agent*

2. Present address — *Adresse actuelle*	3. Address in home country — *Adresse dans le pays d'origine*
7777 Second Street San Francisco, California U.S.A. Telephone number — *Numéro de téléphone* ▶ (415) 999-1111	☐ Same as in question 2 or *Préciser si elle diffère de celle donnée au 2* 99999 John Street Kingston, Jamaica

4. Date of Birth — *Date de naissance*			5. Place of Birth — *Lieu de naissance*			6. Citizen of *Citoyenneté*
D-J	M	Y-A	City/Town — *Ville/Village*	Prov./State — *Prov./État*	Country — *Pays*	
05	03	1958	Clarendon		Jamaica	Jamaica

7. Sex — *Sexe*

☒ Male *Homme* ☐ Female *Femme*

8. Present marital status — *État civil*

☒ Unmarried (never married) *Célibataire* ☐ Engaged *Fiancé(e)* ☐ Married *Marié(e)* ☐ Widowed *Veuf (Veuve)* ☐ Separated *Séparé(e)* ☐ Divorced *Divorcé(e)*

9. Personal details of family members who will accompany me to Canada
Renseignements sur les membres de ma famille qui m'accompagneront au Canada

	Family name *Nom de famille*	First and second names *Prénoms*	Date and place of birth *Date et lieu de naissance*	Relationship to me *Lien de parenté*	Citizenship *Citoyenneté*
a)	None				
b)					
c)					
d)					
e)					
f)					

10. Passport details for myself and for persons listed in question 9
Précisions portées sur le passeport — Visiteur et personnes mentionnées au 9

	First name *Prénom*	Passport number *Nº du passeport*	Country of issue *Pays de délivrance*	Date of issue *Date de délivrance*	Date of expiry *Date d'expiration*
Applicant *Requérant*		ABC 999999	Jamaica	June 27, 1982	June 26, 198-
a)					
b)					
c)					
d)					
e)					
f)					

IMM. 1296 (11-80)

This form has been established by the Minister of Employment and Immigration
Formulaire établi par le Ministre de l'Emploi et de l'Immigration

11. The purpose of my visit to Canada is — *Objet de ma visite au Canada*	12. My present occupation is — *Profession actuelle*
To visit my brother -- a Canadian citizen	Automobile mechanic

13. Name, address and relationship of any person(s) whom I will visit are — *Nom et adresse de toute personne à qui je rendrai visite et lien de parenté*

Name — *Nom*	Address in Canada — *Adresse au Canada*	Relationship to me — *Lien de parenté*
Robert Friendly	777777 Yonge Street, Toronto, Ontario	Brother
Roberta Friendly	Same as above	Sister-in-Law
Robin Friendly	Same as above	Niece

14. I intend to be in Canada between
J'ai l'intention de séjourner au Canada du

	D-J	M	Y-A	and *au*		D-J	M	Y-A
▶	01	08	8-		▶	22	08	8-

15. On this trip, I intend to leave and re-enter Canada
Pendant mon séjour, j'ai l'intention de quitter le Canada et d'y revenir

▶ One   Times — *fois*

16. The approximate date of my "final entry" will be
La date approximative de ma dernière entrée au Canada est

	D-J	M	Y-A
▶	20	08	8-

17. Funds available for my stay in Canada
Je dispose, pour mon séjour, de

$ Cdn. 750.00   *(en dollars canadiens)*

18. Have you or any member of your family ever:
Les questions suivantes s'adressent également au visiteur et à tout membre de sa famille

("x" in the appropriate box)
(*Inscrire "x" dans la case appropriée*)

a) Been treated for any serious physical or mental disorders or any communicable or chronic diseases?
Vous a-t-on jamais traité(e) pour une maladie mentale ou physique grave, ou pour une maladie contagieuse ou chronique?
☐ Yes *Oui* ☒ No *Non*

b) Been convicted of any crime in any country?
Vous a-t-on jamais trouvé(e) coupable d'un acte criminel dans quelque pays que ce soit?
☐ Yes *Oui* ☒ No *Non*

c) Been refused admission to or ordered to leave Canada?
Vous a-t-on jamais refusé l'admission au Canada ou enjoint de quitter le Canada?
☐ Yes *Oui* ☒ No *Non*

d) Been refused a visa to travel to Canada?
Vous a-t-on jamais refusé l'autorisation de séjour au Canada?
☐ Yes *Oui* ☒ No *Non*

e) Obtained a Canadian Social Insurance Number?
Vous a-t-on jamais attribué un numéro d'assurance sociale au Canada?
☐ Yes *Oui* ☒ No *Non*

If the answer to any of the above is "yes", give details below — *Si vous avez répondu "oui" à l'une ou l'autre question ci-dessus, veuillez donner des précisions*

19. During the past five years have you or any family member accompanying you lived in any other country for more than six months?
Au cours des derniers cinq ans, avez-vous vécu dans un autre pays pendant plus de six mois? Ne pas oublier les membres de votre famille qui vous accompagneront au Canada.

▶ ☐ Yes *Oui* ☒ No *Non*

20. If answer to question 19 is "yes" list countries and length of stay
Si la réponse au 19 est affirmative, indiquer le nom de ces pays et la durée du séjour

Country — *Pays*	Length of Stay *Durée du séjour*	Country — *Pays*	Length of Stay *Durée du séjour*

I declare that I have answered all required questions in this application fully and truthfully
Je déclare avoir donné des réponses exactes et complètes à toutes les questions de la présente demande.

June 25, 198-

_____   _____
Signature of Applicant — *Signature du requérant*   Date

▮✚ Employment and Immigration Canada Emploi et Immigration Canada	**File — *Réf.***
	Visa No. — *Visa nᵒ*
APPLICATION FOR	**No. of Entries — *Nombre d'entrées***
TEMPORARY ENTRY TO CANADA *DEMANDE D'AUTORISATION DE*	**Until — *Jusqu'au***
(STUDENT AUTHORIZATION) *SÉJOUR TEMPORAIRE AU CANADA*	
(PERMIS DE SÉJOUR POUR ÉTUDIANT)	**Length of Stay — *Durée du séjour***

APPLICATION FOR

TEMPORARY ENTRY TO CANADA

(STUDENT AUTHORIZATION)

DEMANDE D'AUTORISATION DE

SÉJOUR TEMPORAIRE AU CANADA

(PERMIS DE SÉJOUR POUR ÉTUDIANT)

1. Surname (Family name) *Nom de famille*	First name *Prénom*	Middle name *Autres prénoms*	**Issued on — *Délivré le***
TOWNSEND	JILLIAN	DIANNE	**Officer — *Agent***

2. Present address — *Adresse actuelle*

12345 Beacon Hill
San Francisco, California
U.S.A.

Telephone number — *Numéro de téléphone* ▶ (415) 999-2222

3. Address in home country — *Adresse dans le pays d'origine*

[X] Same as in question 2 or
Préciser si elle diffère de celle donnée au 2

4. Date of Birth — *Date de naissance*			5. Place of Birth — *Lieu de naissance*			6. Citizen of *Citoyenneté*
D-*J*	M	Y-*A*	City/Town — *Ville/Village*	Prov./State — *Prov./État*	Country — *Pays*	
05	03	58	San Francisco	California	U.S.A.	U.S.A.

7. Sex — *Sexe*	8. Present marital status — *État civil*
☐ Male *Homme* [X] Female *Femme*	[X] Unmarried (never married) *Célibataire* ☐ Engaged *Fiancé(e)* ☐ Married *Marié(e)* ☐ Widowed *Veuf (Veuve)* ☐ Separated *Séparé(e)* ☐ Divorced *Divorcé(e)*

9. Personal details of family members who will accompany me to Canada
Renseignements sur les membres de ma famille qui m'accompagneront au Canada

	Family name *Nom de famille*	First and second names *Prénoms*	Date and place of birth *Date et lieu de naissance*	Relationship to me *Lien de parenté*	Citizenship *Citoyenneté*
a)	NONE				
b)					
c)					
d)					
e)					
f)					

10. Passport details for myself and for persons listed in question 9
Précisions portées sur le passeport — Visiteur et personnes mentionnées au 9

	First name *Prénom*	Passport number *Nᵒ du passeport*	Country of issue *Pays de délivrance*	Date of issue *Date de délivrance*	Date of expiry *Date d'expiration*
Applicant *Requérant*		ZZZ 7777777	U.S.A.	April 1, 1985	April, 1, 199-
a)					
b)					
c)					
d)					
e)					
f)					

IMM. 1294 (11-80)

This form has been established by the Minister of Employment and Immigration
Formulaire établi par le Ministre de l'Emploi et de l'Immigration

11. I have been accepted at (attach original of letter of acceptance) — *J'ai été accepté à (joindre l'original de la lettre d'acceptation)*

Name of school *Nom de l'établissement d'enseignement*	Complete address of school in Canada *Indiquer l'adresse au complet de cet établissement au Canada*
York University	Keele Street, North York, Ontario, Canada

12. My course of study will be — *Études en*

Masters of Business Administration

13. Total length of course in — *Durée totale du cours*

Years and/or *An(s)* ▶	Months *Mois* ▶ 12	Starts on — *Du*			Finishes on — *Au*		
		D-J 02	M 09	Y-A 8-	D-J 25	M 08	Y-A 8-

14. The cost of my studies will be (in Canadian dollars)
Coût de mes études (en dollars canadiens) ▶ $9,500.00

Tuition *Frais de scolarité* $ 2,500.00	Room and Board *Pension* $ 5,000.00	Other — *Autres* $ 2,000.00

15. I intend to take — *Je compte emporter au Canada*

Cdn $ 12,000.00 to Canada with me
(en dollars canadiens)

16. My expenses in Canada will be paid by — *Mes dépenses au Canada seront assumées par*

[X] Myself
Moi-même [ ] Other (specify)
D'autres (préciser)

17. As proof of my ability to support myself (and my family, if applicable) I attach — *Pour prouver que j'ai les moyens de subvenir à mes propres besoins (et à ceux de ma famille, s'il y a lieu) je joins*

[X] Bank statement — *Un relevé bancaire*

[ ] Foreign Exchange Control Authorization to transfer funds
Une autorisation de virer des fonds au Canada (nécessaire dans le cas des pays où il existe un contrôle des changes)

[X] Other (specify)
Autres (préciser) Travellers' cheques

18. Have you or any member of your family ever:
Les questions suivantes s'adressent également au visiteur et à tout membre de sa famille

("x" the appropriate box)
(Inscrire "x" dans la case appropriée)

a)	Been treated for any serious physical or mental disorders or any communicable or chronic diseases? *Vous a-t-on jamais traité(e) pour une maladie mentale ou physique grave, ou pour une maladie contagieuse ou chronique?*	[ ] Yes *Oui*	[X] No *Non*
b)	Been convicted of any crime in any country? *Vous a-t-on jamais trouvé(e) coupable d'un acte criminel dans quelque pays que ce soit?*	[ ] Yes *Oui*	[X] No *Non*
c)	Been refused admission to or ordered to leave Canada? *Vous a-t-on jamais refusé l'admission au Canada ou enjoint de quitter le Canada?*	[ ] Yes *Oui*	[X] No *Non*
d)	Been refused a visa to travel to Canada? *Vous a-t-on jamais refusé l'autorisation de séjour au Canada?*	[ ] Yes *Oui*	[X] No *Non*
e)	Obtained a Canadian Social Insurance Number? *Vous a-t-on jamais attribué un numéro d'assurance sociale au Canada?*	[ ] Yes *Oui*	[X] No *Non*

If the answer to any of the above is "yes", give details below — *Si vous avez répondu "oui" à l'une ou l'autre question ci-dessus, veuillez donner des précisions*

19. During the past five years have you or any family member accompanying you lived in any other country for more than six months?
Au cours des derniers cinq ans, avez-vous vécu dans un autre pays pendant plus de six mois? Ne pas oublier les membres de votre famille qui vous accompagneront au Canada ▶ [ ] Yes
Oui [X] No
Non

20. If answer to question 19 is "yes" list countries and length of stay
Si la réponse au 19 est affirmative, indiquer le nom de ces pays et la durée du séjour

Country — *Pays*	Length of Stay *Durée du séjour*	Country — *Pays*	Length of Stay *Durée du séjour*

I declare that I have answered all required questions in this application fully and truthfully
Je déclare avoir donné des réponses exactes et complètes à toutes les questions de la présente demande

Jillian D. Townsend
Signature of Applicant — *Signature du requérant*

July 6, 198-
Date

SAMPLE #26
APPLICATION FOR TEMPORARY ENTRY TO CANADA
(EMPLOYMENT AUTHORIZATION)

	File
▌✦ Employment and Immigration Canada Emploi et Immigration Canada	**Visa No.**
	No. of Entries
APPLICATION FOR	**DEMANDE D'AUTORISATION DE**
TEMPORARY ENTRY TO CANADA	**SÉJOUR TEMPORAIRE AU CANADA**
(EMPLOYMENT AUTHORIZATION)	**(PERMIS DE TRAVAIL)**

	File
	Visa No.
	No. of Entries
	Until
	Length of Stay

1. Surname (Family name) *Nom de famille*	First name *Prénom*	Middle name *Autres prénoms*	Issued on
TOWNSEND	BRUCE	ELLIOT	Officer

2. Present address — Adresse actuelle

55555 Short Street
Silicon Valley
California 99999
U.S.A.

Telephone number — *Numéro de téléphone* ▶

3. Address in home country — Adresse dans le pays d'origine

[X] Same as in question 2 or
Préciser si elle diffère de celle donnée au 2

4. Date of Birth — Date de naissance

D-J	M	Y-A
25	07	8-

5. Place of Birth — Lieu de naissance

City/Town — Ville/Village	Prov./State — Prov./État	Country — Pays
Coral City	California	U.S.A.

6. Citizen of *Citoyenneté*

U.S.A.

7. Sex — Sexe [X] Male Homme [ ] Female Femme

8. Present marital status — État civil

[ ] Unmarried (never married) Célibataire [ ] Engaged Fiancé(e) [X] Married Marié(e) [ ] Widowed Veuf (Veuve) [ ] Separated Séparé(e) [ ] Divorced Divorcé(e)

9. Personal details of family members who will accompany me to Canada
Renseignements sur les membres de ma famille qui m'accompagneront au Canada

	Family name *Nom de famille*	First and second names *Prénoms*	Date and place of birth *Date et lieu de naissance*	Relationship to me *Lien de parenté*	Citizenship *Citoyenneté*
a)	Townsend	Dianne	Coral City, Calif. June 1, 1939	Wife	U.S.A.
b)	Townsend	Robert Bruce	Silicon Valley,Cal. June 2, 1975	Son	U.S.A.
c)					
d)					
e)					
f)					

10. Passport details for myself and for persons listed in question 9
Précisions portées sur le passeport — Visiteur et personnes mentionnées au 9

	First name *Prénom*	Passport number *N° du passeport*	Country of issue *Pays de délivrance*	Date of issue *Date de délivrance*	Date of expiry *Date d'expiration*
	Applicant *Requérant*	ZZZ LL 33333	U.S.A.	March 4, 1984	March 4, 199-
a)	Dianne	AAA BB 22222	U.S.A.	April, 10, 1983	April 10. 199-
b)	Robert Bruce	DDD FF 11111	U.S.A.	June 6, 1985	June 6, 199-
c)					
d)					
e)					
f)					

IMM. 1295 (11-80)

This form has been established by the Minister of Employment and Immigration
Formulaire établi par le Ministre de l'Emploi et de l'Immigration

11. My present occupation is — *Profession actuelle*	12.		Months *Mois*	Years *An(s)*
Vice President, Operations	I have held my present job for *J'occupe mon emploi actuel depuis*			12

13. The name and address of my employer and the type of business are — *Nom et adresse de mon employeur (préciser également le genre d'entreprise)*

The XYZ Oil Company Inc.
3456 J. Street
Silicon Valley, California
U.S.A.

A multinational oil exploration and refining company

14. The name and address of my prospective employer in Canada are: (Attach original copy of offer of employment)
Nom et adresse de mon employeur éventuel au Canada (joindre l'original de l'offre d'emploi)

The XYZ Oil Company Canada Ltd.
4567 G. Street
Edmonton, Alberta
Canada

15. My occupation in Canada will be — *Ma profession au Canada sera*	16. My salary will be — *Mon salaire sera de*
President	$ Cdn. $175,000.00 *(en dollars canadiens)*

17. Estimated amount of money in my possession upon arrival in Canada *Montant approximatif en ma possession à mon arrivée au Canada*	$ Cdn. $50,000.00 *(en dollars canadiens)*

18. I am expected to start my employment on *Je suis censé commencer à travailler le* ▶	D-J 02	M 09	Y-A 8-	19. My employment is expected to finish on *Il est prévu que mon emploi prendra fin le* ▶	D-J 02	M 08	Y-A 8-

20. Have you or any member of your family ever:
Les questions suivantes s'adressent également au visiteur et à tout membre de sa famille

("x" in the appropriate box)
(Inscrire "x" dans la case appropriée)

		Yes *Oui*	No *Non*
a)	Been treated for any serious physical or mental disorders or any communicable or chronic diseases? *Vous a-t-on jamais traité(e) pour une maladie mentale ou physique grave, ou pour une maladie contagieuse ou chronique?*	☐	☒
b)	Been convicted of any crime in any country? *Vous a-t-on jamais trouvé(e) coupable d'un acte criminel dans quelque pays que ce soit?*	☐	☒
c)	Been refused admission to or ordered to leave Canada? *Vous a-t-on jamais refusé l'admission au Canada ou enjoint de quitter le Canada?*	☐	☒
d)	Been refused a visa to travel to Canada? *Vous a-t-on jamais refusé l'autorisation de séjour au Canada?*	☐	☒
e)	Obtained a Canadian Social Insurance Number? *Vous a-t-on jamais attribué un numéro d'assurance sociale au Canada?*	☐	☒

If the answer to any of the above is "yes", give details below — *Si vous avez répondu "oui" à l'une ou l'autre question ci-dessus, veuillez donner des précisions*

21. During the past five years have you or any family member accompanying you lived in any other country for more than six months?
Au cours des derniers cinq ans, avez-vous vécu dans un autre pays pendant plus de six mois? Ne pas oublier les membres de votre famille qui vous accompagneront au Canada.   ▶   ☒ Yes *Oui*   ☐ No *Non*

22. If answer to question 21 is "yes" list countries and length of stay
Si la réponse au 21 est affirmative, indiquer le nom de ces pays et la durée du séjour

Country — *Pays*	Length of Stay *Durée du séjour*	Country — *Pays*	Length of Stay *Durée du séjour*
West Germay	24 months		

I declare that I have answered all required questions in this application fully and truthfully
Je déclare avoir donné des réponses exactes et complètes à toutes les questions de la présente demande.

D.C. Townsend
Signature of Applicant — *Signature du requérant*

April 15, 198-
Date

Employment and Emploi et
Immigration Canada Immigration Canada

VISITOR RECORD   FICHE DU VISITEUR

HEADQUARTERS' USE ONLY - RÉSERVE A L'ADMINISTRATION CENTRALE

SECTION A   41   04   TYPE OF CASE/GENRE DE CAS   23

SURNAME, GIVEN NAMES/NOM DE FAMILLE, PRÉNOMS
VISITOR   RAYMOND   NAME FLAG/INDICA TEUR OUI NON 55

BIRTH DATE/DATE DE NAISSANCE   COUNTRY OF BIRTH/PAYS DE NAISSANCE   COUNTRY OF CITIZENSHIP/CITOYENNETÉ
D J 0 2 M 10 Y A 1952   Jamaica 77   Jamaica 99

SEX/SEXE   MARITAL STATUS/ÉTAT MATRIMONIAL   TOTAL PERSONS NO. TOTAL DE PERS   FAMILY STATUS INDICATOR INDICATEUR DE LA SITUATION PAR RAPPORT A LA FAMILLE
-M/H   1 SINGLE CÉLIBATAIRE   3 WIDOWED VEUF/VEUVE(E)   5 SEPARATED SÉPARÉ(E)   1 PRINCIPAL APPLICANT REQUÉRANT PRINCIPAL   3 DEPENDANT PERSONNE À CHARGE
-F/F 82 M   2 MARRIED MARIÉ(E)   4 DIVORCED DIVORCÉ(E)   84 1   85 0 1   2 SPOUSE CONJOINT   87 1

COMPLETE ADDRESS OUTSIDE CANADA/ADRESSE AU LONG A L'EXTÉRIEUR DU CANADA
BUYERS ST, MONTEGO BAY, JAMAICA   88

NAME AND COMPLETE ADDRESS WHERE YOU CAN BE REACHED IN CANADA/
NOM ET ADRESSE AU LONG OU L'ON PEUT VOUS REJOINDRE AU CANADA
500 VUAGHN CRES., TORONTO, ONTARIO   91

SECTION B   **RECORD OF ENTRY**

TERMS AND CONDITIONS/CONDITIONS

Shall not attend school
Shall not engage in any employment
Shall report any change of address

ACCOMPANYING FAMILY MEMBERS/MEMBRES DE LA FAMILLE QUI VOUS ACCOMPAGNENT		
NAME/NOM	DATE OF BIRTH DATE DE NAISSANCE	RELATIONSHIP LIEN DE PARENTE
None		

STATUS ÉTAT 130

I CERTIFY THAT THE PARTICULARS OF MY IDENTITY ARE CORRECT AND ACCEPT THE TERMS AND CONDITIONS SET OUT HEREIN
JE CERTIFIE QUE LES RENSEIGNEMENTS SUR MON IDENTITÉ SONT EXACTS, ET J'ACCEPTE LES CONDITIONS PRÉCITÉES

VALID UNTIL/DATE D'EXPIRATION
D J 0 M 5 Y A 0 1 8 122
BONDED/CAUTIONNEMENT 1 YES OUI 2 NO NON 128   BOND NUMBER N° DU CAUTIONNEMENT
SIGNATURE OF VISITOR SIGNATURE DU VISITEUR ▶

DATE SIGNED/SIGNE LE
D J 1 M 5 Y A 1 2 129
CANADA IMMIGRATION CENTRE CENTRE D'IMMIGRATION CANADA
Tor. Airport 156
SIGNATURE OF IMMIGRATION OFFICER SIGNATURE DE L'AGENT D'IMMIGRATION ▶

REMARKS/OBSERVATIONS

Coming to visit uncle, Mr. Jack Citizen, over Christmas and New Year's

MEDICAL COMPLETED FORMALITÉS MÉDICALES ACCOMPLIES
1 YES OUI   2 NO NON   148 2
SPECIAL PROGRAM/PROGRAMME SPÉCIAL
N/A   161

DATE OF ORIGINAL ENTRY DATE D'ENTRÉE INITIALE
D J 1 5 M 1 2 Y A 8 — 160
EXTENSION NUMBER/CODE APPROPRIE 186
ORIGINAL SERIAL NUMBER N° DE SÉRIE INITIAL 188

OFFICE FILE NO./N° DE RÉFÉRENCE DU BUREAU
ERROR/ERREUR 191
UTILITIES/LIBRES 203 204 205 206 207 208 209 210 211

M. 1097 (5-78)

(d) proof of sufficient funds to pay your way home (such proof usually takes the form of a bank draft, bank book, letter of credit, or return ticket).

With these documents, the Canadian visa officer will usually issue a visitor's visa, called a Student Authorization, authorizing you to attend school in Canada. You must attend the school that applies on your visa. If you wish to change schools when in Canada, *you must obtain permission before you actually do so.*

A student must obtain a visa before coming to Canada. A student visa *cannot* be issued inside the country. Once a visitor's visa with student authorization has been issued and you are in Canada, extensions can and will be granted inside Canada.

A student will be granted a visa for a period not exceeding one year. If your course is longer than that, and most courses are, you will have to renew your visa each year at an immigration office, and each year you will have to bring a letter from your school stating that you have been admitted for the next year as well as proof of your ability to support yourself.

A recent amendment in policy allows a visa officer to issue a student authorization for the duration of the course (i.e., three or four years). It is rare to receive this since most officials both inside and outside Canada are used to the old system. However, over the next several years, we may see a change in this area and longer visas may be issued abroad or at first renewal in Canada.

c. BUSINESS PEOPLE, ARTISTS, MILITARY, ETC.

If you are coming to Canada to carry on business without being employed in Canada or doing anything for which you would normally expect to be paid, you may enter Canada as a visitor subject to the requirements outlined in section **a.** above. You do not need an employment authorization in advance. A foreign business person, for instance, will normally be allowed to enter Canada for a period not exceeding 90 days provided that he or she makes no sales to the general public.

Similarly, diplomats and United Nations personnel or our allies coming for training will be given permission to work and do not need an employment authorization issued prior to their arrival.

The law regarding artists, such as singers and musicians who come to Canada to perform, is now quite complex. The need to have or not have an employment authorization turns on the nature, duration, and number of performances, and other business surroundings of the artist.

Artists who come to Canada to perform often have to clear their performance with the local Canadian union. In addition, artists who bring things such as expensive instruments and electronic amplification equipment with them will probably have to post a refundable bond ensuring the removal of the equipment from Canada when they depart. This latter problem concerns the Canadian Customs officials and not the immigration authorities.

Artists and performers clearly require the assistance of a knowledgeable Canadian immigration lawyer to assist them in this area.

d. CREW MEMBERS

Last, members of the crews of ships or airplanes are allowed to enter Canada temporarily as visitors without employment authorization as long as their ship or vessel is in Canada. As soon as the plane or ship leaves Canada, any members of the crew who have failed to leave with their ship are deemed to be in Canada illegally.

The only exception to this is the case of those crew members seeking refugee status in Canada, and even they are required to report to the nearest Canadian immigration office as soon as possible.

If you are getting ideas of jumping ship as a refugee, DON'T, unless you can fit into the very narrow Canadian definition of this term. Generally speaking, you must be seeking asylum from persecution directed personally against you by a state or government or as a refugee recognized as such by the United Nations. (See chapter 17 for a much more detailed discussion.)

e. ENTERING CANADA AS A VISITOR

Remember, if you have any doubts before you come to Canada as a non-immigrant, check with a Canadian official either at one of the foreign offices or in Ottawa, Canada.

Getting into Canada as a visitor can be very difficult. Border officials with the Immigration Department are strict and very enforcement-minded. They are very suspicious about an individual's motives for coming to Canada. If possible, have a letter of invitation to Canada from friends or relatives. Be sure to know their name, address, and telephone number. If possible, have one of your relatives or friends at the airport to meet you.

f. OBTAIN A VISA

It bears repeating: get a visa if you are planning to visit Canada.

During a recent summer, approximately 200 non-immigrants per week were detained and either deported or asked to leave Canada immediately without being allowed to visit family or friends. This number has probably increased since then. Some of these people had saved for years to make this trip and they lost everything. Remember, if at all possible, obtain a visitor's visa from the nearest Canadian embassy or consulate before you come on your visit.

People with visas can appeal to the Immigration Appeal Board (see chapter 25).

People without visas can appeal only to the Federal Court of Appeal with more restricted rights of appeal and at a much greater cost (see chapter 26).

g. WHO DOES NOT NEED A VISA?

The following people do not require a visa to come to Canada as non-immigrant visitors:

(a) British citizens or British overseas citizens readmissible to the United Kingdom

(b) Citizens of British dependent territories through birth or descent including Anguilla, Bermuda, British Virgin Islands, Cayman Islands, Falkland Islands, Gibraltar, Hong Kong, Monseratt, Pitcairn, St. Helena, and the Turks and Caicos Islands.

(c) Permanent residents of the United States coming directly from the United States to Canada

(d) People in transit through Canada directly to another country.

The following is a list of countries from which non-immigrant visitors do NOT require visas — subject to my warnings in section a. of this chapter:

Andorra
Antigua and Barbuda
Argentina
Australia
Austria
Bahamas
Barbados
Belgium
Beliz
Botsana
Brunei
Costa Rica
Cyprus
Denmark
Dominica
Federal Republic of Germany
    (West Germany)

Finland
France
Greece
Grenada
Iceland
Ireland
Israel
Italy
Japan
Kenya
Kiribati
Lesotho
Liechtenstein
Luxembourg
Malawi
Malaysia
Malta
Mexico
Monaco
Nauru
Netherlands
New Zealand
Norway
Papua New Guinea
Paraguay
San Marino
Saudi Arabia
Seychelles
Singapore
Solomon Islands
Spain
St. Lucia
St. Kitts and Nevis
St. Vincent
Surinam
Swaziland
Sweden
Switzerland
Tonga
Tuvalu
United States
Uruguay
Vanuatu
Venezuela
Western Samoa
Zambia
Zimbabwe

Although people from almost all the countries of Central and South America and adjacent islands are included among those who, in law, don't require a non-immigrant visa, people visiting Canada from those countries would be well advised to obtain one.

Remember: Anyone coming to visit Canada from a country not listed above must have a visa. If you do not have a visa, you will be turned back at the airport or border.

h. VARYING A VISITOR'S VISA

If you have been admitted to Canada as a visitor in any category — tourist, student, crew member, business person — you can apply at the nearest Canada Immigration Centre to change or cancel the terms of your admission. This could include a tourist asking for an extension of time to visit relatives or to travel in Canada, a student wishing to change schools, or a businesswoman requesting an extension of time to conduct her business.

This application to vary *must be brought before the time you have been allowed in Canada has expired*, and *before* you make any such change (e.g., moving to a new school). You must make the request while you are legally in Canada, and you must obtain permission from Immigration before you act or stay here longer.

If you go to the Immigration Department after the expiry of your time limit or after you have changed schools without permission, you have broken the law; you are then probably an illegal and subject to report and removal or deportation from Canada (see chapter 24).

This same rule also applies to people in Canada with work authorizations (see chapter 21). When you go to your interview for a change or variance in your visitor's permit, you should go with the friend or relative you are visiting.

You must take your passport, proof of funds in Canada, and proof of your return transportation to your homeland. You must have good reasons for your extension and specific plans for the additional time requested. It is also a good idea to have proof of a job to return to in your homeland and a letter authorizing you to take the additional time from your employer. A letter that proves you have employment in your homeland is particularly useful when you come to Canada as a visitor from a Third World country.

Sample #28 is an example of the Application to Vary or Cancel Terms and Conditions of Admission to Canada (IMM #1249) that will be required when you apply for your extension or change.

SAMPLE #28
APPLICATION TO VARY OR CANCEL
TERMS AND CONDITIONS OF ADMISSION

Employment and Immigration Canada   Emploi et Immigration Canada

APPLICATION TO VARY OR CANCEL TERMS AND CONDITIONS OF ADMISSION
DEMANDE DE MODIFICATION OU D'ANNULATION DES CONDITIONS D'ADMISSION

My family name is / Mon nom de famille	My first name is / Mon prénom	My middle name is / Mon second prénom	My sex is – Sexe
VISITOR	JOSEPH	NORMAN	XX Male / Homme ☐ Female / Femme

My date of birth was / Ma date de naissance

Day-Jour	Month-Mois	Year-Année	My place of birth was / Mon lieu de naissance City or town – Ville	Country – Pays	I am a citizen of / Je suis citoyen de
18	May	1953	PARIS	FRANCE	FRANCE

My present mailing address is / Mon adresse postale actuelle	No. and Street / N° et rue	City or town / Ville	Province	Telephone no. – N° de téléphone
	100 Rue de la Republique	Quebec City	Quebec	555-5555

My present marital status is ("X" the appropriate block) NOTE: Any change in marital status must be reported to the office handling your application.
Mon état matrimonial actuel (inscrivez (X) dans la case appropriée) NOTE: Tout changement doit être signalé au bureau chargé de l'étude de votre demande.

XX Single (never married) / Célibataire   ☐ Engaged / Fiancé(e)   ☐ Married / Marié(e)   ☐ Widowed / Veuf (veuve)   ☐ Separated / Séparé(e)   ☐ Divorced / Divorcé(e)

PARTICULARS OF MY SPOUSE AND CHILDREN (IF ANY) ARE – RENSEIGNEMENTS SUR MON CONJOINT ET MES ENFANTS (S'IL Y A LIEU):

Family name / Nom de famille	Given names / Prénoms	Relationship / Lien de parenté	Day Jour	Month Mois	Year Année	City or town of birth / Lieu de naissance (ville)	Citizenship / Citoyenneté
	NOT APPLICABLE						

I was admitted to Canada on / J'ai été admis(e) au Canada le   March 1, 1983   at / à   Montreal, Quebec (Mirabel)

As a / À titre de   ☐ Permanent resident / Résident permanent   XX Visitor until / Visiteur jusqu'au   March 30/8-   Under the following terms and conditions: / En vertu des conditions suivantes:

As a tourist.

And I hereby make application to / Et je demande par les présentes   ☐ cancel / l'annulation   XX vary these terms and conditions for the following reasons: / la modification de ces conditions pour les raisons suivantes:
(Attach seperate sheet if required)   (Joindre une feuille distincte s'il y a lieu)

I WISH AN EXTENSION OF FOUR WEEKS TO TRAVEL TO
VANCOUVER, BRITISH COLUMBIA, TO VISIT AN UNCLE THERE.

Signature of applicant – Signature du requérant   Date

For official use only. / Do not complete. / Réserve   ▶   Application / Demande   ☐ Approved / Approuvée   ☐ Refused / Rejetée   Senior Immigration Officer (or) adjudicator / Agent d'immigration supérieur (ou) arbitre

IMM 1249 (4-82)   THIS FORM HAS BEEN ESTABLISHED BY THE MINISTER OF EMPLOYMENT & IMMIGRATION.
FORMULAIRE ÉTABLI PAR LE MINISTRE DE L'EMPLOI ET DE L'IMMIGRATION

Canada

21
EMPLOYMENT AUTHORIZATIONS

a. THE RULES

Canada has adopted a policy of allowing visitors to work for a specified, temporary period in this country. Unfortunately, the Canadian temporary employment authorization is not very easy to obtain. The application to obtain a work permit must be made by the prospective Canadian employer NOT by the visitor who wishes to find work on a temporary basis while legally in Canada.

Most important is the fact that, as mentioned in chapter 20, the issuing of an employment authorization to a visitor can only be done at a Canadian embassy or consulate with an immigration section (see Appendix 2) *outside* of Canada.

An exception to this rule applies in certain circumstances to U.S. citizens and U.S. permanent residents and also under the Canada/U.S.A. Free Trade Agreement (see chapter 22).

In addition, the employment authorization can be issued only if there has been a prior approval *in Canada* of the temporary job offer. The employment division of the Employment and Immigration Commission in Canada will have to approve the temporary offer by stating that they are unable to locate an available and qualified Canadian or permanent resident to do the job you have been offered on a temporary basis.

Your prospective temporary employer will be required to make an application for you at the nearest Canada Employment Centre. The application form is identical to the one used when seeking an employment approval for an immigrant (see Sample #7).

The only difference in completing the form is that you should indicate that the job is temporary and state the duration of the job. Otherwise, your future temporary employer should complete the form in the same manner as shown on Sample #7 and according to the instructions in chapter 10.

The application must be completed by the employer personally at a local Canada Employment Centre. The form may not be taken away from the premises and will not be sent to employers. They must go there personally.

Thus, the burden is on employers to show the government that they need you. The employment division will spend several weeks, or perhaps months, attempting to find a suitable employee in Canada for your prospective employer. If they do, then the employer will not be given a permit to hire you. Only if the government is unsuccessful in finding a suitable Canadian or permenent resident will you be allowed to work in Canada for a temporary period of time, usually six months and seldom more than twelve months.

As you can see, the onus is on the future visitor who wishes to work in Canada first to find someone who will employ him or her and then to convince that person to go through a fairly complex government procedure in order to obtain permission to hire him or her.

All this must be done before you come to Canada or you must first come to

Canada, locate the job, have the employer apply for you while you return to your homeland and wait for approval since you *cannot* obtain the visa to work in Canada. Sample #29 shows a sample Visitor's Visa with Employment Authorization (IMM #1102), permission to work for a temporary period in Canada.

In my opinion, unless your future employer has obtained employment approval on the EMP #2151 (Sample #7), you will not be granted an employment authorization in Canada.

This system is aimed at curtailing employment — even temporarily — of visitors to Canada. Not very many employers will take the time and effort to obtain a work permit for you and, in addition, suffer the scrutiny of a government department that will attempt to find a Canadian or permanent resident who can do the job.

Since most visitors, especially students, are seeking unskilled and semi-skilled jobs, the opportunity to obtain a temporary work permit is limited. It is the specially skilled and trained worker, often those with a unique knowledge of a particular machine or process, who will find it easier to obtain a temporary work permit because their prospective employer will tolerate the difficulties of making an application in order to obtain the services of a specific individual.

Thus, if you are a student, for example, hoping to come to Canada on a summer visit and work here in order to finance your trip, be sure to have obtained guaranteed employment through one of the student exchange programs co-ordinated through Canadian embassies and consulates abroad.

Also, be sure to check out with a Canadian embassy or consulate the credentials of any tour plan or travel agency that has promised you employment in Canada. Often such promises have no basis

in fact, and may be a means of using you as cheap, illegal labor in Canada.

b. THE EXEMPTIONS

There are exemptions in rare circumstances from the requirement to obtain approval from Employment Canada for any job offer. These exemptions are enumerated in Regulations 19 and 20 to the Immigration Act and include the following individuals:

(a) Diplomats

(b) Visiting armed forces of our allies

(c) Members of the clergy of accredited religious orders and denominations

(d) Performing artists within a group of more than 15 people for a specific concert or tour

(e) Crew members of ships or airplanes

(f) Foreign news correspondents coming to report on a specific event in Canada

(g) People coming to *purchase* goods in Canada

(h) Salespersons for less than 90 days where there are no sales to the general public

(i) Persons coming to provide emergency medical treatment or to preserve life or property

(j) Persons destined to international sporting events as players

(k) Judges or referees for international amateur sporting events or animal shows

(l) Guest speakers at dinners or graduations

(m) Expert witnesses testifying before a Canadian court or tribunal

(n) Medical electives or clinical clerks in medicine coming to *observe* medical procedures

(o) Trainees of multinational corporations coming to *observe* only and not to perform any work or services

(p) U.S. citizens under the Free Trade Agreement (see chapter 22)

The following people are exempt from the requirement to apply from outside Canada for an Employment Authorization. Provided that they are already *legally in Canada,* they and their spouses and unmarried children may apply for an employment authorization:

(a) Diplomats

(b) Armed forces personnel of our allies

(c) Members of the clergy

(d) Foreign news reporters

(e) Foreign government officials on exchange plans

(f) A person already on a currently valid student authorization and his or her unmarried child

(g) A person already on a currently valid employment authorization and his or her unmarried child

(h) Holders of minister's permits and their spouses and unmarried children

(i) Persons required to carry out emergency repairs to industrial equipment

(j) Foreign registered ships' crews operating in Canadian waters

(k) Certain performing artists

(l) Persons awaiting orders-in-council allowing them to obtain permanent resident status *in Canada* such as the spouses of Canadian citizens or permanent residents

(m) Persons found by the immigration authorities or the Immigration and Refugee Board to be convention refugees

(n) Persons who have claims to Canadian citizenship or to be convention refugees who have appeals pending concerning same in the courts who without permission to work would require public assistance (welfare) to subsist.

c. GRADUATING STUDENTS

Foreign students who have attended college or university in Canada on a full-time basis are now permitted to work in Canada for one year following graduation in order to obtain experience and training. Students in this situation must obtain a written job offer and apply for an employment authorization at a Canadian Immigration Centre *within 60 days after graduation.*

This change in Canadian policy appears to mirror similar laws in the United States and affords an opportunity to obtain one year's experience in Canada before returning home. This one-year employment authorization *cannot* be extended and if you return to school after your work experience, for example, to do a master's degree, you cannot have a second year of work experience after your second degree. It is a one time, once only opportunity.

One important factor to remember is that under the point system (see chapter 9), an independent applicant for immigration to Canada must receive at least one point for experience and one point for occupational demand. The one year's experience in Canada *provided that it is in the same occupational category in which you subsequently apply to immigrate to Canada* will qualify for your experience requirement under the point system.

HEADQUARTERS' USE ONLY - *RÉSERVÉ À L'ADMINISTRATION CENTRALE*

SECTION A

4 2

TYPE OF CASE *GENRE DE CAS* (23)

SURNAME, GIVEN NAMES *NOM DE FAMILLE, PRENOMS*

N O R M A N   B A R R Y

NAME FLAG INDICATEUR DU NOM (55)

BIRTH DATE *DATE DE NAISSANCE*

D J 2 5 | M 0 1 | Y A 1 9 4 4

COUNTRY OF BIRTH *PAYS DE NAISSANCE*: ISRAEL (77)

COUNTRY OF CIT. *NSHIP/CITOYENNETE*: ISRAEL (80)

SEX/*SEXE*: 1-M/H 2-F/F (83) 1

MARITAL STATUS *ÉTAT MATRIMONIAL*:
1 SINGLE *CELIBATAIRE*
2 MARRIED *MARIÉ(E)*
3 WIDOWED *VEUF(VEUVE)*
4 DIVORCED *DIVORCÉ(E)*
5 SEPARATED *SÉPARÉ(E)*

TOTAL PERSONS *NO. TOTAL DE PERS.* (84) 2

(85) 0 4

FAMILY STATUS INDICATOR *INDICATEUR DE LA SITUATION PAR RAPPORT À LA FAMILLE*:
1 PRINCIPAL APPLICANT *REQUÉRANT PRINCIPAL*
2 SPOUSE *CONJOINT*
3 DEPENDANT *PERSONNE À CHARGE*
(87) 1

COMPLETE ADDRESS OUTSIDE CANADA *ADRESSE AU LONG À L'EXTÉRIEUR DU CANADA*

Ramat Sharuden, Tel Aviv, Israel.
(88)

NAME AND COMPLETE ADDRESS OF EMPLOYER *NOM ET ADRESSE AU LONG DE L'EMPLOYEUR*

University of Toronto
Faculty of Medicine
Toronto, Canada
(81)

INTENDED OCCUPATION *PROFESSION ENVISAGÉE*

Professor of
Bio-chemistry
(95)

NAME AND COMPLETE ADDRESS WHERE YOU CAN BE REACHED IN CANADA *NOM ET ADRESSE AU LONG OU L'ON PEUT VOUS REJOINDRE AU CANADA*

10 Pervis St. Toronto, Canada

LOCATION OF EMPLOYMENT *LIEU DE TRAVAIL*

Toronto, Ontario

DATE OF ISSUE *DATE DE DÉLIVRANCE* (108) D J 10 | M 0 | Y A 78 -

VISA POST *BUREAU DES VISAS* Tel Aviv (115)

SIGNATURE OF VISA OFFICER *SIGNATURE DE L'AGENT DES VISAS* ▶

SECTION B   **RECORD OF ENTRY**

TERMS AND CONDITIONS/*CONDITIONS*

Shall only teach at the University
of Toronto and attached Teaching
hospitals

Shall not attend school as a student

ACCOMPANYING FAMILY MEMBERS/*MEMBRES DE LA FAMILLE QUI VOUS ACCOMPAGNENT*

NAME/*NOM*	DATE OF BIRTH *DATE DE NAISSANCE*	RELATIONSHIP *LIEN DE PARENTÉ*
Pesia Judith	Feb.24,46	Wife
Daniel Jonathan	Nov 13,70	Son
Allison Heather	July 20 1973	Daughter

STATUS *ÉTAT* (120)

I CERTIFY THAT THE PARTICULARS OF MY IDENTITY ARE CORRECT AND ACCEPT THE TERMS AND CONDITIONS SET OUT HEREIN
JE CERTIFIE QUE LES RENSEIGNEMENTS SUR MON IDENTITÉ SONT EXACTS, ET J'ACCEPTE LES CONDITIONS PRECITÉES.

VALID UNTIL *DATE D'EXPIRATION* (122) D J 1 | M 0 | Y A 98 -

BONDED/*CAUTIONNEMENT*: 1 YES *OUI* 2 NO *NON* (128) 2

BOND NUMBER *Nº DU CAUTIONNEMENT*

SIGNATURE OF VISITOR *SIGNATURE DU VISITEUR* ▶

DATE SIGNED/*SIGNE LE* (129) D J 0 | M 8 | Y A 98 -

CANADA IMMIGRATION CENTRE *CENTRE D'IMMIGRATION CANADA* Tor Air't (135)

SIGNATURE OF IMMIGRATION OFFICER *SIGNATURE DE L'AGENT D'IMMIGRATION* ▶

REMARKS/*OBSERVATIONS*

SECTION C

MEDICAL COMPLETED *FORMALITÉS MÉDICALES ACCOMPLIES*: 1 YES *OUI* 2 NO *NON* (140)

EXEMPTION *DISPENSE RÈGLEMENT* (141)

CANADA MANPOWER CENTRE *CENTRE DE MAIN D'OEUVRE DU CANADA* (144)

IMP 2151 NO *IMP 2151 Nº* (149)

UEI NUMBER *Nº DE L'EMPLOYEUR* (156)

STANDARD IND. CLASS.(S.I.C.) *CLASSIFICATION TYPE DES INDUSTRIES (C.T.I.)* (165)

SPECIAL PROGRAM *PROGRAMME SPÉCIAL*

SOCIAL INSURANCE NUMBER *Nº D'ASSURANCE SOCIAL* (171)

SECTION D

DATE OF ORIGINAL ENTRY *DATE D'ENTRÉE INITIALE* (180) D J | M | Y A

EXTENSION NUMBER/*CODE APPROPRIE* (186)

ORIGINAL SERIAL NUMBER *Nº DE SERIE INITIAL* (188)

MULTIPLE AUTHORIZATION *AUTORISATIONS MULTIPLES*: 1 YES *OUI* 2 NO *NON* (198)

OFFICE FILE NO *Nº DE RÉFÉRENCE DU BUREAU*

ERROR/*ERREUR*

UTILITIES *LIBRES*

M 1102 (5-78)

22

THE CANADA/U.S.A. FREE TRADE AGREEMENT

In January, 1989, Canada and the United States of America entered into a free trade agreement (FTA). The FTA involves not only goods but also services, and chapter 15 of the FTA deals with the movement of U.S. citizens to Canada for a wide range of business purposes on a *temporary basis only*.

The FTA covers four distinct categories of business persons coming to Canada from the United States:

(a) Business visitors (Schedule 1 to FTA)

(b) Traders and investors

(c) Professionals (Schedule 2 to FTA)

(d) Intra-company transferees

The FTA does not replace or restrict the previously existing immigration rules and procedures for the above categories as outlined in chapters 20 and 21. The FTA enhances and expands these provisions as they apply to U.S. citizens (with one possible exception — see below concerning intra-corporate transferees).

Note: The FTA applies only to U.S. citizens coming to Canada. it does not apply to permanent residents (green card holders) of the United States.

Schedule 1 to the FTA lists seven broad areas in which U.S. business visitors to Canada shall be granted entry into Canada without the necessity of obtaining prior employment authorization (a work permit) and without the necessity of obtaining prior labor clearance as outlined in chapter 10. The seven areas are as follows:

(a) Research and design

(b) Growth, manufacture and production

(i) Harvester owner

(ii) Purchasing and production management personnel

(c) Marketing

(i) Market researchers

(ii) Trade fair and promotional personnel

(d) Sales

(i) Taking orders or negotiating contracts for services *but not delivering goods or providing services*

(e) Distribution

(i) Transporting goods

(f) After sales service

(i) Specialized repair, installation, or maintenance pursuant to a contractual obligation or warranty

(g) General service

(i) Professionals not being paid by a Canadian source (other than out-of-pocket expenses such as travel, hotels, food, etc.)

(ii) Management personnel

(iii) Computer specialists

(iv) Financial services personnel

(v) Public relations and advertising personnel

(vi) Tourism personnel — agents, guides, etc.

(vii) Translators and interpreters

All the above categories of U.S. business visitors to Canada will be examined and admitted pursuant to the FTA at a port-of-entry (i.e., airport or land crossing), and will have to provide evidence of U.S. citizenship, proof that they are engaging in one of the seven areas outlined above, and compliance with Canada's immigration laws in general.

Proof of citizenship would be a U.S. citizenship card, passport, or birth certificate. Proof of activities would depend on the nature of the entry but could include copies of contracts, warranties, letter from employer re sales, invitation from Canadian company, trade show brochure, etc.

The general rules under Canadian immigration law concerning intra-company transferees have not been substantially altered by the FTA. In general, the Canadian *Immigration Manual* provides that a person in a senior or managerial category who has a letter from a company carrying on business in Canada that identifies the holder as an employee of a branch, subsidiary, or parent of the company located outside Canada and who seeks to enter Canada to work at a senior executive or managerial level as an intra-corporate transferee for a temporary period, for employment at a permanent and continuing establishment of that company in Canada, is permitted to enter Canada and work for that company for a temporary period without the requirement for a validated Offer of Employment (EMP 2151) from a Canada Employment Centre.

In order to comply with the executive or managerial exemption for intra-corporate transferees, the job in Canada must be defined within the Canadian Classification and Dictionary of Occupations (CCDO) as being within the master title of "general manager." Some persons defined as "manager" *may* be included depending on their responsibilities.

Included in the "general manager" category are senior corporate employees such as president, senior vice-president,

executive vice-president, vice-president, chief executive officer, and the like.

Individuals who have senior-sounding titles but who are more accurately described as "managing supervisors" are excluded from the exemptions. Included in this group are managers of retail and service organizations and working proprietors.

The difficult cases involve those managers who are lower than "general managers" and whose responsibilities include planning, organizing, directing, and controlling the activities of a department, division, program, or office of an industrial, commercial, governmental, or other establishment through subordinates who are at a supervisory level or above.

In general, in order to comply with the definitions and policy outlined above, an employer must take care to establish that there is need for the transferee, that the duties and responsibilities are executive or managerial as defined in the CCDO, and that there will be tangible benefits to Canada resulting from the admission of the transferee.

The FTA has extended Canada's general policy in this area by adding, in the case of U.S. citizens, services in a capacity that involves *specialized knowledge*.

This is a new departure for Canada and there is, as yet, no definition or case law on what constitutes "specialized knowledge." The draft operations policy for Canada under the FTA indicates that "specialized knowledge" means proprietary knowledge of the company's products, service, research equipment, or techniques. What this means is unclear. "Proprietary" may be restricted to "patented" or "copyrighted" but how can you protect a "service" or a "technique"? It will be interesting to see how this area evolves in Canada immigration law as similar to or distinct from U.S. law.

Another interesting question for intra-company transferees is the U.S. requirement under Section 101(a)(15)L of the Immigration and Nationality Act and under the FTA that the transferee must have been employed continuously for one year in one of the enumerated capacities. Canada has never had such a requirement. While the "one-year rule" has been a rule of thumb in Canada, many intra-company transferees have been employed by the parent, subsidiary, or affiliate for substantially less than one year.

A question that must be answered is whether or not the more stringent U.S. and FTA requirements will now apply to the detriment of U.S. citizens being transferred to Canada. It is my understanding that Canada Immigration will not apply the harsher requirements to U.S. citizens and that appears to be reflected in the policy statements which clearly state that if the FTA does not apply then the general rules of immigration will. If the general procedures allow the temporary entry and the FTA does not, then the general rules will be used instead of the FTA.

The procedures concerning intra-corporate transfers of U.S. citizens are very easy. Unlike the normal U.S. L-1 procedures, a U.S. citizen or resident *need not apply* for an Intra-corporate Employment Authorization at a Canadian consulate or embassy abroad, but can do so in person at any point-of-entry in Canada — that is, at a border crossing point or an international airport upon arrival in Canada.

In addition, U.S. citizens and residents do not require a passport if they are visitors coming to work in Canada; however, I highly recommend having a valid passport as a form of identity, as proof of citizenship, and within which an entry stamp can be placed in addition to the issuance of the employment authorization.

It is very important to note that the issuance of an employment authorization to an intra-corporate transferee at the border by an immigration officer is discretionary with the officer and is subject only to the persuasiveness of your presentation. Therefore, it is highly recommended that you have all your documents in order when you arrive at the border.

While a refusal to issue an employment authorization may be appealed to higher levels within the Canada Employment and Immigration Commission, there are normally no appeals of such refusals to the courts unless there has been a denial of natural justice or a refusal of jurisdiction in which case *certiorari* (the right to petition the court to hear a further appeal) and *mandamus* (an order to quash) may be possible.

Again, the FTA will likely change appeal procedures for U.S. citizens (not U.S. permanent residents). It seems to me that a denial of entry to a U.S. citizen seeking to come into Canada under any of the provisions of the FTA, including intra-company transferees, will now be subject to judicial review by way of appeal to the Federal Court of Canada (see chapter 26).

One of the areas where there is significant change under the FTA between Canada and the United States is in the movement of professionals between the two countries for temporary purposes. Prior to the FTA, professionals had a great deal of difficulty moving between the two countries. Canadian lawyers travelling to the United States on behalf of multi-national clients are often questioned at length about who their client is, who is paying them, why an American attorney cannot be retained, and the like. We presume similar problems occur for U.S. attorneys attempting to enter Canada.

The agreement provides for many professionals to move freely between the countries with authorization to work in each country provided the individual is engaged in one of the professions set forth in Schedule 2 to chapter 15 of the FTA.

The professionals covered include accountants, engineers, scientists, research assistants, medical professionals (but not medical doctors except in teaching or research capacities only), dentists, nurses, veterinarians, architects, lawyers, teachers at the university or college level, economists, social workers, vocational counsellors, various horticulturists, computer systems analysts, psychologists, scientific technicians and technologists, and — NOTE — management consultants.

The minimum requirement for any of the professionals listed in Schedule 2 is a baccalaureate degree or professional licensing except in the case of librarians (M.L.S.), journalists (baccalaureate *and* three years' experience), and management consultants (baccalaureate or equivalent professional experience).

The major problems will occur with journalists who do not have a university degree but may have 20 years' or more experience and with scientific technicians and technologists, many of whom both in Canada and the United States did not attend university but rather have a college or polytechnic diploma.

The major loophole, of course, is the management consultant who can have "equivalent experience." Who and what is a management consultant? It is my understanding that the border officials are initially using a five-year rule and requiring reasonably clear documentation to prove experience and background as a management consultant.

Since all these cases will be adjudicated at the border, in the case of management consultants we are telling them to bring as much as possible of the following documents: proof of incorporation, tax returns, letterhead, copies of previous contracts, letters of recommendation, and the like. Also dress the part — do not show up in jeans, sandals, and a sweatshirt even if that is how you always dress.

The implications of this section relating to professionals means that a large number of individuals will merely have to appear at the border indicating they wish to work in one country or the other and show professional qualifications to be able to obtain permission to work in the other country. It is not clear from the FTA whether or not a specific job will even have to be available in one of the countries in order for such employment authorization to be issued, although a letter of invitation or contract for services from a Canadian company would be very helpful.

The last category covered by the FTA is traders and investors. This is an old concept for the United States and has applied to several countries for many years. However, having U.S. traders and investors entering Canada for temporary purposes is a completely new concept for Canadian immigration law.

Traders and investors from the United States will be admitted to Canada under an already-existing Canadian regulation that permits entry into Canada on an employment authorization where employment is pursuant to an international agreement between Canada and a foreign government (see chapters 20 and 21). This is the regulation Canada has decided to use to allow U.S. traders and investors into Canada.

A trader is a U.S. citizen who enters Canada solely for the purpose of carrying on substantial trade in goods and/or services primarily between Canada and the United States or vice versa. Substantial trade refers to both the value and the amount of goods or services. Goods are things: merchandise and commodities. Services include economic activities that are not tangible such as financial advice, banking, insurance, data processing, communications, advertising, design, accounting, and similar activities.

The trader coming to Canada must be involved at an executive, management, or specialized (proprietary) knowledge level similar to those outlined for intra-corporate transferees above.

Substantial trade means more in terms of volume than necessarily in dollar amount. However, a good rule of thumb is that the trade should be in the range of $500 000 with more than half with Canada.

In addition, for both the trader and the investor, the U.S. company must be owned/controlled by U.S. citizens; that is, more than 50% of the shareholders exercising control must be U.S. citizens as must be the trader or investor who is coming to Canada.

An investor is a U.S. citizen who enters Canada for the purpose of committing money to an investment in this country. That means his or her money must be "at risk" in a commercial sense. If the funds have not been risked — that is, the funds are subject to potential loss if the investment fails — then you are not eligible to apply for an employment authorization as an investor.

An investor may be "actively in the process of investing," but this means a present and continuing commitment of money as opposed to a mere intent to invest. To be an investor under the FTA, you must have a legally binding commitment to invest the funds.

What is a "substantial investment"? It must be more than 50% of the amount needed to establish or purchase the business. On the other hand, the actual dollar amount need not necessarily be large. Thus, an investment of $100 000 in which you put in $55 000 at risk would qualify, provided the investment is not your sole source of income. To qualify as an investor, the investment cannot be your only source of income. *You must be able to show other continuing assets and income in the United States.*

Applications to be granted trader or investor status must be made at a Canadian embassy or consulate (see Appendix 2) and be accompanied by a $50 (Canadian) fee in the form of a bank draft or money order. You will also be required to complete form IMM #1295 (see Sample #24). Your spouse and children can accompany you, and your spouse may work in the enterprise but not elsewhere without complying with ordinary immigration procedures. Your children will be permitted to attend school and be issued student authorizations (see chapter 20).

While the border between Canada and the United States of America may be more open under the FTA for the movement of U.S. citizens to Canada, there will be some interesting litigation and bilateral negotiations in the future.

23

LOSS OF PERMANENT RESIDENT STATUS, VISITOR'S STATUS, AND RETURNING RESIDENT PERMITS

a. LOSS OF PERMANENT RESIDENT STATUS

A permanent resident can lose his or her status in 13 different ways.

If *prior to arrival in Canada as a permanent resident* you have done any of the five following actions which you failed to disclose and the Immigration Department discovers, you can be deported.

(a) You have been convicted of an offence that corresponds to any federal offence in Canada punishable by a maximum of more than 10 years in jail.

(b) You are a person who it is believed will commit one or more serious crimes or will engage in organized criminal activity.

(c) You are a person who has or it is believed will engage in espionage.

(d) You are a person who has or it is believed will engage in terrorist activities.

(e) You have been convicted of an offence that corresponds to any federal offence in Canada punishable by indictment for which a maximum term of imprisonment of less than 10 years has been imposed.

You can also be deported if you have done any of the eight following actions *after your arrival in Canada as a permanent resident:*

(a) You have broken any term or condition of your landing (such as not going to a particular city, failing as an entrepreneur to establish the business you said you would, or failing to comply with medical inspection).

(b) You are engaged in the subversion of any government by force.

(c) You have been convicted of any offence while in Canada under any act of the federal Parliament for which you received a jail term of more than six months or for which five or more years imprisonment may be imposed even if it was not so imposed and you only received a monetary fine.

(d) You obtained your permanent resident status in Canada by means of false or forged documents.

(e) You obtained your permanent resident status in Canada by reason of any false or misleading information of a material fact; for example, you told the government you were not married or had no children and in fact this was not true.

(f) You *wilfully* fail to support yourself or any dependent members of your family in Canada. (This would not include an inability to find employment provided you were actually and truly seeking it.)

(g) Subsequent to landing are found to be a person who it is believed on reasonable and probable grounds to have committed war crimes or crimes against humanity.

(h) You leave Canada with the intention of abandoning it as your place of permanent residence. You are deemed to have lost your status if you are out of Canada for more than 183 days unless you have a returning resident permit (see section **c.** below).

b. LOSS OF VISITOR'S STATUS

If you are a visitor to Canada — whether a tourist, business person, crew member, or a person on a student or employment authorization — you can lose your visitor's status in any of the following 21 ways *after arrival in Canada:*

(a) You breach any term of your admission into Canada including —

    (i) overstaying your permitted time,

    (ii) working illegally or changing jobs without permission,

    (iii) attending school illegally or changing schools without permission, or

    (iv) failing to report when required to do so.

(b) You have been issued a Departure Notice and fail to leave when required to do so (see chapter 24).

(c) You have been ordered deported from Canada.

(d) You are suffering from any disease, disorder, disability, or other health impairment that might be or become a public danger or place an excessive demand on our health or social services.

(e) You are unwilling or unable to support yourself thereby becoming a burden to the Canadian taxpayer.

(f) You have been convicted of an offence that corresponds to any federal offence in Canada punishable by a maximum of more than 10 years in jail.

(g) It is believed you will commit one or more serious crimes or will engage in organized criminal activity.

(h) You did or might engage in espionage or subversion of our government.

(i) You did or it is believed will engage in terrorist activities.

(j) You are inadmissible and do not have the consent of the Ministry of Immigration to enter into Canada.

(k) You have been convicted of an offence that corresponds to any federal offence in Canada punishable by indictment for which a maximum term of imprisonment of *less than* 10 years has been imposed.

(l) You have been convicted of two or more offences that correspond to any federal offence in Canada punishable by summary conviction.

(m) You cannot or do not comply with any requirement or conditions under the Immigration Act that apply to you.

(n) You engage in subversion by force of *any* government.

(o) You have been convicted while in Canada of *any* offence under the Criminal Code (either summary or indictable) or convicted of any indictable offence under any other act of Parliament or convicted of any offence under the Immigration Act (see chapter 27).

(p) You entered Canada at other than a proper entry point.

(q) You obtained your visitor's status in Canada by means of a false or forged document.

(r) You obtained your visitor's status by means of any false or misleading information of a material fact (for instance, you said you are the vice-president of a large company and you are not).

(s) You were previously deported from Canada and you have returned without the personal permission of the Minister of Immigration.

(t) You came into Canada as the member of a crew on a ship, bus, train, airplane, etc., and failed to leave on the vehicle when it left Canada.

(u) You wilfully failed to support dependent members of your family while in Canada.

Chapters 24, 25, and 26 deal with the right to a hearing and rights of appeal of permanent residents and visitors who break any of the above immigration laws.

c. RETURNING RESIDENT PERMITS

I cannot turn to the area of removal from Canada and appeals without first discussing at greater length sections 24 and 25 of the Immigration Act. These are so important with respect to landed immigrants that I have reproduced them in full below:

> 24. (1) A person ceases to be a permanent resident when:
>
> (a) that person leaves or remains outside Canada with the intention of abandoning Canada as that person's place of permanent residence; or
>
> (b) a deportation order has been made against that person and such order is not quashed or the execution thereof is not stayed pursuant to subsection 73
>
> (2) Where a permanent resident is outside Canada for more than one hundred and eighty-three days in any one twelve month period, he shall be deemed to have abandoned Canada as his place of permanent residence unless that person satisfies an immigration officer or an adjudicator, as the case may be, that he did not intend to abandon Canada as his place of permanent residence.
>
> 25. (1) Where a permanent resident intends to leave Canada for any period of time or is outside Canada, that person may in prescribed manner make an application to an immigration officer for a returning resident permit.
>
> (2) Possession by a person of a valid returning resident permit issued to that person pursuant to the regulation is, in the absence of evidence to the contrary, proof that the person did not leave or remain outside Canada with the intention of abandoning Canada as his place of permanent residence.

Under these two sections, the primary way to lose your permanent resident status is by intending to give up Canada as your place of permanent residence (at any time (section 24(1)(a)). This means if you leave Canada even for a period of time less than 183 days and you become a permanent resident of the United States (with a green card), take a job there, and rent an apartment, you will probably have lost your permanent resident status in Canada.

The very difficult situation occurs under section 24(2) where even if you do not intend to abandon Canada as your place of residence, you are deemed by law to have done so if you are out of Canada more than 183 days. In the first situation — out less than 183 days — the burden of proving you have abandoned Canada is on the government. On the other hand, if you are out more than 183 days, the burden of proof is on you to show by your actions that you did not intend to abandon Canada as your place of permanent residence. In both cases, a hearing will be held before an adjudicator as described in chapter 24 and you will be allowed to have a lawyer represent you. Also, if you lose you will have a right of appeal to the Immigration and Refugee Board (see chapter 25).

You can avoid the problem of a court case if you apply for a returning resident permit (see Sample #30) before you leave Canada if you know you will be gone more than three or four months. I strongly recommend that if you will be out of the country more than three months, you apply for the permit at your nearest Canada Immigration Centre.

When you go to obtain the permit you have to show the officer some document giving the reason why you will be gone and prove your intention to return. This might include a temporary contract to teach abroad or do research abroad for a year or two; it might be a letter from your Canadian employer transferring you abroad to a branch office for a period of time; it might be the death of a parent and the need to return to your homeland to handle the estate and property.

I cannot stress too strongly the need to obtain such a permit. It should also be mentioned that if you go abroad intending to return shortly and circumstances result in your having to remain outside of Canada for a longer period of time than you anticipated, you can apply for a returning resident permit at a Canadian embassy or consulate abroad.

Sample #31 is an example of a returning resident permit (IMM #1288). You will note that the permit has a place for a passport-sized photograph and you will be required to provide two photographs — one for the permit and one for the Immigration Department.

A returning resident permit may only be issued for a period not exceeding 12 months and with special permission (which is very difficult to obtain) may be extended for an additional 12 months or originally issued for a period of 24 months.

SAMPLE #30
APPLICATION FOR A RETURNING RESIDENT PERMIT

Employment and Immigration Canada   Emploi et Immigration Canada

CANADA IMMIGRATION   *IMMIGRATION CANADA*

APPLICATION FOR A RETURNING RESIDENT PERMIT
DEMANDE DE PERMIS DE RETOUR POUR RÉSIDENT PERMANENT

All the information to be provided on this form is needed to determine whether a returning resident permit may be issued as authorized by the Immigration Act, 1976 and regulations thereunder. For more details on uses and the rights for inspecting and correcting the information, refer to the Federal Information Bank Index, available in Canada at Post Offices and most libraries.

Tous les renseignements qui devront figurer sur ce formulaire viseront à déterminer si un permis de retour pour résident permanent peut être délivré aux termes de la Loi sur l'immigration de 1976 et du Règlement qui s'y rattache. Si vous désirez obtenir des précisions quant à l'utilisation des renseignements et au droit de les vérifier et de les corriger, veuillez consulter le catalogue des banques fédérales de données que vous pouvez consulter au Canada dans les bureaux de poste et dans la plupart des librairies.

Applicant must include 2 recent passport size photographs, showing a full front view of the head and shoulders without head covering, taken against a plain white background, on single weight unglazed (matte finish) paper; photographs should normally measure 2 x 2¾ inches (50 x 70mm) including ½ inch (13mm) blank signature space at the bottom which forms part of the photographic print.

Do not pin, staple or glue photograph to application form. This will be done at the immigration office.

Le requérant doit inclure deux photos format passeport récentes montrant très bien, de face, la tête, sans couvre-chef, ainsi que les épaules, et prises sur fond uni et blanc, sur papier de simple épaisseur, fini non glacé (mat); les photos doivent d'ordinaire mesurer 2" x 2 ¾" (50mm x 70mm), y compris une bande blanche de ½" au bas, réservée à la signature et faisant partie de l'épreuve photographique.

Ne pas épingler, brocher ou coller la photographie sur le formulaire. Le bureau d'immigration s'en chargera.

SURNAME
NOM DE FAMILLE — RESIDENT

GIVEN NAMES
PRÉNOMS — DANIEL JOHN

DATE AND COUNTRY OF BIRTH
DATE ET PAYS DE NAISSANCE — Day/Jour 31 Month/Mois 05 Year/Année 1950 West Germany

CITIZEN OF
CITOYENNETÉ — West Germany

PERMANENT ADDRESS
ADRESSE PERMANENTE — Street — Rue: 1 Saint Clare Street

City — Ville: Toronto   Province/State *Province/État*: Ont   Postal/Zip Code *Code postal/Zip*: ZIP 0G0

Country — Pays: Canada   Telephone No. — Tél.: 416 999 3333

DATE AND PLACE OF LANDING
LIEU ET DATE DE L'OCTROI DU DROIT D'ÉTABLISSEMENT — Day/Jour 17 Month/Mois 04 Year/Année 80 Montreal

Reason for temporary absence from Canada
Raisons motivant l'absence temporaire du Canada — Transferred for one year to company's head office in Dallas, Texas for the purpose of management training and experience.

DATE AND PLACE OF DEPARTURE FROM CANADA
LIEU ET DATE DU DÉPART DU CANADA — Day/Jour 14 Month/Mois 03 Year/Année 8- Vancouver

PROPOSED DATE OF INTENDED RETURN TO CANADA
DATE PRÉVUE DU RETOUR AU CANADA — Day/Jour 01 Month/Mois 03 Year/Année 8-

February 15, 198-
Date

Daniel J. Resident
Signature of applicant — *Signature du requérant*

FOR OFFICE USE ONLY — *RÉSERVÉ À L'USAGE DU BUREAU*

Returning resident permit no.
N° de permis du résident de retour _____   issued on *délivré le* _____

Permit valid until
Date d'expiration du permis _____   Permit extended on *Prolongation du permis le* _____   until *jusqu'au* _____

Issuing office — *Bureau qui a délivré le permis* _____   Immigration Officer — *Agent d'immigration* _____

IMM 1227 (5-78)   THIS FORM HAS BEEN ESTABLISHED BY THE MINISTER OF EMPLOYMENT AND IMMIGRATION
FORMULAIRE ÉTABLI PAR LE MINISTRE DE L'EMPLOI ET DE L'IMMIGRATION

SAMPLE #31
RETURNING RESIDENT PERMIT

 Employment and Immigration Canada   Emploi et Immigration Canada

CANADA IMMIGRATION   *IMMIGRATION CANADA*

RETURNING RESIDENT PERMIT
PERMIS DE RETOUR POUR RÉSIDENT PERMANENT

Permit No.
Nº du permis

Name – *Nom*
Daniel John Resident

Date of Birth – *Date de naissance*	Country of Birth – *Pays de naissance*	Citizenship – *Citoyenneté*
May 31, 1950	West Germany	West German

Permanent Address in Canada – *Adresse permanente au Canada*
1 Saint Clare St. Toronto, Ontario

AFFIX PHOTOGRAPH

IMPRINT OFFICE STAMP ON A PORTION OF PHOTO AND PERMIT.

APPLICANT'S SIGNATURE SHOULD APPEAR ON STRIP AT BOTTOM OF PHOTO.

_____

INSÉRER LA PHOTOGRAPHIE

APPLIQUER LE TIMBRE DU BUREAU IR UN COIN DE LA PHOTO ET JU PERMIS.

LE RÉSIDENT PERMANENT DOIT IMPOSER SA SIGNATURE SUR LA BANDE AU BAS DE LA PHOTO.

VALIDITY OF PERMIT – *DURÉE DE VALIDITÉ DU PERMIS*

Date of Issue – *Date de la délivrance*	Valid until – *Date d'expiration*
February 28, 198–	February 28, 198–

Office of Issue
Bureau qui a délivré le permis
Toronto East

Signature of Issuing Officer
Signature de l'agent qui a délivré le permis

Permit Extended until
Permis prolongé jusqu'au

Date of Extension – *Date de prolongation*	Office of Extension – *Bureau qui a accordé la prolongation*

Signature of Officer Granting Extension *Signature de l'agent qui a accordé la prolongation*	Extending Office Stamp – *Timbre du bureau qui a accordé la prolongation*

Signature of Permit Holder
Signature du titulaire du permis

IMM 1228 (8-77)

THIS FORM HAS BEEN ESTABLISHED BY THE MINISTER OF EMPLOYMENT AND IMMIGRATION
FORMULAIRE ÉTABLI PAR LE MINISTRE DE L'EMPLOI ET IMMIGRATION

24

DEPORTATION, REMOVAL, EXCLUSION, AND ENFORCED DEPARTURE

a. GENERAL

Visitors, permanent residents, and immigrants at the border and inside Canada can all be the subject of a hearing in which they can be refused admission or re-admission into Canada or be forced to leave Canada by means of one of several methods.

You would expect that in order to be removed from Canada you would have to do something very serious, especially in the case of a permanent resident. While this is true, you may also be removed from Canada for minor infractions of the law including the Immigration Act and the Regulations. You should review chapter 23 to see just how many ways you can lose your permanent resident or visitor status. This chapter deals with what happens after you fall into one of the 13 ways a permanent resident can lose his or her status and the 21 ways a visitor can lose his or her status.

b. COMMENCEMENT OF THE INQUIRY PROCEDURE

If you fall into one of the categories listed in sections a. and b. of chapter 23, an immigration officer to whom your situation becomes known is required to write a report to the Deputy Minister of Immigration concerning your situation. These reports, usually under section 27(1) and 27(2) of the Immigration Act, outline the reasons why the officer believes you should not be allowed to remain in Canada.

These reasons could be as a result of your conviction for a criminal offence, or for working without an employment authorization, or for overstaying your visit. Samples #32 and #33 are sample reports under sections 27(1) and 27(2) respectively. As you can see from these forms, they do not provide a great deal of information.

The deputy minister or his or her local representative, usually the officer-in-charge of the Immigration Centre, reviews the report, and will decide whether or not an immigration inquiry is necessary. At this point, there is no outside input into this person's decision. The decision is based on the report and perhaps the file itself. In almost all cases, once a report has been written, it will be followed by a decision to hold an inquiry.

Following the decision to hold an inquiry, the deputy minister or his or her representative will forward a Direction for Inquiry (Form IMM #1246 — see Sample #34) to a senior immigration officer. This direction orders the officer to arrange an inquiry. A senior immigration officer (SIO) is appointed to the position. Usually these officers will also hold the position of case presenting officer (CPO) and will represent the minister before the adjudicator at your hearing.

■✦ Employment and Immigration Canada   Emploi et Immigration Canada

CANADA IMMIGRATION

REPORT UNDER SUBSECTION 1
OF SECTION 27 OF THE IMMIGRATION ACT, 1976

*RAPPORT ÉTABLI AUX TERMES DU PARAGRAPHE 1
DE L'ARTICLE 27 DE LA LOI SUR L'IMMIGRATION DE 1976*

TO: Deputy Minister of Employment and Immigration
POUR: Le sous-ministre de l'emploi et de l'immigration

File
N° de référence _____

In accordance with subsection 27(1) of the Immigration Act, 1976 I have to report that,
Conformément au paragraphe 27(1) de la Loi sur l'immigration de 1976, je dois signaler que,

Surname
Nom de famille
JONES

Given names
Prénom(s)
SAMUEL GORDON

Date and Country of Birth
Date et pays de naissance
30 06 1954   Great Britain

Citizen of
Citoyen de
GREAT BRITAIN

is a permanent resident who:
est un résident permanent qui:

1. Has been convicted of the offence of armed robbery.

This report is based on information in my possession as follows:
Le présent rapport se fonde sur les renseignements suivants qui se trouvent en ma possession:

1. Certified certificate of conviction dated January 24, 198-
   issued by the Clerk of the County Court of the Judicial
   District of York in the Province of Ontario stating that
   one Samuel Gordon Jones was convicted of the offence of
   armed robbery by a jury on January 15, 198- and was
   sentenced to a period of six years in jail.

Dated at
Daté à Toronto

in the Province of
dans la Province de Ontario

this
ce 22

day of
jour de March   19 8-

IMM. 1241 (12-77)

Immigration Officer - *Agent d'immigration*

161

SAMPLE #33
REPORT UNDER SECTION 27(2)

I✦I Employment and Immigration Canada

CANADA IMMIGRATION

REPORT UNDER SUBSECTION 2
OF SECTION 27 OF THE IMMIGRATION ACT, 1976

TO: Deputy Minister of Employment and Immigration
POUR: Le sous-ministre de l'emploi et de l'immigration

File no.
N° de référence _____

In accordance with subsection 27(2) of the Immigration Act, 1976 I have to report that,
Conformément au paragraphe 27(2) de la Loi sur l'Immigration de 1976, je dois signaler que:

Surname
Nom de famille

`V I S I T O R`

Given names
Prénom(s)

`R O N A L D   J O H N`

Date and Country of Birth
Date et pays de naissance

`2 2 0 7 19 4 2`   `J A M A I C A`

Citizen of
Citoyen de

`J A M A I C A`

is a person in Canada, other than a Canadian citizen or a permanent resident, who:
qui se trouve au Canada, est une personne autre qu'un citoyen canadien ou un résident permanent, qui:

ENTERED Canada on July 25, 198– and engaged in
employment without being in possession of an
employment authorization

This report is based on information in my possession as follows:
Le présent rapport se fonde sur les renseignements suivants qui se trouvent en ma possession:

1. The statement of the person concerned to Immigration
   officer Jonathan Jones
2. The statement of the employer Mr. Harvey Fielder
3. The cancelled cheques for wages obtained from the employer

Dated at
Daté à _____ Winnipeg _____

in the Province of
dans la Province de _____ Manitoba _____

this
ce _____ 23 _____

day of
jour de _____ December _____ 19 8–

_____
Immigration Officer — Agent d'immigration

162

SAMPLE #34
DIRECTION FOR INQUIRY

Employment and Immigration Canada **Emploi et Immigration Canada**
IMMIGRATION MANUAL **GUIDE DE L'IMMIGRATION**

Employment and **Emploi et**
Immigration Canada **Immigration Canada**

CANADA IMMIGRATION

**DIRECTION FOR INQUIRY UNDER
SUBSECTION 27(3) OF THE
IMMIGRATION ACT**

File 4520-7-5555

TO: Senior Immigration Officer _____

Russell Smith

I have reviewed the report dated _____
submitted pursuant to subsection 27( ) of the
Immigration Act concerning

JONES
Surname

Samuel Gordon
Given names

and I consider that an Inquiry is warranted.

Pursuant to subsection 27 (3) of the Immigration Act, I
hereby direct that an Inquiry be held to determine if
the above mentioned is a person described in
paragraph(s)

27 (2) (a) _____ of the said Act.

Dated at _____ Toronto

in the Province of Ontario

This _____ 16th _____ day of June 19 9-

_____
Deputy Minister of Employment and
Immigration

IMMIGRATION CANADA

***DIRECTIVE PRÉVOYANT LA TENUE D'UNE ENQUÊTE
AUX TERMES DU PARAGRAPHE 27(3) DE LA LOI
SUR L'IMMIGRATION***

N° de référence _____

POUR: Agent principal _____

J'ai étudié le rapport fait le _____
*qui a été présenté conformément au paragraphe 27( )
de la loi sur l'immigration concernant*

_____
Nom

_____
Prénoms

et j'estime que la tenue d'une enquête est justifiée.

*Conformément au paragraphe 27(3) de la Loi sur
l'immigration, j'ordonne, par les présentes, qu'une
enquête soit tenue pour déterminer si la personne
précitée est visée à l'alinéa*

_____ *de ladite Loi.*

Fait à _____

dans la province de _____

ce _____ *jour de* _____ 19 _____

_____
Le Sous-ministre d'Emploi et Immigration Canada

THIS FORM HAS BEEN ESTABLISHED BY THE
MINISTER OF EMPLOYMENT AND IMMIGRATION

*CE FORMULAIRE A ÉTÉ ÉTABLI PAR LE
MINISTRE D'EMPLOI ET IMMIGRATION*

Canada

IMM 1246 FP-1 (10-88) 8

1

163

When the Direction for Inquiry is received, the SIO will immediately prepare and sign a Notice of Inquiry (Form IMM #1243 — see Sample #35). This form will indicate whether or not you are in detention (see section c. below) and further direct an adjudicator to hold a hearing on a specific date. This notice, along with the original report, will be sent to the adjudicator and will be served on the subject of the hearing, that is, you, known as the "person concerned."

If you have any dependent family members who might be included in your removal from Canada, they are entitled to be at your hearing, to be represented by independent counsel, and to be heard. Such family members will receive a Notice of Inquiry to Family Members (Form IMM #1248 — see Sample #36).

c. DETENTION AND RELEASE

If you are a visitor to Canada in any category (see chapter 20) and you are refused admission to Canada at the border (this also includes an airport), you may be arrested and held in custody pending an inquiry. Similarly, a permanent resident who has been serving a jail sentence may also be held in custody following completion of that sentence pending an inquiry. In both cases, you would be arrested and held by means of an immigration arrest warrant (Form IMM #420 — see Sample #37).

While under arrest, you might be held in a local jail or at an Immigration Detention Centre — usually part of a local hotel of very poor quality in which you will be locked and guarded by a private security force. Your release from custody may be allowed at the first instance by the SIO who may allow your release upon conditions or refuse your release. If you are released, the conditions usually include the requirement to report to the immigration office at specific times and usually requires a cash bond to be put up for you by your friends and relatives and the requirement that you

report any change of address. Sample #38 is an example of a release by an SIO.

If you are not released by the SIO, the adjudicator can order your release. Sample #39 is a request from the SIO to the adjudicator to review your detention. This review will usually take place at the opening of your inquiry and be reviewed every seven days.

If you are released by the SIO or adjudicator, you will be required, as will any person signing for you, to sign various documents. If you are released on your own without anyone having to sign as guarantor for you, you will have to sign a bond for conditional release. If you are released as a result of someone signing for you (surety) and promising to pay if you fail to appear, he or she will be required to sign a bond.

Whether you will be released or not and how much or little will be required of you and your guarantors, if necessary, will depend on the seriousness of the reason for which you have been arrested. It should not be necessary to say but at this point *you need a lawyer* — not a friend, minister, priest, relative, or anyone else, but a lawyer, competent and knowledgeable in immigration law.

d. THE INQUIRY

The inquiry will be held by an adjudicator. He or she is a senior member of the Immigration Department whose job is to decide whether or not you should be removed from Canada and the method of removal. The adjudicator sits as a sort of quasi or semi-judge — but remember, he or she is an employee of the Immigration Department and, although most adjudicators attempt to be fair and equitable, they are not trained in the law and their background in earlier years with the department often leads them to favor the case presenting officer.

SAMPLE #35
NOTICE OF INQUIRY

▮✦▮ Employment and Immigration Canada   Emploi et Immigration Canada
IMMIGRATION MANUAL   GUIDE DE L'IMMIGRATION

▮✦▮ Employment and   Emploi et
Immigration Canada   Immigration Canada

NOTICE OF INQUIRY UNDER THE IMMIGRATION ACT	**AVIS D'ENQUÊTE AUX TERMES DE LA LOI SUR L'IMMIGRATION**
File 4520-7-5555	N° de référence _____
TO: An Adjudicator	POUR: Arbitre
In Accordance with the provisions of the Immigration Act.	Conformément aux dispositions de la Loi sur l'immigration
I hereby cause an inquiry to be held pursuant to section _____ 26	J'ordonne qu'une enquête soit tenue en application de l'article _____
concerning Samuel Gordon JONES Given Name(s) Surname	concernant _____ Prénom(s) Nom
who is alleged to be described in paragraph(s) 27 (2) (a)	qui serait visé à (aux) l'alinéa(s) _____
You are requested to preside at an inquiry which is scheduled to be held on	Vous êtes prié(e) de présider l'enquête qui doit se tenir le
7 March ___ 199– at 10 a.m. Date Time	_____ 19 ___ à ___ Date Heure
at 66 Main Street, Toronto Place	à _____ Endroit
Dated at Toronto	Fait à _____
in the Province of Ontario	dans le province de _____
this 26th day of February 19 9–	ce _____ jour de _____ 19 ___.
Russell Smith Senior Immigration Officer	_____ Agent principal

IMM 1243 EP-I (10-88) B

Canada

1

I✦I Employment and Immigration Canada   Emploi et Immigration Canada
IMMIGRATION MANUAL   **GUIDE DE L'IMMIGRATION**

I✦I Employment and
Immigration Canada   Emploi et
Immigration Canada

CANADA IMMIGRATION

NOTICE OF AN INQUIRY TO FAMILY MEMBERS

IMMIGRATION CANADA

AVIS D'ENQUÊTE SIGNIFIÉ AUX MEMBRES DE LA FAMILLE

File: 4520-7-5555   N° de référence _____

TO: Mrs. Mary Martha Jones   POUR

Address: 100 Jonathon Street   Adresse:
Toronto, Ont. M6B 7A8

This is to advise you that an inquiry is to be held in accordance   Les présentes ont pour objet de vous aviser qu'une enquête doit

with 27 (2) (a) of the Immigration   être tenue conformément au _____ de la Loi sur

Act, as amended concerning _____   l'immigration, telle que modifiée, concernant _____

Samual Gordon JONES   _____

The purpose of the inquiry is to determine whether   L'enquête vise à établir si

Samuel Gordon JONES   _____

shall be admitted to or allowed to remain in Canada. The basis for   doit être admis(e) ou autorisé(e) à demeurer au Canada. L'enquête
the inquiry is a report/direction under subsection 26   se fonde sur un rapport/une directive dont fait mention le paragraphe
of the Act. A copy of the document is attached.   _____ de la Loi. Vous trouverez ci-joint
un double du document.

If a deportation order or a conditional deportation order or   Si une mesure d'expulsion ou une ordonnance d'expulsion conditionnelle
departure notice or a conditional departure notice is issued to   ou un avis d'interdiction de séjour ou un avis d'interdiction de séjour
Samuel Gordon JONES   conditionnelle est délivré à
you may be included in the order or notice and be required to leave   vous pouvez être inclus(o) dans la mesure, l'ordonnance ou l'avis et
Canada. You are requested to attend the inquiry on   être prié(e) de quitter le Canada. Veuillez vous présenter à l'enquête
qui se tiendra

7 March 199-   at 10 a.m.   le _____ à _____
Date   Time   Date   Heure

at 66 Main Street, Toronto   à _____
Place   Lieu

The Act provides you with the right to obtain the services of a   Aux termes de la Loi, vous pouvez, retenir les services d'un avocat,
barrister or solicitor or other counsel and to be represented by   d'un procureur ou de tout autre conseil, pour vous représenter
such counsel at the inquiry. Attached is a Notice (IMM. 689) which   à l'enquête. Vous trouverez ci-joint un avis (IMM. 689) qui fait
outlines your right to counsel.   état de votre droit de vous faire représenter.

You have the right to participate fully at the inquiry by examining   Vous avez le droit de participer pleinement à l'enquête, à savoir
evidence, cross-examining witnesses and producing evidence.   examiner les preuves, contre-interroger les témoins et produire des
preuves.

Dated at Toronto   Fait à _____

in the Province of Ontario   dans la province de _____

this 27th day of February 19 9-   ce _____ jour de _____ 19 ____

Russell Smith

Authorized Officer and Title   Agent autorisé et titre

THIS FORM HAS BEEN ESTABLISHED BY THE   CE FORMULAIRE A ÉTÉ ÉTABLI PAR LE
MINISTER OF EMPLOYMENT AND IMMIGRATION   MINISTRE DE L'EMPLOI ET DE L'IMMIGRATION

IMM 1248 EP-P (01-89) B

07-89

1

SAMPLE #37
WARRANT FOR ARREST

 Employment and Immigration Canada   Emploi et Immigration Canada

Canada Immigration

WARRANT FOR ARREST

(under Subsection (1) of Section 103 of the Immigration Act, 1976)

TO EVERY OR ANY IMMIGRATION OR PEACE OFFICER.

WHEREAS (an examination)   an Inquiry   under the provisions of the Immigration Act, 1976 is to be held respecting ___Theodore Bernard___

(or)

WHEREAS   a deportation order   an exclusion order   has been made under the Immigration Act, 1976 against_____,
I hereby command you to arrest the said person and detain him, in accordance with the provisions of the Immigration Act, 1976.

Dated at __Edmonton__ this __14th__ day of __November__ , 199-__ .

_____
Authorized Officer and Title

This form has been established by the Minister of Employment and Immigration

IMM. 420 (6-78)

167

```
                         DETENTION REVIEW


On the    19th      day of  November     198-  I reviewed the detention

of (Name)   Jack Louis                    at   Tor West

Detention Centre pursuant to 104(5) of the Immigration Act, 1976.

I have served him/her with the following documents:


 XX Notification of Right to Counsel

 XX Vienna Convention Notification

 XX Copy of 27 Report, Direction for Inquiry and Notification to Appear
    for Inquiry.

I have not offered release.

OR

I offered release subject to the following terms and conditions:

(Amount and type of Bond)   $3 000.00 cash bond

(Date to appear for Inquiry/Removal)    November 26, 198-

(Other conditions)


     Must continue to reside at 111 Canyon Street, Toronto
     Must report once per week on Tuesdays between 8 a.m.
     and 4 p.m. to this office



                         Date Nov. 22, 198- Time 2:30 p.m.
                         Date                Time



 Release effected

 48-hour period expires           J.M. Officer
                                  Senior Immigration Officer
```

NOTICE OF DETENTION REVIEW

TO: An Adjudicator

You are requested to conduct a review of the detention of

_____ Theodore Bernard _____   August 16, 1945 ___
(Name)   (Date of birth)

at 11:30 a.m. ___ on ___ Friday, November 16, 198- _____ at
    (Time)   (Date)

_____ Edmonton Common Jail _____.
                    (Place of detention)

The above person was detained for Immigration Warrant - Illegal entry
                                        (Reason)   into Canada

at 9:30 a.m. ___ on ___ November 14, 198- _____.
    (Time)   (Date)

SUBJECT ADVISED   XX

COUNSEL ADVISED   XX

NO COUNSEL OF RECORD _____

                                    _J.M. Officer_____
                                    Senior Immigration Officer

cc. CPO Supervisor

The adjudicator does not know anything about your case at the beginning except your name. All he or she has seen is the Direction for Inquiry (Sample #34) and the Notice to Family Members (Sample #36), if applicable. The case presenting officer (CPO), another employee of the Immigration Commission, will present the evidence first at the hearing. Unfortunately, you will most likely be the first witness! You have no choice. The CPO will file the various reports and directions and then will call you as the first witness. You cannot refuse to testify and must do so under oath or affirmation. A refusal to testify is itself an offence under the Immigration Act.

The CPO must present all his or her evidence and witnesses first. Your lawyer will have the right to cross-examine (question) any witnesses.

Then you can present your witnesses and evidence. The CPO will have the right to question them. If you want to have witnesses come to the hearing who refuse to come voluntarily, the adjudicator has the power to order them to appear. Sample #40 is a sample of such an order.

As mentioned above, if you have dependent family members, such as a wife and minor children, each of them is entitled to be represented at his or her own expense by a lawyer. In the case of these relatives, the issue will be not whether they did anything wrong, but whether they should be included in any deportation order because they are dependent on you for their support.

Following all evidence, the CPO and your lawyer will be allowed to argue the law as to why you should or should not be removed from Canada. The adjudicator who has listened to all the witnesses and all the presentations and read all the material will then make the decision.

The possible results include a removal order which consists of either a deporta-tion order or an exclusion order and a departure notice. Each of these possible orders will be examined in the following sections.

e. DEPORTATION ORDERS AND EXCLUSION ORDERS

A deportation order (see Sample #41) is one of the two removal orders under the Immigration Act — the other is an exclusion order (see Sample #42).

The adjudicator *must* make an order of deportation against you if you are seeking to come into Canada as a visitor or as a returning resident and you are or have become a member of an inadmissible category. You are in an inadmissible category if you have done one of the following:

(a) Been convicted of an offence punishable by 10 years or more in jail

(b) Have or will engage in organized crime

(c) Have or will engage in espionage

(d) Have or will engage in acts of terrorism

(e) Have or will subvert any government

(f) Have been convicted of an offence punishable by indictment for which the maximum penalty is less than 10 years in jail

(g) Have been convicted of two or more offences punishable by summary conviction

(h) Have returned to Canada having been deported, or before the time of an exclusion order expires without the permission of the Minister of Immigration

(i) Have not left Canada on or before the date specified in a Departure Notice

(j) Are suspected of having committed war crimes or crimes against humanity

SAMPLE #40
SUMMONS TO A WITNESS

Employment and Immigration Canada   Emploi et Immigration Canada
IMMIGRATION MANUAL   **GUIDE DE L'IMMIGRATION**

Immigration Canada   Immigration Canada

SUMMONS TO A WITNESS   *ASSIGNATION À UN TÉMOIN*

(THE IMMIGRATION ACT, as amended)   *(LA LOI SUR L'IMMIGRATION, telle que modifiée)*

File No. – *N° de référence*

Jennifer Kathleen Helper
Name of Witness – *Nom du témoin*

TO
POUR

7000 Ontario Street, Halifax, N.S.
Address – *Adresse*

Whereas in accordance with _____
of the Immigration Act, as amended,

Attendu que, conformément aux dispositions du _____
de la Loi sur l'immigration , telle que modifiée,

☐ an Inquiry   ☐ *une enquête*

☒ a Hearing   ☐ *une audience*
is to be held concerning   *doit être tenue concernant*

Name of person concerned – *Nom de l'intéressé(e)*

LOLA ILLEGAL

and it has been made to appear that you are likely to give material evidence.   *et qu'il semble que vous seriez en mesure de produire des témoignages pertinents.*

This is therefore to command you to attend at   *Les présentes ont donc pour objet de vous enjoindre de comparaître à*

Location – *Endroit*

724 Castle Street
Halifax, N.S.

On the 6th day of June 9- at 2 o'clock in the after
ce jour de à h

to give evidence concerning the said matter, and to bring with you any written matter in your possession or under your control that relates to the said matter and, more particularly, without restricting the generality of the foregoing, the following items:

pour témoigner au sujet de ladite question, et d'apporter tout document écrit en votre possession ou sous votre responsabilité qui a trait à ladite question et, plus particulièrement, sans restreindre la portée de ce qui précède les documents suivants:

Birth certificate

Passport

Employment records

You are warned that failure, without lawful excuse, to attend the said inquiry/hearing is an offence under the Act.

Sachez que si vous négligez d'être présent(e) à ladite enquête/audience, sans excuse légitime, vous enfreindrez la Loi.

Dated at Halifax   in the province of Nova Scotia this 11th day of May 9-
Fait à   *dans la province de*   *ce*   *jour de*   19

Joseph Brown

Signature of Adjudicator – *Signature de l'arbitre*

THIS FORM HAS BEEN ESTABLISHED BY THE MINISTER OF EMPLOYMENT AND IMMIGRATION
FORMULAIRE ÉTABLI PAR LE MINISTRE DE L'EMPLOI ET DE L'IMMIGRATION

IMM 1232 EP-P (01-89) B

Canada

07-89

1

171

SAMPLE #41
DEPORTATION ORDER

Employment and Immigration Canada — Emploi et Immigration Canada

DEPORTATION ORDER — *MESURE D'EXPULSION*

V 010 440 032

HEADQUARTERS' USE ONLY - *RÉSERVÉ À L'ADMINISTRATION CENTRALE*

CASE SERIAL NO. - *Nº DE CAS INITIAL*

CLIENT ID - *ID DU CLIENT*

OFFICE FILE NO. - *Nº DE RÉFÉRENCE DU BUREAU*

5 3

SURNAME - *NOM*
IL LE GA L

GIVEN NAMES - *PRÉNOMS*
LO LA

DATE OF BIRTH - *DATE DE NAISSANCE* 2 27 99
COUNTRY OF BIRTH / *PAYS DE NAISSANCE* U.S.A.

COUNTRY OF CITIZENSHIP - *CITOYEN DE*
U.S.A.

ON THE BASIS OF THE EVIDENCE ADDUCED AT THE INQUIRY HELD UNDER THE PROVISIONS OF THE IMMIGRATION ACT AS AMENDED.

D'APRÈS LA PREUVE PRODUITE À L'ENQUÊTE TENUE AUX TERMES DE LA LOI SUR L'IMMIGRATION TELLE QUE MODIFIÉE

☐ I HEREBY ORDER THAT YOU BE DEPORTED PURSUANT TO SUBSECTION

☐ *J'ORDONNE PAR LES PRÉSENTES QUE VOUS SOYEZ EXPULSÉ(E) CONFORMÉMENT AU PARAGRAPHE*

☐ I HEREBY CONDITIONALLY ORDER THAT YOU BE DEPORTED PURSUANT TO PARAGRAPH _____ BECAUSE YOU ARE A PERSON DESCRIBED IN

☐ *J'ORDONNE CONDITIONNELLEMENT PAR LES PRÉSENTES QUE VOUS SOYEZ EXPULSÉ(S) CONFORMÉMENT À L'ALINÉA _____ PARCE QUE VOUS ÊTES UNE PERSONNE VISÉE À*

PURSUANT TO SUBSECTION 32.1(5) OF THE IMMIGRATION ACT, AS ENACTED BY S.C. 1988, C. 35, NO CONDITIONAL DEPORTATION ORDER MADE AGAINST A CLAIMANT IS EFFECTIVE UNLESS AND UNTIL.

A) THE CLAIMANT WITHDRAWS THE CLAIM TO BE A CONVENTION REFUGEE;
B) THE CLAIMANT IS FINALLY DETERMINED UNDER THIS ACT TO HAVE ABANDONED THE CLAIM TO BE A CONVENTION REFUGEE;
C) THE CLAIMANT IS FINALLY DETERMINED UNDER THIS ACT NOT TO BE A CONVENTION REFUGEE; OR
D) THE CLAIMANT IS DETERMINED AT AN INQUIRY REOPENED PURSUANT TO SUBSECTION 48.07(1) NOT TO HAVE A RIGHT UNDER SUBSECTION 4(2.1) TO REMAIN IN CANADA.

SUBSECTION 32.1(1) DEFINES A CLAIMANT AS A PERSON WHO CLAIMS TO BE A CONVENTION REFUGEE AND WHOSE CLAIM HAS BEEN REFERRED TO THE REFUGEE DIVISION

EN VERTU DU PARAGRAPHE 32.1(5) DE LA LOI SUR L'IMMIGRATION, ÉDICTÉ PAR L.C. 1988, CH. 35, UNE ORDONNANCE D'EXPULSION CONDITIONNELLE NE DEVIENT EXÉCUTOIRE QUE SI SE RÉALISE L'UNE OU L'AUTRE DES CONDITIONS SUIVANTES.

A) *LE DEMANDEUR DE STATUT RENONCE À SA REVENDICATION DU STATUT DE RÉFUGIÉ AU SENS DE LA CONVENTION;*
B) *LE DÉSISTANT DU DEMANDEUR DE STATUT A ÉTÉ, EN CETTE MATIÈRE, DÉFINITIVEMENT ÉTABLI;*
C) *LE STATUT RÉFUGIÉ AU SENS DE LA CONVENTION A ÉTÉ DÉFINITIVEMENT REFUSÉ AU DEMANDEUR DE STATUT;*
D) *IL A ÉTÉ DÉTERMINÉ, LORS D'UNE ENQUÊTE ROUVERTE AUX TERMES DU PARAGRAPHE 48.07(1), QUE LE DEMANDEUR DE STATUT N'AVAIT PAS, EN APPLICATION DU PARAGRAPHE 4(2.1), LE DROIT DE DEMEURER AU CANADA.*

LE PARAGRAPHE 32.1(1) DÉFINIT UN DEMANDEUR DE STATUT COMME ÉTANT UNE PERSONNE QUI REVENDIQUE LE STATUT DE RÉFUGIÉ AU SENS DE LA CONVENTION ET DONT LA REVENDICATION EST DÉFÉRÉE À LA SECTION DU STATUT.

DATE ▸ 9 June9— TIME / *L'HEURE* ▸ 10 am AT ▸ Halifax N.S. ADJUDICATOR *ARBITRE* ▸

I FULLY UNDERSTAND THE ABOVE DECISION. I ALSO FULLY UNDERSTAND, THAT I MUST NOT COME INTO CANADA WITHOUT THE WRITTEN CONSENT OF THE MINISTER OF EMPLOYMENT AND IMMIGRATION AT ANY TIME AFTER THE DAY ON WHICH I AM REMOVED FROM OR OTHERWISE LEAVE CANADA.

JE COMPRENDS PARFAITEMENT LA DÉCISION INDIQUÉE CI DESSUS. EN OUTRE JE COMPRENDS PARFAITEMENT QU'APRÈS LA DATE DU J'AURAI ÉTÉ RENVOYÉ(E) DU CANADA OU CELLE OÙ J'AURAI PAR AILLEURS QUITTÉ LE CANADA JE NE DEVRAI PAS Y REVENIR SANS L'AUTORISATION ÉCRITE DU MINISTÈRE DE L'EMPLOI ET DE L'IMMIGRATION

NAME / *NOM* Lola Illegal SIGNATURE ▸ Lola Illegal DATE ▸ June 9, '9—

I HAVE FAITHFULLY AND ACCURATELY INTERPRETED IN THE — *J'AI INTERPRÉTÉ FIDÈLEMENT ET EXACTEMENT EN*

LANGUAGE THE INFORMATION PROVIDED ABOVE. — *LES RENSEIGNEMENTS PRÉCITÉS.*

NAME / *NOM* ▸ SIGNATURE ▸ DATE ▸

DATE SIGNED / *SIGNÉ LE* OFFICE OF ISSUE - *BUREAU DE DÉLIVRANCE*

IMM 1215 EP-P (01-89) B

Canada THIS FORM HAS BEEN ESTABLISHED BY THE MINISTER OF EMPLOYMENT AND IMMIGRATION. THIS DOCUMENT IS THE PROPERTY OF THE GOVERNMENT OF CANADA *FORMULAIRE ÉTABLI PAR LE MINISTRE DE L'EMPLOI ET DE L'IMMIGRATION LE PRÉSENT DOCUMENT EST LA PROPRIÉTÉ DU GOUVERNEMENT DU CANADA*

ADJUDICATOR *ARBITRE* **1**

PURSUANT TO SUBSECTION 32.1(5) OF THE IMMIGRATION ACT, THIS CONDITIONAL DEPORTATION ORDER IS EFFECTIVE AS OF _____

EN VERTU DU PARAGRAPHE 32.1(5) DE LA LOI SUR L'IMMIGRATION, LA PRÉSENTE MESURE D'EXPULSION CONDITIONNELLE EST EXÉCUTOIRE À COMPTER DU _____

DATE _____ AT / *À* _____

OFFICER SIGNATURE - *SIGNATURE*

THIS FORM HAS BEEN ESTABLISHED BY THE MINISTER OF EMPLOYMENT AND IMMIGRATION. THIS DOCUMENT IS THE PROPERTY OF THE GOVERNMENT OF CANADA *FORMULAIRE ÉTABLI PAR LE MINISTRE DE L'EMPLOI ET DE L'IMMIGRATION LE PRÉSENT DOCUMENT EST LA PROPRIÉTÉ DU GOUVERNEMENT DU CANADA*

Canada
07-89

PROGRAM DATA, NHQ *DIVISION DES DONNÉES, ADMINISTRATION CENTRALE* **3**

1

SAMPLE #42
EXCLUSION ORDER

Employment and Immigration Canada
EXCLUSION ORDER

Emploi et Immigration Canada
MESURE D'EXCLUSION

V 030 264 242

HEADQUARTERS' USE ONLY - RÉSERVÉ À L'ADMINISTRATION CENTRALE

| 5 | 4 | | |

CASE SERIAL NO. - N° DE CAS INITIAL

CLIENT ID - ID DU CLIENT

OFFICE FILE NUMBER
N° DE RÉFÉRENCE DU BUREAU

SURNAME - NOM
► I,L,L,E,G,A,L

GIVEN NAMES - PRÉNOMS
► L,O,L,A

DATE OF BIRTH
DATE DE NAISSANCE
D-J | M | Y-A
2,5 0,1 1,9 37

COUNTRY OF BIRTH / PAYS DE NAISSANCE
United States

COUNTRY OF CITIZENSHIP / CITOYEN DE
United States

ON THE BASIS OF THE EVIDENCE ADDUCED AT THE INQUIRY HELD UNDER THE PROVISIONS OF THE IMMIGRATION ACT AS AMENDED.

D'APRÈS LA PREUVE PRODUITE À L'ENQUÊTE TENUE AUX TERMES DE LA LOI SUR L'IMMIGRATION TELLE QUE MODIFIÉE.

☐ I HEREBY ORDER THAT YOU BE EXCLUDED PURSUANT TO SUBSECTION _____ OF THAT ACT

☐ J'ORDONNE PAR LES PRÉSENTES QUE VOUS SOYEZ EXCLU(E) CONFORMÉMENT AU PARAGRAPHE _____ DE LA LOI

☒ I HEREBY CONDITIONALLY ORDER THAT YOU BE EXCLUDED PURSUANT TO PARAGRAPH _____ OF THAT ACT

☐ J'ORDONNE CONDITIONNELLEMENT PAR LES PRÉSENTES QUE VOUS SOYEZ EXCLU(E) CONFORMÉMENT À L'ALINÉA _____ DE LA LOI

BECAUSE YOU ARE A PERSON DESCRIBED IN

PARCE QUE VOUS ÊTES UNE PERSONNE VISÉE À

PURSUANT TO SUBSECTION 32.1(5) OF THE IMMIGRATION ACT, AS ENACTED BY S. C. 1988, C. 35, NO CONDITIONAL EXCLUSION ORDER MADE AGAINST A CLAIMANT IS EFFECTIVE UNLESS AND UNTIL,

A) THE CLAIMANT WITHDRAWS THE CLAIM TO BE A CONVENTION REFUGEE;
B) THE CLAIMANT IS FINALLY DETERMINED UNDER THIS ACT TO HAVE ABANDONED THE CLAIM TO BE A CONVENTION REFUGEE;
C) THE CLAIMANT IS FINALLY DETERMINED UNDER THIS ACT NOT TO BE A CONVENTION REFUGEE; OR
D) THE CLAIMANT IS DETERMINED AT AN INQUIRY REOPENED PURSUANT TO SUBSECTION 48.07(1) NOT TO HAVE A RIGHT UNDER SUBSECTION 4(2.1) TO REMAIN IN CANADA.

SUBSECTION 32.1(1) DEFINES A CLAIMANT AS A PERSON WHO CLAIMS TO BE A CONVENTION REFUGEE AND WHOSE CLAIM HAS BEEN REFERRED TO THE REFUGEE DIVISION.

EN VERTU DU PARAGRAPHE 32.1(5) DE LA LOI SUR L'IMMIGRATION, ÉDICTÉ PAR L. C. 1988, CH. 35, UNE ORDONNANCE D'EXCLUSION CONDITIONNELLE NE DEVIENT EXÉCUTOIRE QUE SI SE RÉALISE L'UNE OU L'AUTRE DES CONDITIONS SUIVANTES:

A) LE DEMANDEUR DE STATUT RENONCE À SA REVENDICATION DU STATUT DE RÉFUGIÉ AU SENS DE LA CONVENTION;
B) LE DÉSISTEMENT DU DEMANDEUR DE STATUT A ÉTÉ, EN CETTE MATIÈRE, DÉFINITIVEMENT ÉTABLI;
C) LE STATUT DE RÉFUGIÉ AU SENS DE LA CONVENTION A ÉTÉ DÉFINITIVEMENT REFUSÉ AU DEMANDEUR DE STATUT;
D) IL A ÉTÉ DÉTERMINÉ, LORS D'UNE ENQUÊTE ROUVERTE AUX TERMES DU PARAGRAPHE 48.07(1), QUE LE DEMANDEUR DE STATUT N'AVAIT PAS, EN APPLICATION DU PARAGRAPHE 4(2.1), LE DROIT DE DEMEURER AU CANADA.

LE PARAGRAPHE 32.1(1) DÉFINIT UN DEMANDEUR DE STATUT COMME ÉTANT UNE PERSONNE QUI REVENDIQUE LE STATUT DE RÉFUGIÉ AU SENS DE LA CONVENTION ET DONT LA REVENDICATION EST DÉFÉRÉE À LA SECTION DU STATUT

DATE ►   TIME
              L'HEURE ►   AT ►

ADJUDICATOR
ARBITRE ►

I FULLY UNDERSTAND THE ABOVE DECISION. I ALSO FULLY UNDERSTAND, THAT I MUST NOT COME INTO CANADA WITHOUT THE WRITTEN CONSENT OF THE MINISTER OF EMPLOYMENT AND IMMIGRATION AT ANY TIME DURING THE TWELVE MONTH PERIOD IMMEDIATELY FOLLOWING THE DAY ON WHICH I AM REMOVED FROM OR OTHERWISE LEAVE CANADA.

JE COMPRENDS PARFAITEMENT LA DÉCISION INDIQUÉE CI-DESSUS. EN OUTRE JE COMPRENDS PARFAITEMENT QUE DURANT LES DOUZE MOIS QUI SUIVRONT IMMÉDIATEMENT LA DATE OÙ J'AI ÉTÉ RENVOYÉ(E) DU CANADA OU CELLE OÙ J'AI PAR AILLEURS QUITTÉ LE CANADA JE NE DOIS PAS Y REVENIR SANS L'AUTORISATION ÉCRITE DU MINISTRE DE L'EMPLOI ET DE L'IMMIGRATION.

NAME ►
NOM
SIGNATURE ►
DATE ►

I HAVE FAITHFULLY AND ACCURATELY INTERPRETED IN THE _____ LANGUAGE THE INFORMATION PROVIDED ABOVE.

J'AI INTERPRÉTÉ FIDÈLEMENT ET EXACTEMENT EN _____ LES RENSEIGNEMENTS PRÉCITÉS.

NAME ►
NOM
SIGNATURE ►
DATE ►

DATE SIGNED
SIGNÉ LE   (148)
D-J | M | Y-A

OFFICE OF ISSUE - BUREAU DE DÉLIVRANCE   (156)

MM 1214 EP-P (01-89) B   **Canadä**

THIS FORM HAS BEEN ESTABLISHED BY THE MINISTER OF EMPLOYMENT AND IMMIGRATION
THIS DOCUMENT IS THE PROPERTY OF THE GOVERNMENT OF CANADA
FORMULAIRE ÉTABLI PAR LE MINISTRE DE L'EMPLOI ET DE L'IMMIGRATION
LE PRÉSENT DOCUMENT EST LA PROPRIÉTÉ DU GOUVERNEMENT DU CANADA

ADJUDICATOR
ARBITRE 1

PURSUANT TO SUBSECTION 32.1(5) OF THE IMMIGRATION ACT, THIS CONDITIONAL EXCLUSION ORDER IS EFFECTIVE AS OF _____ **JAN 1, 199-**

EN VERTU DU PARAGRAPHE 32.1(5) DE LA LOI SUR L'IMMIGRATION, LA PRÉSENTE MESURE D'EXCLUSION CONDITIONNELLE EST EXÉCUTOIRE À COMPTER DU _____

DATE **Nov. 12/9-** AT **Port Town**

S. Martin
OFFICER SIGNATURE - SIGNATURE

THIS FORM HAS BEEN ESTABLISHED BY THE MINISTER OF EMPLOYMENT AND IMMIGRATION
THIS DOCUMENT IS THE PROPERTY OF THE GOVERNMENT OF CANADA
FORMULAIRE ÉTABLI PAR LE MINISTRE DE L'EMPLOI ET DE L'IMMIGRATION
LE PRÉSENT DOCUMENT EST LA PROPRIÉTÉ DU GOUVERNEMENT DU CANADA

MM 1214 EP-P (01-89) B   **Canadä**

If a deportation order is made against you (see Sample #41) you *cannot return to Canada* without the permission of the Minister of Immigration *before* you come; if you return without the permission, you are subject to a maximum penalty of two years in jail.

If you are a visitor or returning permanent resident *at the border* seeking admission into Canada and you do not fall into one of the above categories but do fall into any of the other categories listed as inadmissible classes in chapter 12, the adjudicator *must* make an exclusion order (see Sample #42) against you. An exclusion order means that you must remain outside of Canada for a period of 12 months following the date of the order but thereafter will not be prevented from legally returning to Canada.

In the case of a visitor who does not require the making of a deportation order or exclusion order, the adjudicator may, having regard to all the circumstances and believing you will leave Canada on a specified date, issue a Departure Notice (see section f. below).

In the case of a permanent resident, the adjudicator *must* make a deportation order against you if you fall into any of the categories described in chapter 23, section a.

f. DEPARTURE NOTICE

A Departure Notice may be issued to a visitor as outlined above if the adjudicator believes you will leave Canada when you say you will. A Departure Notice is usually issued to overstaying visitors. If you are issued a Departure Notice, there will be *no* prohibition to your legally returning to Canada at a future date as there is with both the deportation and exclusion orders.

If you are given a Departure Notice, you will be required to make and pay for your travel arrangements back to where you came from. Sample #43 is a typical travel arrangement notice. You will be required to go to the immigration office and confirm that you are leaving by showing them your airline ticket, etc.

g. MINISTER'S PERMITS

A special permit issued by the Minister of Employment and Immigration will permit anyone who is not admissible to Canada to enter into the country and permit anyone who is subject to deportation or exclusion to remain in Canada. These permits are issued only in special circumstances. These include, at times, the inland sponsorship of family class members who are illegally in Canada for a long period of time, certain individuals who have medical problems, the return to Canada of someone previously deported many years ago under the old act for perhaps overstaying, and other such cases.

The minister's permit is issued at the discretion of the minister and he or she may at any time vary its terms or cancel it without notice.

In addition, the minister, after cancelling the permit, may order a person to leave Canada by a specific date or may order such a person deported or excluded from Canada without the right to an inquiry before an adjudicator.

h. SECURITY DEPORTATIONS

There are also provisions in the act for the deportation from Canada of permanent residents who are declared to be a risk to the security of Canada. In such cases, a report will be written concerning you and sent to a special advisory board on security matters to the minister, one of whose members is a retired Supreme Court judge.

This board will hear your response in person and with counsel to the allegations, but will not reveal the source of the allegations.

Since the hearings before this board are *not* held in public and since I have not appeared before this board, I cannot describe its functions and procedures to you. In fact, it has sat on only three or four occasions since it came into being on April 10, 1978.

Needless to say, if you are found to be a security risk, the board will recommend to the minister that you be deported and the government will order you deported *without* right of appeal to any court.

i. REVOCATION OF INLAND SPONSORSHIP

If a person has filed a sponsorship for his or her spouse who is in Canada and decides to revoke (take back the sponsorship) *prior to the spouse receiving his or her permanent resident status*, then the family class spouse is in serious trouble. The same revocation can be done for the sponsorship of any family class member by a sponsor.

At the present time, if your sponsorship is revoked, you have almost no alternative but to leave Canada. This is the current position of the Immigration Commission. I take the position that a sponsor should not be allowed to take back a sponsorship undertaking he or she has signed. It is a legal contract. Often the child, spouse, or parent may have been here several years and is well established in Canada in his or her own right.

If this happens to you and you do not leave Canada voluntarily, you will be subject to the inquiry process described in the beginning of this chapter just as any other overstaying visitor, and you should obtain the services of a knowledgeable immigration lawyer.

Employment and Immigration Canada
Emploi et Immigration Canada

Date: December 1, 19

TO: JENNIFER ILLEGAL

Dear Ms. Illegal

A Departure Notice has been served on you which requires you to leave Canada by

December 11, 19 -

Please make the necessary travel arrangements for your departure and advise this Commission of such arrangements by presenting them, as well as your valid passport to:

    Supervisor, Verification of Departure Unit
    Third Floor
    480 University Avenue
    Toronto, Ontario

on Monday   the 10th   of December   19
between the hours of 9:00 and 11:00 a.m. or 2:00 and 4:00 p.m.

Further documentation will be issued to you at that time.

J. M. Officer
Immigration Officer

25
APPEALS TO THE IMMIGRATION AND REFUGEE BOARD

The revisions of the refugee procedures in Canada as outlined in chapter 17 have resulted in a complete new appeal procedure as of January 1, 1989. As of that date, a new appeal tribunal known as the Immigration and Refugee Board was created. This board replaces the old Immigration Appeal Board.

The new Immigration and Refugee Board has two divisions: an Immigration Appeal Division and a Convention Refugee Determination Division. The Convention Refugee Determination Division has 65 full-time members and additional part-time members. Currently this division has approximately 100 members across Canada. The Appeal Division can have up to 30 permanent members; at the present time it has 18 members. It is not necessary that members of either division be lawyers — in fact, the new law requires that only 10% of the members of the Refugee Division and a majority of the chairpersons and vice-chairpersons be lawyers. Although not required, most of the current members of the Appeal Division are legally trained. I shall deal with the jurisdictions of the two new divisions separately.

a. JURISDICTION OF THE APPEAL DIVISION

The Appeal Division is a court of record which sits with three members to hear appeals but may sit with only one member if all the people concerned agree to it. Unless you have an ironclad case, always take three judges. Also, if you are in the Appeal Division, you should have a lawyer.

The Appeal Division hears the appeals of individuals who have been ordered removed from Canada as follows:

(a) Persons who are permanent residents of Canada and are inside Canada

(b) Persons who are in possession of a returning resident permit (see chapter 23)

(c) Persons seeking admission to Canada (at a border) who are in possession of a valid visa

(d) Persons declared to be convention refugees by the Minister of Immigration and against whom a removal order has been made on other grounds

(e) A Canadian citizen or permanent resident who has sponsored a member of the family class (see chapter 4) and the sponsorship has been refused by a visa officer overseas or in Canada.

Some general comments should be made about each of these categories. In the case of an appeal from a removal order by a permanent resident, there will be no right of appeal if the removal order was based on a finding by the special advisory board that you are a security risk.

Persons who are in possession of valid returning resident permits obviously had to have been permanent residents when they obtained the permit prior to leaving Canada or when they were outside of Canada if they obtained the permit abroad.

For a person who claims to be a permanent resident, who has an IMM #1000 (see Sample #9) but does not have a returning resident permit and who has been outside of Canada more than 183 days, the right of appeal to the Appeal Division is not yet clear.

The old Immigration Appeal Board held in one case that it has the jurisdiction to review a decision by an adjudicator that a person has lost permanent resident status by being out of the country more than 183 days or a finding by an adjudicator that a "former" permanent resident has abandoned his or her intention to reside in Canada (see chapter 23). The IAB claims the right to decide if a person has lost the status in Canada as a permanent resident. The board has gone on to say that if they make a ruling favorable to the person concerned then that person is entitled to come into Canada as a permanent resident. This is an over-simplification of a complex jurisdictional position the IAB has taken.

On the other hand, the federal government, through the Immigration Commission, has taken the position that once an adjudicator has ruled that a person has lost permanent resident status in Canada, there is no right of appeal to the old IAB and there is no jurisdiction for the old IAB to hear the case. The government takes the position that any appeal must be to the Federal Court of Appeal by way of section 28 of their legislation (see chapter 26).

The government appealed this question to the Federal Court and lost. This means the old IAB has jurisdiction to hear appeals of persons whom the government claims have lost their permanent resident status.

In my opinion, this court case should apply to the Appeal Division of the new Immigration and Refugee Board.

If you arrive in Canada with a visa — such as a visitor's visa — and are refused admission by an immigration officer whose decision is upheld by an adjudicator, you have a right of appeal to the Appeal Division. This is why you should obtain a visa if you can. A visitor without a visa has no right of appeal to the Appeal Division.

The Immigration Commission can also appeal to the Appeal Division from a decision of an adjudicator that is favorable to you, that is, a decision that says you are allowed to come into Canada. The Commission does not appeal very often.

In the case of appeals by permanent residents and people in possession of a returning permit, the Immigration Appeal Board may hear the appeal on any ground (argument) based on law or any combination of fact and law. Sample #44 shows the Notice of Appeal you would use.

In addition, if the Appeal Division decides that there is no basis in law for your appeal, it may look at all the circumstances of your situation and that of your family, friends, relatives, and how you came to be in trouble.

If the Appeal Division in its wisdom and discretion decides you should not be removed from Canada, it can cancel the deportation or exclusion order or suspend its being carried out for a period of time to see if you stay out of trouble.

Of course, the Appeal Division can uphold the removal order. There is no appeal from the decision of the Appeal Division not to exercise its humanitarian jurisdiction. There is an appeal on question of law only from the Appeal Division to the Federal Court of Appeal (see chapter 26).

In the case of an appeal to the Appeal Division of a person in possession of a valid visa (a visitor's visa, student authorization, employment authorization, etc.), there is a right of appeal similar to that outlined above on a ground of law or fact or mixed law and fact. In addition, there is a right of appeal based on the existence of humanitarian and compassionate considerations that the person should not be removed from Canada.

The phrase "humanitarian and compassionate considerations" appears to be somewhat more restrictive than the phrase "having regard to all the circumstances of the case" which relates to permanent residents and people in possession of returning resident permits.

The Appeal Division also has jurisdiction to hear an application for a release from detention of anyone held in custody on an immigration warrant.

The Immigration and Refugee Board has the same power to release as does the Immigration Commission. Sample #45 shows an Application for Release from Detention made to the Immigration and Refugee Board.

b. JURISDICTION OF THE REFUGEE DIVISION AND NATURE OF ITS HEARINGS

The Refugee Division has sole and exclusive jurisdiction to hear cases in which an individual has been determined to have a credible basis for a claim to refugee status made at an immigration inquiry (see chapter 17). The Refugee Division meets informally and is not bound by normal courtroom procedures. The hearings are held in private and it is very difficult for anyone including the media to force an open hearing if you object.

The hearing is held before two members of the board neither of whom can be the IRB member who sat at the "credible basis" portion of the immigration inquiry (see chapter 17).

Remember, if you were found not to have a credible basis for your refugee claim at your inquiry, you have no rights of appeal to the IRB.

You have the right to request a hearing before only one board member. Only a fool would do so unless your claim was being conceded to by the government.

The Refugee Division will determine whether or not you are a convention refugee as defined in the United Nations Convention on Refugees. YOU HAVE TO CONVINCE ONLY ONE OF THE TWO MEMBERS TO WIN.

A convention refugee is defined as any person who —

> (a) by reason of a well-founded fear of persecution for reasons of race, religion, nationality, membership in a particular social group, or political opinion,
>
> (i) is outside the country of the person's nationality and is unable or, by reason of that fear, is unwilling to avail himself of the protection of that country, or
>
> (ii) not having a country of nationality, is outside the country of the person's former habitual residence and is unable or, by reason of that fear, is unwilling to return to that country.

In my opinion, a refugee appeal requires the services of an experienced lawyer. Often you will need the testimony of an acknowledged expert witness on the actions of the government of your homeland toward individuals such as yourself.

In Canada, an "expert witness" is not just anybody, but must be someone recognized by the court as being extremely knowledgeable about your country — often a professor specializing in the political science of your country or a former lawyer or governmental official from your homeland.

Arranging for these witnesses, choosing them, and preparing the questions to be asked when such experts give testimony at your hearing usually requires the assistance of competent legal advisors and not the well-intentioned assistance of friends. In a case such as this, you are fighting for your freedom and your future and perhaps your very life and that of your family; you would not let a butcher take out your appendix, would you?

SAMPLE #44
NOTICE OF APPEAL

APPEAL DIVISION

NOTICE OF APPEAL

Section 70 of the Immigration Act,
as enacted by R.S.C. 1985 (4th Supp.) c. 28, s. 18

_____ , Appellant

THE MINISTER OF EMPLOYMENT AND IMMIGRATION , Respondent

TAKE NOTICE:
That I hereby appeal to the Immigration and Refugee Board, Appeal
Division, pursuant to section 70 of the Immigration Act, as enacted
by R.S.C.1985, (4th Supp.) c. 28, s. 18 from a removal order or a
conditional removal order made against me or confirmed on the___
____ day of_____,19__.

Dated at_____ on the _____day of_____,19__.

_____
Appellant

Service thereof acknowledged this _____ day of_____
_____,19__.

_____
Adjudicator

That I

(check appropriate box(es))

☐ wish to be present at the hearing of the appeal to make oral
submission to the Appeal Division;

☐ request the Appeal Division to provide at the hearing an
interpreter proficient in the _____ language;

☐ wish to file written submissions with the Appeal Division;

☐ wish to have my hearing conducted in ☐ English ☐ French.

That I authorize the following person to represent me as my counsel
of record:

Mr. ☐
Mrs. ☐ _____
Miss ☐
Ms. ☐

Address_____
     street   apt #   City   Province Postal code

Occupation_____ Tel:_(___)____-_____
                     (area code) Tel.Number

My address is as follows:

Mr. ☐

Mrs. ☐ _____

Miss ☐

Ms. ☐

Address_____
          street   apt #   City   Province Postal code

Occupation_____ Tel: (___)_____-_____
                                 (area code) Tel.Number

IMPORTANT

You <u>must</u> serve this Notice of Appeal on the Adjudicator who made the removal order or made or confirmed a conditional removal order against you, or file with a copy of the removal order or conditional removal order with the Appeal Division, within <u>seven days</u> of the service of the removal order or notice of confirmation of the conditional removal order on you.

You are required to notify the Appeal Division at_____ if you wish to change the method of presentation of your appeal, and of any <u>changes of address,</u> and of any changes in the name and address of your counsel.

<u>WARNING</u>: Pursuant to Section 76 as enacted by R.S.C. 1985, (4th Supp.) c.28, s.18 of the Immigration Act, if you fail to communicate with the Appeal Division, upon being requested to do so, or if you fail to inform the Appeal Division of your most recent address, the Appeal Division may declare your appeal to be abandoned.

FILED ON

01

SAMPLE #45
APPLICATION FOR RELEASE FROM DETENTION

<u>APPEAL DIVISION</u>

<u>APPLICATION FOR RELEASE FROM DETENTION</u>

<u>Immigration Act, Section 78 (R.S.C. 1985, CI-2)</u>

_____, Appellant

THE MINISTER OF EMPLOYMENT AND IMMIGRATION   , Respondent

I,_____, having
appealed to the Immigration and Refugee Board, Appeal Division by
notice of appeal dated the_____ day of
19___ hereby make application to the Appeal Division pursuant to
Section 78 of the Immigration Act, (R.S.C. 1985,CI-2) for release
from detention under such terms and conditions as the Appeal Divion
may impose.

My submissions to the Appeal Division are attached hereto:

    Pursuant to subrule 38 (1) of the Immigration Appeal Division
Rules, I attach the following:

    (check appropriate box(es))

    ☐   written submissions in support of the application;

    ☐   a copy of the removal order or conditional removal order;
        and

    ☐   a copy of any order of the Federal Court of Appeal
        granting the applicant leave to appeal from a decision
        of the Appeal Division, as well as a copy of any notice
        of appeal filed in accordance with that leave.

Dated at _____ on the ___ day of
_____,19__. | FILED ON

_____
          Applicant

Service thereof acknowledged
this _____ day of_____,19__.

_____
       Immigration Officer

If you lose your appeal to the Refugee Division, you may appeal to the Federal Court of Canada, Appellate Division. The appeal to this court can only be on a point of law and other technical situations (see chapter 26).

c. THE NATURE OF THE HEARING BEFORE APPEAL DIVISION

The hearing before the Appeal Division is judicial in nature. While you may be represented before the board as at the immigration inquiry by anyone you wish, I cannot stress too strongly that you should have a lawyer to be your counsel and, if possible, one familiar with courtroom practice and immigration law.

What happens on an appeal to the Appeal Division and what powers does the board have?

The Appeal Division sits with three members. As a superior court, it has the power to compel the attendance of witnesses and can order the production and examination of anything whatsoever (see Sample #46).

The board is not bound by the strict rules of evidence used in other courts. It can hear and receive any additional information in whatever manner the board desires, and give it whatever weight or credit it wishes.

If you are an applicant who wishes to come to Canada, the obligation to prove that you should be entitled to become a permanent resident is on you, the appellant.

If you are already a permanent resident, the obligation is shifted to the government to prove to the board that the deportation order is valid and that you should lose your permanent resident status.

At the beginning of your hearing, you or your counsel will have an opportunity to present your case first.

You have the right to testify under oath concerning yourself — your past actions, your present situation, and your future hopes. You can present evidence of what you have done in Canada and give evidence of what you want to do in the future. You can call upon your employer, your friends, your relatives, and a member of the clergy to testify about you.

If you have a business, you could call on a chartered accountant to testify about its financial position.

The representative of the government, who may or may not be a lawyer, has the right to cross-examine, that is, ask questions of both you and your witnesses, in an attempt to discredit in some way the testimony you are giving to the board.

After the board has heard you and all your witnesses, the government can call its own witnesses if it so desires. The government very seldom exercises its right to do this.

At the close of the government's case, first you or your lawyer, and then the government representative, will have an opportunity to argue as to why you should or should not be allowed to remain in Canada.

In making its decision, the Appeal Division must first decide whether or not the order of deportation made against you is valid.

As an example of this procedure, let us say that you have been ordered deported from Canada because you are a permanent resident and police records indicate that a person with your name has been convicted of the theft of an automobile.

The Appeal Division must first either allow your appeal or dismiss your appeal. For example, your appeal would be allowed if the person who stole the automobile had, in fact, the same name as you but their identity was confused with yours.

SAMPLE #46
SUMMONS

<u>APPEAL DIVISION</u>

File #_____

<u>SUMMONS</u>

<u>Rule 31(1) of the Immigration Appeal Division Rules</u>

_____ , Appellant/Applicant

_____ , Respondent

ELIZABETH THE SECOND, by the Grace of God of the United Kingdom, Canada and Her other Realms and Territories Queens, Head of the Commonwealth, Defender of the Faith, **GREETING.**

TO:_____

WE COMMAND YOU to attend before Our Immigration and Refugee Board, Appeal Division at:

on the _____ day of _____,19__, at _____ AM/PM and so from day to day until your attendance is, no longer required,

      1) **TO GIVE** evidence at the request of _____
_____;

      2) **AND ALSO** to bring with you and produce any document, book or paper that you have or control that is relevant to the proceeding and more particularly the following:
_____
_____
_____

      AND if you fail to comply with this summons a warrant for your apprehension may be issued.

_____   ISSUED BY:_____
      date   Registrar

If, in fact, you were the person who stole the automobile, the Appeal Division would dismiss your appeal; that is, find that the order of deportation was valid.

d. WHAT ARE HUMANITARIAN CONSIDERATIONS?

If the board dismisses your appeal, the Canadian government has seen fit to give the board the power, at its discretion, to stop the order of deportation, to quash the order of deportation, or to stay (suspend) the order of deportation.

When will the board exercise these discretionary powers? In the case of a permanent resident, such as the one described above, the board will look at all the circumstances of the case, and if it believes that the crime was an isolated incident, will usually stop the deportation.

Since the first edition of this book was published in 1974, there have been sufficient cases to make certain generalizations concerning the attitude of the old IAB and the new IRB in the area of humanitarian considerations.

If you are a permanent resident who is in trouble, the board's attitude will often depend on the seriousness of the matter. For simple possession of marijuana or hashish, shoplifting, theft under $200, or common assault, the board will usually stay the order of deportation for a period of time — perhaps 12 to 18 months. This means that the board will order that the deportation not be carried out at the present time. If you get into no further trouble during the period of the stay, then the board will likely cancel the order of deportation; this is like a period of probation.

However, if the nature of the offence is very serious, such as armed robbery, rape, robbery, fraud, or breach of trust, the board might decide to let the order of deportation stand and be carried out. Other factors involved in making the decision will be whether the offence is a first one or a second or third. Also considered will be your family, if any, especially your spouse and children.

If you, as a permanent resident, are unfortunate enough to be sent to jail for six months or longer, what you do in prison to improve yourself will be considered by the Appeal Division. Such improvements would include school upgrading, technical courses, and certificates you have received, as well as your conduct while in prison.

All in all, the Appeal Division has very wide powers of discretion either to order your removal from Canada, allow you to stay, or to stay on a form of probation for a period of time.

e. SPONSORSHIP APPEALS TO THE APPEALS DIVISION

Section 77 of the act provides for appeals to the Appeal Division if you are a Canadian citizen or permanent resident sponsoring a member of the family class (i.e., one of the following):

(a) Parents or grandparents

(b) Husband or wife

(c) Fiancé or fiancée

(d) Unmarried children

(e) Unmarried orphans under 18 who are brothers, sisters, nieces, nephews, or grandchildren of sponsor (see chapter 4).

The appeal can be started only after the immigration (visa) officer abroad has refused the immigration to Canada of your relative on the grounds that either you or your relative does not meet the requirements of sponsorship.

The two most common grounds of refusal are inability to prove by way of documentation your relationship with your family class relative, and your inability to financially support your family class relative.

Often a long period of time (as much as a year or more) will pass from the date you sponsor your family class relative to the date you will receive the refusal in Canada. At that time you should file a Notice of Appeal under Section 77 (see Sample #47) which is a notice of appeal for sponsors to the IRB — Appeal Division.

The appeal to the board can be one of law or fact or mixed law and fact. In addition, the board has a humanitarian and compassionate jurisdiction to grant relief and allow your relatives to come to Canada.

The hearing before the Appeal Division is similar to those described above and you should have a lawyer represent you. If the IRB allows your appeal, the case will be re-opened and continued by the Immigration Commission without regard to the reasons the application was refused in the first instance.

This means it is possible, though not likely, that your relative could be refused a second time for different and new reasons not previously used. Of course, the Appeal Division could uphold the officer's decision and not allow your appeal.

In the example given above, the relationship of your relative could be a question of law or fact or both. It would be a question of law if your adopted, orphaned nephew qualifies as a family class member. It would be a question of fact as to whether this child was the same one who was in fact adopted by your now-deceased aunt and uncle.

After you have filed your Notice of Appeal and before the appeal is heard by the Appeal Division, you will receive a summary of the information upon which the refusal of your sponsorship is based. It will be this presentation you must overcome with your testimony and the testimony of experts in the law and customs of your country, if necessary.

APPEAL DIVISION

NOTICE OF APPEAL

Section 77 of the Immigration Act, (R.S.C. 1985, CI-2)

_____, Appellant
(Sponsor)

THE MINISTER OF EMPLOYMENT AND IMMIGRATION , Respondent

TAKE NOTICE:
That I hereby appeal to the Immigration and Refugee Board, Appeal Division, from the refusal of the sponsored application for landing made by

RELATIONSHIP TO SPONSOR	NAME	DATE OF BIRTH
_____	_____	_____
_____	_____	_____
_____	_____	_____
_____	_____	_____
_____	_____	_____

I was informed of the reasons for the refusal on the _____ day of _____,19__, by letter dated the _____ day of _ _____,19__.

This appeal dated at_____ on the_____ day of_____ _____,19__.

_____
Appellant

Service thereof acknowledged this _____ day of_____ _____,19__.

_____
Immigration Officer

That I

(check appropriate box(es))

☐ wish to be present at the hearing of the appeal to make oral submission to the Appeal Division;

☐ request the Appeal Division to provide at the hearing an interpreter proficient in the _____ language;

☐ wish to file written submissions with the Appeal Division;

☐ wish to have my hearing conducted in ☐ English ☐ French.

That I authorize the following person to represent me as my counsel of record:

Mr. ☐

Mrs. ☐ _____

Miss ☐

Ms. ☐

Address_____
       street   apt #   City   Province Postal code

Occupation_____ Tel: (____) ____-____
                             (area code) Tel.Number

My address is as follows:

Mr. ☐

Mrs. ☐ _____

Miss ☐

Ms. ☐

Address_____
       street   apt #   City   Province Postal code

Occupation_____ Tel: (____) ____-____
                             (area code) Tel.Number

IMPORTANT

You <u>must</u> serve this Notice of Appeal on an Immigration officer or file it with the Appeal Division within **THIRTY DAYS** from the date on which you were informed of the reasons for the refusal of the sponsored application for landing.

You are required to notify the Appeal Division at_____
_____ if you wish to change the method of presentation of your appeal and of any changes of address, and of any changes in the name and address of your counsel.

FILED ON

26

APPEALS TO THE FEDERAL COURT OF CANADA

The Federal Court of Canada Trial or Appellate Division (the Federal Court of Appeal), is the second highest court in Canada and is the court to which appeals concerning the actions of federal government employees, boards, and tribunals are made. This, then, is the court to which some appeals from the decisions of immigration officers and adjudicators (see chapter 24) and the Immigration and Refugee Board (see chapter 25) are made.

You can either appear in the Federal Court of Appeal in person or be represented by a lawyer. You may NOT have a friend, relative, consultant, or advisor represent you in this court — it can only be a lawyer or yourself.

The cost of going to this court in terms of legal fees is not small and will depend on the complexity of your case (the time involved in preparing and presenting it) and the fee schedule of the particular lawyer you choose. There is no set schedule of fees for lawyers in immigration matters and you are well-advised to seek lawyers knowledgeable in this area of law and discuss their fees in advance. Usually lawyers will require a retainer in advance for a case like this — it will usually amount to a couple of thousand dollars or more. A retainer is not a full fee; it is an advance on fees and out-of-pocket expenses such as photocopying, long-distance calls, and court fees.

Section 84 of the Immigration Act provides that if the government appeals a decision that you have won either before an adjudicator or the Immigration and Refugee Board, the government will have to pay your lawyer's fees. If, however, you wish to appeal a decision you lost, the government will not pay your lawyer's fees even if you win unless ordered to do so by the court.

There are two ways of arriving at the Federal Court of Canada in an immigration case. The first is by an appeal from a decision of the Immigration and Refugee Board; the second is by an appeal from the decision of an adjudicator, visa, or immigration officer (where there is no appeal to the IRB) under section 28 of the Federal Court Act. I shall deal with each method of appeal separately.

a. APPEALS FROM THE IMMIGRATION AND REFUGEE BOARD

Where you have a right of appeal to the Immigration and Refugee Board from the decision of an adjudicator (i.e., you are a permanent resident, possess an immigrant or non-immigrant visa, or are claiming either refugee status or Canadian citizenship), you must take your appeal first to the Appeal Division of the Immigration and Refugee Board. If you lose your appeal at the board, you may appeal to the Federal Court of Appeal under section 83 of the Immigration Act.

Such appeal can be made only on the basis that the board has made an error on a point of law or that the board for some reason had no legal jurisdiction to hear your case. An appeal based on law or jurisdiction can only be made by someone trained in the law. Remember that you cannot appeal to the Federal Court of Appeal a decision of the Immigration and Refugee Board not to exercise humanitarian considerations in your case. Compassionate jurisdiction is solely that of the Appeal Division of the Immigration and Refugee Board.

An appeal to the Federal Court is not made by right, but requires an application for permission to appeal called an application for leave to appeal. This application is made to and decided by a single judge of the court. The application is made in writing only and must be made within 15 days of the decision being appealed from.

If your application for leave to appeal is refused, there is NO right of appeal to a higher court of that decision under any circumstances.

If leave is granted, then the lawyer will be required to file a complete written argument of the points of law he or she wishes to argue. The rules of the Federal Court set out how the argument is to be made in general terms, including sections containing the facts of the case; the points for argument; the argument; the orders sought; the list of legal precedents relied upon; and so on.

Note: The law as of January 1, 1989, states *there is no appeal of a decision of an adjudicator and/or an IRB member not to make a credible basis finding in a refugee claim.*

b. APPEALS FROM AN ADJUDICATOR, VISA OR IMMIGRATION OFFICER DIRECTLY TO THE FEDERAL COURT

Those classes of people who cannot appeal to the Immigration and Refugee Board and from there to the Federal Court of Appeal can appeal from the decision of the adjudicator directly to the Federal Court Trial Division under section 18 of the Federal Court Act.

The right of appeal in these cases is much narrower than in the former. These cases would involve people who arrive in Canada as visitors at the border and are refused entry because the immigration officer believes that they are not real visitors, but intend to remain in Canada illegally after their visit and work without permission. Also included are people who overstay their two- or three-week visit and remain in Canada illegally.

As a result of the amendments to the Immigration Act on January 1, 1989, these appeals are now made to a single judge of the Federal Court of Canada, Trial Division, and no longer to the Federal Court of Appeal. As with appeals from the Immigration and Refugee Board, all these appeals with the exception of those outlined below also require an application for leave to appeal to be made in writing only to a judge of the Trial Division of the Federal Court pursuant to section 18 of the Federal Court Act.

An appeal to the Federal Court Trial Division under section 18 can be made on any point of law or of jurisdiction. Under section 18 of the Federal Court Act, an appeal can be made only if the adjudicator failed to observe the laws of natural justice, erred in law, or made a finding of fact in a capricious manner.

The Federal Court of Canada has largely interpreted its jurisdiction under section 18 as that of a review of the procedures used by the adjudicator (i.e., that you had a fair hearing); that you had the right to have counsel of your own choosing present; that you had the right to call witnesses on your behalf; that you had the right to give testimony on your behalf; that you had the right to have an interpreter if you cannot speak English; and the like.

The denial of any of these basic principles of justice will result in the Federal Court questioning the deportation order. This does not prevent a new hearing being convened by the immigration authorities, but it does give you the time to leave Canada without the blemish of a deportation order, which would prevent you from ever returning to Canada as a visitor or an immigrant without the permission of the Minister of Employment and Immigration.

In a section 18 appeal, the Federal Court only looks at a transcript of the hearing and hears argument based on it alone. The court does not hear verbal testimony except under the most unusual of circumstances and has only heard such testimony in an immigration case once or twice to my knowledge since the court was created in 1970.

The court will not substitute its opinion of the evidence before it for that of the adjudicator, unless such decision was so perverse and capricious as to border on the absurd. In practice, this means that even if the Federal Court comes to a different decision, the court will not change the adjudicator's decision unless the officer has denied you one of the basic principles of justice or has made a decision, based on the facts available, that was so absurd as to warrant its reversal. This means there must be no evidence upon which the adjudicator could have based the decision he or she made. Such cases are few and far between.

Last, if the adjudicator has made an error in applying the law to your case, the Federal Court has the power, although not often used under a section 18 application, to cancel the deportation order, interpret the law for the adjudicator, and send the case back to the adjudicator for a proper disposition or make the final decision itself.

A leave application in writing is NOT required when you are appealing a decision of an immigration officer or a visa officer overseas not to issue either an immigrant or visitor visa, student or employment authorization, returning resident permit, or appeals by sponsors in family class refusals. In these situations, you can file an appeal within 15 days of the decision to the Trial Division of the Federal Court of Canada.

The problem here is how can you file an appeal in 15 days if your friend or relative overseas has been refused a visa. Given communication problems in most of the Third World, it is quite possible that knowledge of the refusal will take more than 15 days to get to your relative or friend, let alone from them to you. This problem will likely be the subject of a court case in the near future.

27
PENALTIES AND FINES FOR VIOLATION OF IMMIGRATION LAWS

In addition to the possibility of deportation outlined in chapter 24, any person — including a Canadian citizen — is subject to fines and/or imprisonment for a breach of the Immigration Act.

Illegal actions that can result in your prosecution under the Immigration Act are as follows:

(a) Coming into the country at other than a regular immigration entry point

(b) Failure to appear at an immigration office when summoned there

(c) Refusal to testify under oath when required to do so

(d) Knowingly making a false offer of employment to a potential immigrant

(e) Claiming that you can influence an immigration officer by the payment of a bribe

(f) Inducing someone to violate the Immigration Act or its regulations in any manner whatsoever

(g) Using forged or false documents to enter Canada

(h) Knowingly making a false or misleading statement at any immigration examination or hearing for the purpose of entering Canada

(i) As a member of a crew, failing to leave Canada with the vehicle in which you entered

(j) Escaping custody

(k) Failing to comply with any term or condition imposed upon admission to Canada

(l) Remaining in Canada without the written consent of an immigration officer after your visitor's status (time in Canada) has expired

(m) Knowingly inducing, aiding, or abetting anyone to contravene or break any section of the Immigration Act or Regulations

(n) Last, and most important, as a Canadian citizen, permanent resident, or company, knowingly employing anyone who is not a Canadian citizen, permanent resident, or visitor with a valid employment authorization and similar offences inducing people to break Canada's immigration laws.

Such prosecution will be before a provincial court judge or magistrate, and you will be entitled to be represented by a lawyer. If you are charged, it is in your best interest to hire a lawyer to defend you.

The government can proceed by way of summary conviction (usually a first offence) or by way of indictment (usually a second or subsequent offence). *If you are convicted summarily, you are subject to a maximum fine of not more than $1 000 (it could be less) or to a jail term of not more than six months, or to both fine and imprisonment.*

If you are convicted by way of indictment, you are subject to a maximum fine of not more than $5 000 or to a jail term of not more than two years, or to both!

Remember that these penalties are *in addition* to the possibility of deportation as outlined in chapter 24.

Since the recent crackdown on illegal immigrants — including those who return after deportation — there have been many more prosecutions under this section.

With the amendments to the Immigration Act in 1989, including all the new procedures concerning refugees and especially allegedly fake refugee claims (see chapter 17), the government has created some new offences under the Immigration Act, 1976, other than the ones listed above. The most important of these new offences relates to anyone who knowingly organizes or assists or helps anyone to come into Canada who does not have a valid passport, travel document, and proper Canadian visa. Such a person is guilty of an offence and *subject to a fine or indictment of up to $10 000 or up to five years in jail or both and on summary conviction to a fine of up to $2 000 or up to six months in jail or both.*

If the scheme involves 10 or more persons being brought to Canada without valid papers then *the fine can be up to $500 000 or up to 10 years in jail or both.* This applies both to the organizers of the scheme and to the master or pilot of any vehicle used to carry out the scheme.

Similarly, there are other new offences with *penalties of up to $10 000 in fines and up to five years in jail or both,* to cover people who knowingly advise people to make false refugee claims.

These sections are aimed supposedly at organized immigrant smuggling and other schemes to breach Canadian law. Unfortunately, the wording of the section is so poor and vague that it could also catch legitimate immigrant aid societies such as the churches, Amnesty International, the Polish Congress, Jewish Immigrant Aid Society, and others. A challenge to these and other sections is presently in the Federal Court of Canada and will likely take several years to work its way through to the Supreme Court of Canada. We will let you know the outcome in the next edition of this book.

28
CONCLUSION

It is apparent that, while there has been an increase in the number of immigrants coming to Canada in the various independent categories over the past 5 years, the fact is that 26 500 families in 1990 who are not either refugees or in the family class is a very small number of people from the whole world.

Therefore, prospective immigrants will have to be able to offer much more than their willingness to struggle for a new life in Canada. You must have a job — one that cannot be filled by a Canadian — or be on the demand list of occupations. You will need to use the efforts of your friends, relatives, and lawyers to help locate employment and prepare and present your various applications to the government if you ever hope to succeed in your efforts.

Good luck.

MAP OF CANADA

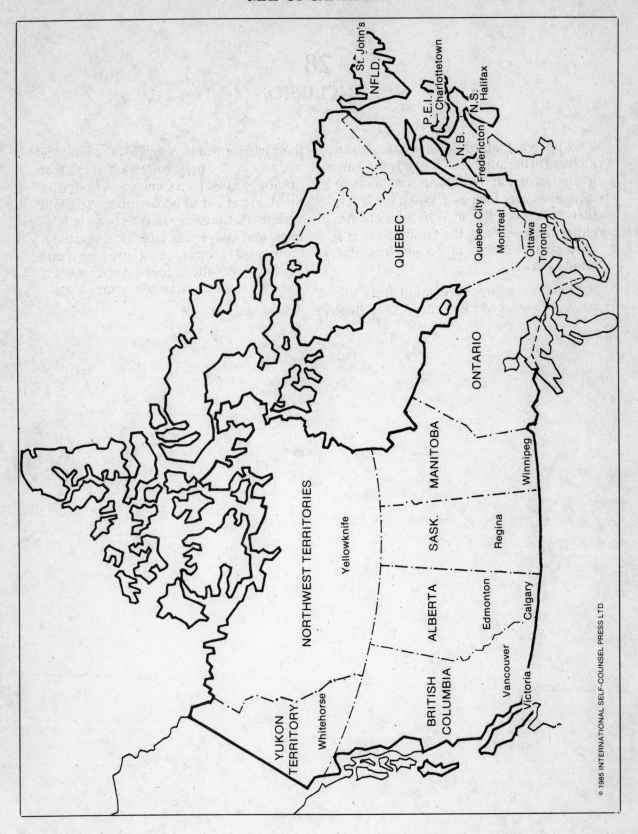

APPENDIX 1
LOCATIONS OF CANADIAN EMBASSIES AND CONSULATES

Abidjan (Ivory Coast)

Algiers (Algeria)

Accra (Ghana)

Addis Ababa (Ethiopia)

Amman (Jordan)

Ankara (Turkey)

Athens (Greece)

Atlanta (U.S.A.)

Baghdad (Iraq)

Bangkok (Thailand)

Beirut (Lebanon)
    (temporarily closed, 1985)

Belgrade (Yugoslavia)

Berne (Switzerland)

Bogota (Colombia)

Bonn (West Germany)

Boston (U.S.A.)

Brasilia (Brazil)

Bridgetown (Barbados)

Brussels (Belgium)

Bucharest (Romania)

Budapest (Hungary)

Buenos Aires (Argentina)

Buffalo (U.S.A.)

Cairo (Arab Republic of Egypt)

Canberra (Australia)

Caracas (Venezuela)

Chicago (U.S.A.)

Colombo (Sri Lanka)

Copenhagen (Denmark)

Dakar (Senegal)

Dallas (U.S.A.)

Dar-es-Salaam (Tanzania)

Detroit (U.S.A.)

Dhaka (Bangladesh)

Dublin (Ireland)

Georgetown (Guyana)

Guatemala City (Guatemala)

The Hague (Netherlands)

Harare (Zimbabwe)

Helsinki (Finland)

Hong Kong

Islamabad (Pakistan)

Jakarta (Indonesia)

Jeddah (Saudi Arabia)

Kiev (U.S.S.R.) (1990)

Kigalia (Rwanda)

Kingston (Jamaica)

Kinshasa (Republic of Zaire)

Kuala Lumpur (Malaysia)

Kuwait City (Kuwait)

Lagos (Nigeria)

Libreville (Gabon)

Lima (Peru)

Lisbon (Portugal)

London (U.K.)

Los Angeles (U.S.A.)

Madrid (Spain)

Manila (Philippines)

Mexico City (Mexico)

Minneapolis (U.S.A.)

Moscow (U.S.S.R.)

Nairobi (Kenya)

New Delhi (India)

New York (U.S.A.)

Oslo (Norway)

Paris (France)

Peking (People's Republic of China)

Port-au-Prince (Haiti)
Port of Spain (Trinidad and Tobago)
Prague (Czechoslovakia)
Pretoria (South Africa)
Quito (Ecuador)
Rabat-Agdal (Morocco)
Rome (Italy)
San Francisco (U.S.A.)
San Jose (Costa Rica)
Santiago (Chile)
Seattle (U.S.A.)

Seoul (Korea)
Singapore
Stockholm (Sweden)
Tel Aviv (Israel)
Tokyo (Japan)
Tunis (Tunisia)
Vienna (Austria)
Warsaw (Poland)
Washington, D.C. (U.S.A.)
Wellington (New Zealand)
Yaounde (Cameroon)

APPENDIX 2
MAILING ADDRESSES OF CANADIAN EMBASSIES AND CONSULATES WITH FULL IMMIGRATION SERVICES

ARGENTINA

Canadian Embassy
Immigration Section
Casilla de Correo 1598
Buenos Aires, Argentina

Areas of responsibility:
Brazil, Falkland Islands, Paraguay, Uruguay

AUSTRALIA

Canadian Consulate General
8th Floor, A.M.P. Centre
50 Bridge Street
Sydney, NSW 2000
Australia

Areas of responsibility:
American Samoa, British Solomon Islands, Christmas Islands, Cook Islands, Loyalty Islands, New Hebrides Condominium, Solomon Islands, Tonga, Tuvalu Islands, Wallis Islands, Western Samoa, Fiji, French Polynesia, Gilbert Islands, New Zealand, Papua New Guinea, and other Pacific Islands south of the Equator

AUSTRIA

Canadian Embassy
Immigration Section
Dr. Karl Lueger Ring 10
A-1010 Vienna, Austria

Areas of responsibility:
Albania, Czechoslovakia

BANGLADESH

The Canadian High Commission
G.P.O. Box 569
Dhaka, Bangladesh

BARBADOS

Canadian High Commission
Commonwealth Development Corp.
P. O. Box 404
Bridgetown, Barbados

Areas of responsibility:
Antigua, Dominica, Dominican Republic, Grenada, Montserrat, Puerto Rico, St. Kitts-Nevis-Anguilla, St. Lucia, St. Vincent, Virgin Islands (British & U.S.)

BELGIUM

Ambassade du Canada
Service de l'Immigration
2 de Tervuren Avenue
1004 Bruxelles, Belgium

Areas of responsibility:
Luxembourg

BRAZIL

Consulate General of Canada
Immigration Section
Caixa Postal 01-4996
01.499 Sao Paulo, Brazil

CHILE

Canadian Embassy
Immigration Section
Casilla 427
Santiago, Chile

Areas of responsibility:
Bolivia, Peru

CHINA

Canadian Embassy
10 San Li Tun Road
Chao Yang District
Beijing, China

COLUMBIA

Canadian Embassy
Immigration Section
Apartado Aereo 53531
Bogota 2, Colombia

Areas of responsibility:
Ecuador, Venezuela

COSTA RICA

Canadian Embassy
Apartado Postal 10303
San Jose, Costa Rica

DENMARK

Canadian Embassy
Immigration Section
Kr. Bernikowsgade 1
1105 Copenhagen K, Denmark

Areas of responsibility:
Iceland

EGYPT, ARAB REPUBLIC OF

Canadian Embassy
Immigration Section
Kasr el Doubara Post Office
Garden City, Cairo
Arab Republic of Egypt

Areas of responsibility:
Libya, Sudan

FINLAND

Canadian Embassy
P. O. Box 779
00101 Helsinki 10, Finland

FRANCE

Canadian Embassy
35 av. Montaigne
75008 Paris viii^e, France

GERMANY (FEDERAL REPUBLIC)

Canadian Embassy
Immigration Section
Godesberger Allee 119
5300 Bonn, Federal Republic of Germany

GREECE

Canadian Embassy
Immigration Section
4 Ioannou Ghennadiou Street & Ypsilantoo
Athens 11521, Greece

GUATEMALA

Canadian Embassy
P. O. Box 4000
Guatemala, C.A.

GUYANA

Canadian High Commission
Box 10880
Georgetown, Guyana

HAITI

Ambassade du Canada
Service de l'Immigration
C.P. 826
Port-au-Prince, Haiti

Areas of responsibility:
Guadaloupe, Martinique, Saba, St. Eustatius, St. Maarten, St. Martin

HONG KONG

Commission for Canada
Immigration Section
P. O. Box 11142 G.P.O.
Hong Kong

Areas of responsibility:
Macao, People's Republic of China, Taiwan, Tibet, Vietnam (Socialist Republic of)

HUNGARY

Canadian Embassy
Visa Section
Budakeszi, ut 32
Budapest H-1121, Hungary

INDIA

Canadian High Commission
Immigration Section
P. O. Box 5207
New Delhi, India

Areas of responsibility:
Andaman and Nicobar Islands,
Bangladesh, Bhutan, Laccadive, Nepal, Sri
Lanka, Minicoy and Aminidivi Islands,
Maldives

IRELAND

Canadian Embassy
Immigration Section
65 St. Stephen's Green
Dublin 2, Ireland

ISRAEL

Canadian Embassy
Box 6410
Tel Aviv 61063, Israel

Areas of responsibility: Cyprus

ITALY

Canadian Embassy
Immigration Section
Via G.B. de Rossi, 27
00161 Rome, Italy

Canadian Consulate General
Via Vittor Pisani, 19
20124 Milan, Italy

IVORY COAST

Ambassade du Canada
Service de l'Immigration
01 C.P. 4104
Abidjan, Ivory Coast

Areas of responsibility:
Angola, Benin, Cameroon, Cape Verde Is-
land, Central African Empire, Chad,
Equatorial Guinea, Gabon, Gambia,
Ghana, Guinea, Guinea-Bissau, Liberia,
Mali, Mauritania, Niger, Nigeria, Sao
Tome & Principe, Senegal, Sierra Leone, St.
Helena, Togo, Upper Volta

JAMAICA

Canadian High Commission
Immigration Section
P.O. Box 1500
Kingston 10, Jamaica

Areas of responsibility:
Bahamas, Cayman Islands, Turks and
Caicos Islands

JAPAN

Canadian Embassy
Immigration Section
3-38 Akasaka 7-chome
Minato-ku
Tokyo 107, Japan

Areas of responsibility:
Guam, Ryukyu Islands, Trust Territory of
the Pacific Islands, other Pacific islands
north of the Equator

KENYA

Canadian High Commission
Immigration Section
P. O. Box 30481
Nairobi, Kenya

Areas of responsibility:
Burundi, Comoro Island, Congo, Crozet
Island, Djibouti, Ethiopia, Malagasy
Republic, Malawi, Mauritius, Mozam-
bique, Reunion, Rwanda, Tanzania, Ugan-
da, Zaire, Zambia, Kerguelen Archipelago,
Seychelles, Somai Republic

KOREA

Canadian Embassy
Immigration Section
P. O. Box 6299
Seoul 100, Korea

KUWAIT

Canadian Embassy
Immigration Section
P.O. Box 25281
(Safat) Kuwait City, Kuwait

LEBANON

At the time of writing, this embassy was
temporarily closed. All cases are being
referred to Damascus, Syria.

MALAYSIA

Canadian High Commission
Immigration Section
P. O. Box 10990
50732 Kuala Lumpur, Malaysia

MEXICO

Canadian Embassy
Immigration Section
Apartado Postal 105-05
11580 Mexico D.F., Mexico

Areas of responsibility:
Belize, Costa Rica, Cuba, El Salvador, Guatemala, Honduras, Nicaragua, Panama, Panama Canal Zone

MOROCCO

Ambassade du Canada
Service de l'Immigration
C.P. 709
Rabat-Agdal, Morocco

NETHERLANDS

Canadian Embassy
Immigration Section
Sophialaan 7
The Hague, Netherlands

PAKISTAN

Canadian Embassy
Immigration Section
P. O. Box 1042, G.P.O.
Islamabad, Pakistan

Areas of responsibility:
Afghanistan

PERU

Canadian Embassy
Casilla 1212
Lima, Peru

PHILIPPINES

Canadian Embassy
Immigration Section
P.O. Box 971, Commercial Centre
Makati, Rizal
Metro Manila, Philippines

POLAND

Canadian Embassy
Immigration Section
Ulica Matejki 1/5, Strodmiescle
00-481 Warsaw, Poland

Areas of responsibility:
German Democratic Republic

PORTUGAL

Canadian Embassy
Immigration Section
Rua Rosa Araujo 2, Sixth Floor
Lisbon 1200, Portugal

Areas of responsibility:
Azores, Madeira

SAUDI ARABIA

Canadian Embassy
P. O. Box 5050
Jeddah 31422, Saudi Arabia

Areas of responsibility:
Bahrain, Iraq, Kuwait, Oman, People's Democratic Republic of Yemen, Yemen Arab Republic, Qatar, Saudi Arabia, United Arab Emirates

SINGAPORE

Canadian High Commission
Immigration Section
P. O. Box 845, Robinson Road
Singapore 9016

Areas of responsibility:
Brunei, Indonesia

SOUTH AFRICA

Canadian Embassy
Immigration Section
P.O. Box 26016, Arcadia
Pretoria 0007, South Africa

Areas of responsibility:
Botswana, Lesotho, Namibia, Rhodesia, Swaziland

SPAIN

Canadian Embassy
Immigration Section
Apartado 587
Madrid 28080, Spain

Areas of responsibility:
Andorra, Gibraltar, Western Sahara

SRI LANKA

Canadian High Commission
P. O. Box 1006
Colombo, Sri Lanka

SWEDEN

Canadian Embassy
Immigration Section
P.O. Box 16129
S-10323 Stockholm 16, Sweden

SWITZERLAND

Canadian Embassy
Immigration Section
P. O. Box 1261
3001 Berne, Switzerland

Areas of responsibility:
Liechtenstein

SYRIA

Canadian Embassy
P. O. Box 3394
Damascus, Syria

THAILAND

Canadian Embassy
Immigration Section
P. O. Box 2090
Bangkok 10500, Thailand

Areas of responsibility:
Burma, Democratic Kampuchea, Laos

TRINIDAD AND TOBAGO

Canadian High Commission
Immigration Section
Box 1246
Port-of-Spain, Trinidad

Areas of responsibility:
Aruba, Bonaire, Curacao, French Guiana,
Guyana, Surinam

TURKEY

Canadian Embassy
Nenehatum Caddesi No. 75
Gaziosmanpasa
Ankara, Turkey

UNITED KINGDOM

Canadian High Commission
Immigration Section
1 Grosvenor Square
London W1X 0AB, England

U.S.A.

Canadian Consulate General
Immigration Section
400 South Tower
One CNN Center
Atlanta, Georgia 30303
U.S.A.

Areas of responsibility:
States of Alabama, Arkansas, Florida,
Georgia, Louisiana, South Carolina, Ten-
nessee, Mississippi, North Carolina

Canadian Consulate General

Immigration Section
Suite 400, Copley Center
3 Copley Street
Boston, Massachusetts 02116
U.S.A.

Areas of responsibility:
St. Pierre and Miquelon, Maine, Mas-
sachusetts, New Hampshire, Rhode Island,
Vermont

Canadian Consulate General
Immigration Section
1 Marine Midland Center, Ste. 3550
Buffalo, New York 14208
U.S.A.

Areas of responsibility:
Western and Northern New York State

Canadian Consulate General
Immigration Section
310 South Michigan Avenue, Ste. 1200
Chicago, Illinois 60604
U.S.A.

Areas of responsibility:
Illinois, Indiana, Iowa, Kansas, Kentucky,
Missouri, Nebraska and lower Wisconsin

Canadian Consulate
Immigration Section
St. Paul Tower, Suite 1700
750 North St. Paul Street
Dallas, Texas 75201
U.S.A.

Areas of responsibility:
Oklahoma, Texas

Canadian Consulate
Immigration Section
600 Renaissance Center, Suite 1100
Detroit, Michigan 48243
U.S.A.

Areas of responsibility:
Lower Michigan and the State of Ohio

Canadian Consulate General
Immigration Section
300 South Grand Avenue
Los Angeles, California 90071
U.S.A.

Areas of responsibility:
States of Arizona and New Mexico; in California, the counties of Imperial, Kern, Los Angeles, San Diego, San Luis Obispo, Santa Barbara, Ventura, Orange, Riverside, San Bernadino and Clark County in Nevada

Canadian Consulate
Immigration Section
701 Fourth Avenue South
Minneapolis, Minnesota 55415
U.S.A.

Areas of responsibility:
States of Minnesota, North Dakota, South Dakota, Wisconsin

Canadian Consulate General
Immigration Section
1251 Avenue of the Americas
New York, New York 10020
U.S.A.

Areas of responsibility:
Bermuda, States of Connecticut, Delaware, Maryland, New Jersey, Pennsylvania, District of Columbia, and Eastern New York, Virginia, West Virginia

Canadian Consulate General
Immigration Section
50 Fremont Street, Suite 2100
One Maritime Plaza
San Francisco, California 94105
U.S.A.

Areas of responsibility:
State of California (except 10 Los Angeles countries), Colorado, Hawaii, Nevada (except Clark County), Utah, Wyoming

Canadian Consulate General
Immigration Section
412 Plaza 600
Sixth & Stewart
Seattle, Washington 98101
U.S.A.

Areas of responsibility:
Alaska, Idaho, Oregon, Washington and Western Montana

Canadian Embassy
Immigration Section
501 Pennsylvania Avenue N.W.
Washington, D.C. 20001
U.S.A.

U.S.S.R.

Canadian Embassy
Consular & Visa Section
23 Starokonyushenny Pereulok
Moscow, U.S.S.R.

YUGOSLAVIA

Canadian Embassy
Immigration Section
Kneza Milosa 75
11000 Belgrade, Yugoslavia

Areas of responsibility:
Bulgaria, Romania, Turkey

APPENDIX 3
QUEBEC IMMIGRATION OFFICES ABROAD

BANGKOK

Immigration Quebec
Ambassade du Canada
C.P. 2090
Bangkok, Thailand
Telephone: 234-1561
Telex: 2671 (DOMCAN)

Burma, Thailand, Vietnam, Kampuchea, Laos, India, Nepal, Bangladesh, Pakistan, Bhutan and Sri Lanka.

BOSTON

Immigration Quebec
Exchange Place
53 State Street, 19th Floor
Boston, Massachusetts
U.S.A. 02109

Boston, The New England States and St. Pierre and Miquelon.

BRUSSELS

Service d'immigration du Quebec
Delegation generale due Quebec
46, avenue des Arts
1040, Bruxelles, Belgique

Belgium, Luxembourg, The Netherlands, Federal Republic of Germany, Austria, Hungary, Czechoslovakia, Tel Aviv's Territory (Israel & Cyprus), Berne's Territory (Switzerland & Liechtenstein)

BUENOS AIRES

Immigration Quebec
Ambassade du Canada
C.P. 1598
Buenos Aires, Argentine
Telephone: (01) 329081
Telex: 21383 (DOMCAN)

Argentina, Chile, Uruguay, Paraguay, Bolivia, Brazil, and Peru.

HONG KONG

Service d'immigration du Quebec
Delegation du Quebec
Piece 1716
Centre Admiralty, Tour I
Hong Kong

Australia, China, Mongolia, Japan, New Zealand, The Philippines, South Korea, North Korea, Indonesia, Malaysia, Hong Kong, Singapore, Taiwan, and Macao.

LISBON

Immigration Quebec
Ambassade du Canada
Praca Marquis de Pombal 14
Lisbonne, Portugal
Telephone: 537038
Telex: 12377 (DOMCAN)

Portugal, Spain, the Azores, Madeira and the Canaries.

LONDON

Service d'immigration du Quebec
Delegation generale du Quebec
59, Pall Mall
Londres SW1 5JH, Grande Bretagne

Afghanistan, German Democratic Republic, Denmark, Finland, Iceland, Poland, U.S.S.R., United Kingdom, Ireland, Norway, Sweden, Pretoria's Territory (South Africa, Namibia, Swaziland, Lesotho, Botswana, Zimbabwe), Nairobi's Territory (East Africa, Madagascar, and Ile Maurice).

MEXICO

Service d'immigration du Quebec
Delegation du Quebec
Avenida Taine 411
Colonia Bosques de Chapultepec 11580
Mexico, D.F. Mexique

Aruba, Mexico, Costa Rica, Cuba, Curacao, El Salvador, Ecuador, Guatemala, French Guiana, Guyana, Honduras, Panama, Nicaragua, St. Martin, Saint Maarten, Surinam, Trinidad & Tobago, and Venezuela.

MONTREAL - DSSE

Ministere des Communautes culturelles et de l'immigration Montreal-Etranger
355, rue McGill
Montreal, Quebec
H2Y 2E8

United States (except New York, Boston and Buffalo) and Greenland.

NEW YORK

Service d'immigration du Quebec
Delegation generale du Quebec
Centre Rockefeller
17 - 50^e rue ouest
New York, N.Y., U.S.A. 10111

Bermuda, Buffalo and New York

PARIS

Immigration Quebec
66, rue Pergolese
75016 - Paris, France
Telephone: 502-1410
Telex: 620 401 (DELEBEC)

France

PORT-AU-PRINCE

Service d'immigration du Quebec
Delegation du Quebec
13, rue Baussan
B.P. 2243
Port-au-Prince, Haiti (W.I.)

Antigua & Barbuda, Belize, St. Lucia, St. Vincent and the Grenadines, Haiti, Jamaica, Puerto Rico, Martinique, Guadeloupe, Barbados, Grenada, Dominica, the Dominican Republic, St. Kitts-Nevis (also known as St. Christopher-Nevis), Montserrat, British Virgin Islands, and the U.S. Virgin Islands.

ROME

Immigration Quebec Ambassade du Canada
30 Via Zara
Rome, Italie
Telephone: (6) 844-0158Kuwait, Qatar and Bahrain.
Telex: 61056 (DOMCAN)

Yugoslavia, Italy, San Marino, Malta, Greece, Arab Emirates, North and South Yemen, Oman, Romania, Bulgaria, Turkey, Cyprus, Albania, Egypt, Libya, Sudan, Saudi Arabia, Iraq,

SYRIA

Immigration Quebec
a/s de l'Ambassade du Canada
C.P. 3394
Damas, Syria

Damascus' Territory (Syria, Lebanon, Jordan and Iran).

APPENDIX 4
FEES FOR IMMIGRATION SERVICES

In March, 1986, the Canadian government began a cost recovery program for immigration services, visas, and other documents. Put simply, Canada began to charge fees for various services. Some of these fees were raised in April, 1990.

1. Permanent resident application — Non-business $250
   Independent worker
   Family class
    Assisted relative
2. Permanent resident application — Business $500
   Entrepreneur
   Investor
   Self-employed
3. Visitor's visa
   Initially . . . . No Fee
   Extension $75
4. Employment authorizations $75
5. Verification of permanent residence status when document lost
   or request to amend error in permanent residence document,
   i.e., birth date $50

APPENDIX 5
SOURCES OF SELECTED PUBLICATIONS

The following is a list of offices that offer publications relating to starting a business in Canada or one of its provinces. Publications are available by writing to the appropriate office. (See also *Starting a Successful Business in Canada,* another title in the Self-Counsel Series).

1. Federal Business Development Bank

FBDB Services for Business Anywhere in Canada

Minding Your Own Business

Small Business News

Publications can be ordered from:
Federal Business Development Bank
Management Services
P.O. Box 6021
Montreal, Quebec
H3C 3C3

2. Department of Regional Industrial Expansion (federal)

DRIE is the principal department of government for encouraging investment in viable industrial undertakings in manufacturing, resource processing, tourism, and small business. Information and helpful publications are available from:

Department of Regional Industrial
    Expansion
Business Information Centre
235 Queen Street
Ottawa, Ontario
K1A 0H5

3. Alberta (provincial)

Selected publications on how to establish and operate businesses in Alberta may be obtained by writing to:

Alberta Manpower
Park Square
10001 Bellamy Hill
Edmonton, Alberta
T5J 3W5

4. British Columbia (provincial)

An information package available in numerous languages may be obtained from:

Ministry of Industry and Small Business
    Development
Suite 315, Robson Square
800 Hornby Street
Vancouver, British Columbia
V6Z 2C5

5. Ontario (provincial)

Starting a Small Business in Ontario

Copies of this publication may be obtained by writing to:

Small Business Operations Division
Ministry of Industry and Trade
Hearst Block, Queen's Park
Toronto, Ontario
M7A 2E1

APPENDIX 6
ADDRESSES OF PROVINCIAL OFFICES

The following is a list of the provincial ministries or departments responsible for approving entrepreneurial applications:

1. Alberta

Manager, Immigration
Alberta Career Development
    & Employment
14th Floor, Park Square
10001 Bellamy Hill
Edmonton, Alberta
T5J 3W5

2. British Columbia

Ministry of Economic Development
P. O. Box 19
750 Pacific Boulevard S.
Vancouver, British Columbia
V6B 5E7

3. Manitoba

Entrepreneurs and self-employed:
Assistant Deputy Minister
Trade and Industry Division
Department of Industry, Trade
    and Technology
101-155 Carlton Street
Winnipeg, Manitoba
R3C 3H8

4. New Brunswick

New Brunswick Department of Labour
    Planning Division
470 York Street
P.O. Box 6000
Fredericton, New Brunswick
E3B 5H1

5. Newfoundland

Deputy Minister
Department of Labour and Manpower
Beothuck Building
Crosbie Place
St. John's, Newfoundland
A1C 6C9

6. Nova Scotia

Chief, Recruitment and Selection
Metropolitan Place
99 Wyse Road, 5th Floor
P. O. Box 1350
Dartmouth, Nova Scotia
B2Y 4B9

7. Ontario

Ministry of Industry, Trade
    & Technology
Immigrant Entrepreneur Section
Investment Branch
900 Bay Street
Hearst Block, Queen's Park
Toronto, Ontario
M7A 2E1

8. Prince Edward Island

Manager, Immigration
P.E.I. Region
199 Grafton Street
P. O. Box 8000
Charlottetown, Prince Edward Island
C1A 8K1

9. Quebec

Ministere des Communautes culturelles
et de l'immigration du Quebec
Service aux Entrepreneurs/Investisseurs
355 Rue McGill, 10eme etage
Montreal, Quebec
H2Y 2E8

10. Saskatchewan

Trade Programmes Branch
Saskatchewan Economic Development
and Trade
Bank of Montreal Building
3rd Floor, 2103-11th Avenue
Regina, Saskatchewan
S4P 3V7

OTHER TITLES IN THE SELF-COUNSEL SERIES

THE BUSINESS GUIDE TO EFFECTIVE SPEAKING
Making presentations, using audio-visuals, and dealing with the media
by Jacqueline Dunckel and Elizabeth Parnham

Give dynamic speeches, presentations, and media interviews. When you are called upon to speak in front of your business colleagues, or asked to represent your company in front of the media, do you communicate your thoughts effectively? Or do you become tongue-tied, nervous, and worry about misrepresenting yourself and your business?

Effective communication has always been the key to business success, and this book provides a straightforward approach to developing techniques to improve your on-the-job speaking skills. This book is as easy to pick up and use as a quick reference for a specific problem as it is to read from cover to cover. Whether you want to know how to deal with the media, when to use visual aids in a presentation, or how to prepare for chairing a meeting, this book will answer your questions and help you regain your confidence. $7.95

Contents include:
- Preparing your presentation
- When and where will you speak?
- Let's look at visual aids
- Let's hear what you have to say: rehearsing
- How do you sound?
- What is your body saying about you?
- Confidence and self-control
- Packaging the presenter

BUSINESS ETIQUETTE TODAY
A guide to corporate success
by Jacqueline Dunckel

Mind your manners and get ahead! Knowing when to open the door for a colleague or how to accept a gift can sometimes mean the difference between being pigeon-holed in your current position or being offered that attractive promotion. But times have also changed, and the rules once relied on are not always appropriate today. With the growing number of women in company boardrooms and the move toward more international business, a new style of behavior is often called for.

This book is as easy to pick up and use as a quick reference before that special event as it is to read cover to cover. $7.95

Contents include:
- To begin at the beginning — the etiquette of employment
- Department decorum
- Telephone manners
- Meeting manners and boardroom behavior
- Introductions and conversation
- Cultural courtesy
- Table manners
- Eating in and dining out
- Giving and receiving — the etiquette of business gifts
- Put it in writing
- Manners on the road

CHAIRING A MEETING WITH CONFIDENCE

An easy guide to rules and procedure

by Kevin Paul, B.A., M.A.

The author uses everyday language to demystify the art of conducting a meeting in a fair, orderly, and efficient manner. This is not a rules book, but a simple guide on how to run a meeting according to the rules of order. Your meetings can become an effective tool in dealing with the business of the day and the venue for discussion that is productive and to the point. $7.95

PREPARING A SUCCESSFUL BUSINESS PLAN

A practical guide for small business

by Rodger Touchie, B.A., M.B.A.

At some time, every business needs a formal business plan. Whether considering a new business venture or rethinking an existing one, an effective plan is essential to success. From start to finish, this working guide outlines how to prepare a plan that will win potential investors and help achieve business goals.

Using worksheets and a sample plan, readers learn how to create an effective plan, establish planning and maintenance methods, and update their strategy in response to actual business conditions. $14.95

Contents include:

- The basic elements of business planning
- The company and its product
- The marketing plan
- The financial plan
- The team
- Concluding remarks and appendixes
- The executive summary

ORDER FORM

All prices are subject to change without notice. Books are available in book, department, and stationery stores. If you cannot buy the book through a store, please use this order form.
(Please print)

Name _____

Address _____

_____

Charge to:

❑Visa   ❑ MasterCard

Account Number _____

Validation Date _____

Expiry Date_____

Signature _____

❑**Check here for a free catalogue which outlines all of our publications.**

IN CANADA

Please send your order to the nearest location:
Self-Counsel Press, 1481 Charlotte Road
North Vancouver, B. C. V7J 1H1

Self-Counsel Press, 2399 Cawthra Road,
Unit 25, Mississauga, Ontario L5A 2W9

IN THE U.S.A.

Please send your order to:
Self-Counsel Press Inc., 1704 N. State Street
Bellingham, WA 98225

YES, please send me:

_____copies of **Business Guide to Effective Speaking**, $7.95

_____copies of **Business Etiquette Today,** $7.95

_____copies of **Chairing a Meeting With Confidence**, $7.95

_____copies of **Preparing a Successful Business Plan**, $14.95

Please add $2.50 for postage & handling.
WA residents: Please add 7.8% sales tax.
Canadian residents: As of January 1, 1991, please add 7% GST to your order.